Sex Trafficking of Children Online

THE APPLIED CRIMINOLOGY
ACROSS THE GLOBE SERIES

Series Editor: Kimberly A. McCabe, University of Lynchburg, mccabe@ lynchburg.edu

Crime and safety continue to be among the top issues facing the global world and the discipline of applied criminology addresses those issues. *The Applied Criminology across the Globe* series is designed to address the ever-growing need for current and accurate information on a variety of subjects as related to applied criminology. The books in this series provide the readers with monographs that are able to inform and educate individuals on crime and criminal behaviors.

Books in the Series

Sex Trafficking of Children Online: Modern Slavery in Cyberspace, by Beatriz Susana Uitts

Policing and Public Trust: Exposing the Inner Uniform, by Eccy de Jonge

Sex Trafficking of Children Online

Modern Slavery in Cyberspace

Beatriz Susana Uitts

ROWMAN & LITTLEFIELD
Lanham • Boulder • New York • London

Published by Rowman & Littlefield
An imprint of The Rowman & Littlefield Publishing Group, Inc.

4501 Forbes Boulevard, Suite 200, Lanham, Maryland 20706
www.rowman.com
86-90 Paul Street, London EC2A 4NE, United Kingdom

Copyright © 2022 by The Rowman & Littlefield Publishing Group, Inc.

British Library Cataloguing in Publication Information Available

Library of Congress Cataloging-in-Publication Data
Names: Uitts, Beatriz Susana, 1986– author.
Title: Sex trafficking of children online : modern slavery in cyberspace / Beatriz
   Susana Uitts.
Description: Lanham : Rowman & Littlefield, [2022] | Series: Applied criminology
   across the globe | Based on author's thesis (doctoral - Saint Thomas University
   (Miami, Fla.). School of Law, 2019) issued under title: Cyber trafficking of children
   : an international legal response to online child sexual exploitation. | Includes
   bibliographical references and index. | Summary: "This book argues that forms of
   online child sexual exploitation equate to slavery-like practices under international law
   and that States have a responsibility to punish offenders as such, based on a careful
   review of relevant legal instruments and standards"—Provided by publisher.
Identifiers: LCCN 2022005713 (print) | LCCN 2022005714 (ebook) |
   ISBN 9781538146941 (cloth) | ISBN 9781538146958 (epub)
Subjects: LCSH: Human trafficking (International law) | Child trafficking—Law and
   legislation. | Child sexual abuse—Law and legislation. | Online sexual predators—
   Legal status, laws, etc.
Classification: LCC KZ7155 .U38 2022 (print) | LCC KZ7155 (ebook) |
   DDC 345/.02551—dc23/eng/20220531
LC record available at https://lccn.loc.gov/2022005713
LC ebook record available at https://lccn.loc.gov/2022005714

♾️™ The paper used in this publication meets the minimum requirements of American
National Standard for Information Sciences—Permanence of Paper for Printed Library
Materials, ANSI/NISO Z39.48-1992.

For your love and support—Ross, Sofi, and Max

Contents

Preface

The Internet has become one of the most widely used means for people to accomplish their daily activities. Unfortunately, this powerful tool of the modern world is also being misused to facilitate criminal activities, including human trafficking and related exploitation.

As Internet access continues to expand rapidly across the world, children face greater risks than ever before of being lured, recruited, or transferred for sexual exploitation. Offenders exploit children and use them as commodities to be traded and sold. The situation has been further exacerbated by the COVID-19 pandemic.

Although the Internet is not inherently harmful, it can be used as a facilitating instrument for cybercriminals to develop forms of exploitation. Offenders enjoy the benefits of cyberchannels—unrestricted by national borders or geographical boundaries—without leaving the privacy of their home. In particular, the Internet allows them to camouflage their identity while committing cybercrimes involving child sexual exploitation. In this way, the Internet creates new opportunities for offenders and has led to a growth in human trafficking activities. In addition, parallel to the rapid change prompted by the Internet is the evolving nature of harmful and abusive acts against children online.

This book discusses these evolving cybercriminal activities and identifies criminalization gaps and challenges for the criminal justice system. It engages with various research and materials to examine obstacles at the national level that complicate and impede criminal investigations and prosecutions that seek to interrupt and combat online criminals and criminal networks. It is essential that nations understand the dynamics of these crimes and increase international collaboration among law enforcement partners; it is also critical that sound policymaking be enacted across countries. A common legal framework would lead to adequate national legislation, more effective detection and punishment of cyberoffenders, improved prevention efforts, and quicker identification and assistance of potential child victims, thus improving the global community response.

This book sheds light on the striking links between online sex trafficking, modern slavery, and online child sexual exploitation. Using a human rights multistakeholder approach, this book explores how child predation and trafficking have been shaped by Internet use and recommends novel solutions to holistically address this online problem for the sake of enhancing the protection of children's human rights and dignity in cyberspace.

Online sex trafficking of children is a human rights issue because they are being treated as sexually exploitative objects. This book provides helpful insights for lawmakers, legal practitioners, scholars, law enforcement officers, child advocates, and students interested in human rights law, criminal law, and child protection. This book's recommendations aim to address constraints on state action to protect children online and help end forms of online child sexual exploitation by identifying them as slavery-like practices and condemning them as such. Overall, this book demonstrates the urgent need for action from the international community and its member states and encourages the adaptation of legal and policy frameworks to today's rapidly changing realities.

Acknowledgments

Examining a topic as complex as child sex trafficking in cyberspace, although disturbing, has been extremely rewarding. This book draws inspiration from two sources. The first is my legal and advocacy work over the years, including serving vulnerable populations and victims and survivors of human trafficking. In addition, this book was inspired by research undertaken during my time in the doctorate of the science of law (JSD) program in intercultural human rights at St. Thomas University College of Law.

It is a pleasure and honor to thank Professor Siegfried Wiessner, who taught me to appreciate the importance of the law as a vehicle to address human needs and aspirations in order to establish a public order of human dignity. From the very beginning when I first began my master of laws (LLM) in intercultural human rights in 2011, his support has been constant. His advice and insightful feedback have truly been indispensable to the development of the concepts explored in this book.

Furthermore, I am deeply grateful to Professor Roza Pati for her invaluable guidance and mentorship. I owe my graduate fellowship with the John J. Brunetti Human Trafficking Academy of St. Thomas Law School to her. During my time as a student in the LLM and JSD programs, this fellowship provided an opportunity to research human trafficking and to continue to work to advance the dignity and inalienable rights of every person.

I would like to express my thanks to Professor Roy Balleste. His unwavering support, advice, and legal guidance provided an invaluable contribution to this book for which I will be forever grateful.

In addition, I owe a debt of gratitude to the library staff at St. Thomas University Law Library for their wonderful support in acquiring the many books so critical to my research. Their efforts contributed immeasurably to the final version of this book by helping me ensure it would be current with the latest materials and information.

I would also like to thank Ishka Rogbeer, my citation editor, for her excellent work on the reference system and notes for this book.

I am indebted to the editorial and production staff at Rowman & Littlefield. In particular, I thank associate acquisitions editor Becca Beurer for her support and guidance during the entire editorial process.

Thanks to my parents for their enduring faith, tireless support, and encouragement.

Thanks are due above all to my husband, Ross, and to our children, Sofia and Max. This book would not exist without Ross's unfailing love and unconditional support, and Sofi and Max's happy distractions always rested my mind from the intensity of my research. The three of you are my greatest blessings and reason for being.

List of Abbreviations

AFP. Australian Federal Police
APOV. Abuse of a position of vulnerability
C3. Corporación Centro de Consultoría y Conflicto Urbano
CCPCJ. Commission on Crime Prevention and Criminal Justice
CHR. United Nations Commission on Human Rights
CoE. Council of Europe
COP. Child Online Protection Initiative
CRC. United Nations Committee on the Rights of the Child
CSAM. Child sexual abuse material
CSEC. Commercial sexual exploitation of children
CSEM. Child sexual exploitation material
Directive 2011/93/EU. EU Law, "Directive 2011/93/EU of the European Parliament and of the Council of 13 December 2011 on Combating the Sexual Abuse and Sexual Exploitation of Children and Child Pornography, and Replacing Council Framework Decision 2004/68/JHA," *Official Journal of the European Union* 335 (2011).
EC3. European Cybercrime Centre
ECHR. European Convention on Human Rights
ECOSOC. Economic and Social Council
ECtHR. European Court of Human Rights
EFC. European Financial Coalition (against Commercial Sexual Exploitation of Children Online)
EMPACT. European Multidisciplinary Platform Against Criminal Threats
EuroISPA. European Internet Services Providers Association
Europol. European Union Agency for Law Enforcement Cooperation
FOSTA. Allow States and Victims to Fight Online Sex Trafficking Act
GCA. Global Cybersecurity Agenda
GCI. Global Cybersecurity Index
GDPR. General Data Protection Regulation
GGE. United Nations Group of Governmental Experts

HRC. United Nations Human Rights Council

HRCttee. United Nations Human Rights Committee

ICAC. Internet Crimes against Children

ICANN. Internet Corporation for Assigned Names and Numbers

ICC. International Criminal Court

ICCPR. International Covenant on Civil and Political Rights; UNGA, "International Covenant on Civil and Political Rights," entered into force March 23, 1966, U.N.T.S. 999.

ICE. U.S. Immigration and Customs Enforcement

ICESCR. International Covenant on Economic, Social, and Cultural Rights; UNGA, "International Covenant on Economic, Social and Cultural Rights," entered into force January 3, 1976, U.N.T.S. 993.

ICJ. International Court of Justice

ICMEC. International Centre for Missing and Exploited Children

ICTs. Information and communications technologies

ICTY. International Criminal Tribunal for the former Yugoslavia

ICSE. International Child Sexual Exploitation Database

IGF. Internet Governance Forum

ILC. International Law Commission

ILO. International Labour Organization

INHOPE. International Association of Internet Hotlines

Interpol. International Criminal Police Organization

IOCTA. Internet Organised Crime Threat Assessment

IP. Internet protocol

ISPs. Internet service providers

ITU. International Telecommunication Union

IWF. Internet Watch Foundation

Lanzarote Committee. Council of Europe Committee of the Parties to the Lanzarote Convention

Lanzarote Convention. Council of Europe Convention on Protection of Children against Sexual Exploitation and Sexual Abuse; CoE, "Convention on the Protection of Children against Sexual Exploitation and Sexual Abuse," entered into force October 25, 2007, CoE T.S. 201.

LoN. League of Nations

NCMEC. National Center for Missing and Exploited Children

NGO. Nongovernmental organization

NSPCC. National Society for the Prevention of Cruelty to Children

OHCHR. Office of the United Nations High Commissioner for Human Rights

OP-CRC-SC. Optional Protocol to the Convention on the Rights of the Child on the Sale of Children, Child Prostitution and Child Pornography; UNGA, "Optional Protocol to the Convention on the Rights of the Child on the Sale of Children, Child Prostitution and Child Pornography," entered into force January 18, 2002, U.N.T.S 2171.

OP-CRC-SC Guidelines. UNCRC, "Guidelines Regarding the Implementation of the Optional Protocol to the Convention on the Rights of the Child on the Sale of Children, Child Prostitution and Child Pornography," CRC/C/156, September 10, 2019.

P2P. Peer-to-peer

Palermo Protocol. Protocol to Prevent, Suppress and Punish Trafficking in Persons, Especially Women and Children; UNGA, "Protocol to Prevent, Suppress and Punish Trafficking in Persons Especially Women and Children, Supplementing the United Nations Convention against Transnational Organized Crime," entered into force December 25, 2003, U.N.T.S. 2237.

SDGs. Sustainable development goals

SESTA. Stop Enabling Sex Traffickers Act

Supplementary Slavery Convention. ECOSOC, "Supplementary Convention on the Abolition of Slavery, the Slave Trade, and Institutions and Practices Similar to Slavery," entered into force April 30, 1957, U.N.T.S. 3822.

TIP. "Trafficking in Persons" (report)

UDHR. Universal Declaration of Human Rights; UNGA, Resolution 217 A (III), Universal Declaration of Human Rights, December 10, 1948.

UNCRC. United Nations Convention on the Rights of the Child; UNGA, "Convention on the Rights of the Child," entered into force September 2, 1990, U.N.T.S. 1577.

UNGA. United Nations General Assembly

UNGIFT. United Nations Global Initiative to Fight Human Trafficking

UNODC. United Nations Office on Drugs and Crime

UNSG. United Nations secretary-general

UNTOC. United Nations Convention against Transnational Organized Crime; UNGA, "United Nations Convention against Transnational Organized Crime," entered into force September 29, 2003, U.N.T.S. 2225.

VCLT. Vienna Convention on the Law of Treaties; UN, "Vienna Convention on the Law of Treaties," signed May 23, 1969, U.N.T.S. 1155.

VGT. Virtual Global Taskforce

WPGA. WeProtect Global Alliance

WSIS. World Summit on the Information Society

Introduction

The crime of human trafficking has permeated our world today, leaving no country immune to exploitation and modern forms of slavery including practices that victimize children. Moreover, this crime has grown into a multibillion-dollar industry.[1] Perpetrators of this crime engage in any scheme necessary, individually or in groups, to accomplish their exploitative goals. The recruitment and trading of minors in sex trafficking activities continue to occur, for example, through word of mouth, on the streets, in casinos, and at truck stops. However, traffickers now use the Internet and digital technology as well to facilitate every aspect of human trafficking to place children in slavery or sexual exploitation.[2] In cyberspace, perpetrators can recruit, advertise for, contact, and control child victims; communicate with other like-minded individuals and networks; arrange sexual encounters; capture child abuse material that may result in coercion and sexual extortion of children; and transfer criminal proceeds.[3] Additionally, criminals' online interactions may facilitate a subculture of child sexual abuse and exploitation.

Due to the COVID-19 pandemic, a massive closing of schools and physical distancing measures have boosted the importance of online platforms and online communities. For children, online platforms provide opportunities to support their learning, socialization, and play including while in isolation. However, along with these positive potentials, this powerful tool can expose them to risks such as sexual exploitation online. According to the National Center for Missing and Exploited Children (NCMEC), reports received by CyberTipline increased 106 percent in the United States in 2020 of potential incidents of child pornography, child sex trafficking, and online solicitation of children—rising from almost 1 million reports in March 2019 to just over 2 million in March 2020.[4] A similar increase in suspicious activities of this nature was noticed worldwide.[5] In addition, the Human Rights Institute found that of recruiting incidents in active child sex trafficking cases on social media in the United States in 2020, 65 percent occurred on Facebook, 14 percent on Instagram, and 8 percent on Snapchat.[6] Notably, the UK's Internet

Watch Foundation (IWF) in its 2020 report stated that the Internet shows child sexual abuse imagery once every three minutes.[7]

This book describes the growing use of the Internet for trafficking and child sexual exploitation purposes. These online offenses include the use of children for pornographic performances and materials, including the depiction of babies and toddlers in extreme sexual content.[8] Furthermore, these offenses may relate to the sexual exploitation of children for prostitution, including involving children in commercial or commodified sexual activities and sex travel and tourism. In addition, this book brings attention to online practices that may become trafficking situations such as mail-order brides and child marriages with exploitation of the child involved. Internet-facilitated child marriages as a form of trafficking may represent a form of noncommercial sexual exploitation of children because the perpetrator typically aims for sexual gratification instead of sexual exploitation of the child for profit, such as in prostitution. Similarly, the sale of children for illegal adoption with the purpose of exploitation can occur through the Internet.

In light of children's rights enshrined in international law, a child's consent to these online acts and activities is legally irrelevant. He or she is a victim of exploitation and, therefore, should not be treated as a criminal. In these criminal acts, perpetrators exploit the vulnerabilities and the age of child victims, treating them as commodities or depicting them in images and videos as objects for sexual exploitation. Moreover, new manifestations of exploitation associated with trafficking reveal the exercise of one or more ownership powers over children, consequently reaching the threshold required of slavery.

These new modalities of crime demonstrate a vast and complicated problem that affects all countries. It is difficult even to gauge the extent of this crime given the way the Internet obscures it. Today the Internet has become an essential part of children's lives, at increasingly younger ages, and the time they spend online is rising with tablet and mobile phone use.[9] This may expose more children to online risks. Additionally, as children get older they are likely to use the Internet more extensively, further increasing these dangers.[10]

Children are at risk of these exploitative practices worldwide but the predominant type of practice may differ by country. For example, children playing games on the Internet may be enticed by offenders in online forums or dating sites. In addition, children can be sold and trafficked by the people they love and trust the most, such as their parents. Indeed, criminals often take advantage of a family's poverty to involve parents in the exploitation of their own children. In this way, the perpetrators of these crimes range from the solitary child predator on a website to an organized crime group using sophisticated international logistics and information technology techniques. Child victims of these acts may be too scared or too brainwashed to report them, often suffering psychological harm from these traumatic situations that strip them of their humanity.

The human dignity of children should never be placed in jeopardy even in cyberspace. Online sex trafficking offenses present new challenges for our international child-protective framework.[11] One primary challenge is the lack of a clear definition in national criminal laws of illegal actions that result in the exploitation of children on the Internet. Deficiencies in detection and reporting mechanisms, investigation and prosecution of perpetrators, prevention and protection of child victims, and international cooperation are also hurdles.[12] To provide a robust foundation to address these issues, states must implement consistent policy measures addressing the sexual exploitation of children and including practices in cyberspace.

In particular, the criminalization of forms of child trafficking and sexual exploitation in cyberspace complicates the interpretation and implementation of international legal instruments. For example, United Nations treaties pertaining to the topic—such as the UN Optional Protocol to the Convention on the Rights of the Child on the Sale of Children, Child Prostitution and Child Pornography (OP-CRC-SC) and the UN Protocol to Prevent, Suppress and Punish Trafficking in Persons, Especially Women and Children (Palermo Protocol)—do not specifically address cyberspace exploitation of children.[13] Given the period in which these legally binding instruments were adopted, their legal provisions regarding offenses for the purposes of sexual exploitation of children did not address the cybercriminal practices that children face today. At that time, Internet technologies were less developed and less widespread and the drafters of these instruments were hence not concerned by the possibility that such offenses might proliferate in cyberspace.[14] All acts intended to focus on cyberspace exploitation of children require precise legal definitions at the national level. States must ban new forms of online sexual exploitation, delineating with certainty these online crimes in their domestic legislation and demonstrating no tolerance for them in their national legal systems and practice. It was the urgency of sufficiently protecting children against criminal exploitative actions in cyberspace that drove me to write this book.

As duty bearers under international human rights law, nations have the responsibility to protect their children from harm and infringement of their human rights everywhere as well as in cyberspace. Based on their obligations under international human rights law, states are required to act with due diligence to prevent any practices that infringe on the human rights of children in cyberspace and to investigate and punish offenders. A human rights–based approach to online sex trafficking requires an understanding of what constitutes violations of children's rights to ensure that states meet their obligation to protect the victims of these violations.[15] Moreover, adoption of this human rights approach requires a balance between, on the one hand, each child's right to protection from harm and, on the other, the right to freedom of expression and privacy of children and other users of the Internet.

This book is divided into three parts. Part I (chapters 1–3) establishes how already existing law and jurisprudential principles clearly establish the legal connection between slavery and human trafficking, on the one hand, and various activities associated with the online sexual exploitation of children, on the other. I demonstrate that existing frameworks are fully relevant and applicable to the online sexual exploitation of children, and I then elaborate on this reasoning. I also discuss the novel legal complexities posed by the Internet in respect of such considerations. Part II (chapters 4–6) then details the forms such online sexual exploitation of children can take, showing the ways each form demonstrates a clear violation of fundamental human rights and human dignity. This requires sociological analysis of the criminal networks, activities, technologies, and processes involved in these practices to clarify the practical challenges legal mechanisms need to address. Part III (chapters 7–8) then initially returns to a theoretical framework that helps clarify how these practical challenges can be defined and understood in a jurisprudential perspective before providing practical recommendations based on this theoretical framework. The theoretical framework adopted is the New Haven School articulation of the basis and inviolability of human dignity. The practical recommendations proceed from this basis and frame the pertinent principles identified in part I in the form of both already existing national laws and a draft for an international treaty for the prevention, prohibition, and penalization of online activity for the purpose of the sexual exploitation of children.

Chapter 1 examines the practice of slavery in its traditional sense and the evolved definition of slavery and key cases in international criminal law, regional human rights law, and the inter-American system. Chapter 2 provides a thorough analysis of human trafficking and how it has been translated into an online context, spelling out the continuities between this and slavery-like practices already addressed by binding international legal instruments. Chapter 3 discusses the legal complexities posed by the Internet—as both a boon to freedoms such as those of expression and association but also a means whereby abhorrent violations of human rights can be facilitated—and considers the challenges these pose for responses to online activity for the purpose of the sexual exploitation of children.

Chapter 4 explores the types of trafficking activities, new and established, facilitated by the Internet that may involve elements of ownership over a child. It discusses the importance of legally considering the transference and acquisition of children on the Internet in relation to forms of sexual exploitation. Chapter 5 examines online grooming, its exploitative nature, and its use as an element of trafficking. In further detail, chapter 6 discusses child vulnerabilities and the root causes of this online problem. In addition, it presents the principle of the irrelevancy of the consent of children involved in exploitation, including exploitative sexual acts online. Then the chapter explores the general characteristics of cyberoffenders, their motives, and their modus operandi for these illegal activities.

Chapter 7 appraises the use of human dignity as a foundation for establishing international law on child exploitation in cyberspace. It underscores the importance of combating these practices within a strong human rights framework that balances child safety online with rights to freedom of expression and privacy. Finally, chapter 8 provides policy and practice recommendations to fight online sexual exploitation of children in the context of human trafficking. Recommendations are based on states' obligations under international law to prevent and eliminate this cybercrime.

Online sex trafficking is a human rights issue that involves new and evolving manifestations of sexual exploitation of children. Therefore, it demands more effective responses from governments to improve the efficiency of national policy frameworks, foster international cooperation, and engage the private sector. States cannot act alone in the fight against these Internet-related crimes. These crimes constitute a dynamic phenomenon that requires multistakeholder collaboration, particularly in the Internet industry and including Internet service providers (ISPs), search engine companies, and social media platforms. In this respect, based on a framework of corporate social responsibility, responsibility for detecting and reporting these crimes to the competent authorities falls on the Internet industry. Taken together, these efforts should help make the Internet a safer and more secure environment for children and the world.

This form of criminality is a direct threat to not only children but the entire world. The advancement of children's rights online is an issue that affects all humanity from the individual to the community of nations. It is our duty to shoulder this burden and tackle the problem of online child sexual exploitation head-on.

NOTES

1. See International Labour Organization (ILO), *Profits and Poverty: The Economics of Forced Labour* (Geneva: ILO, 2014), 13, 15, 27.

2. Staca Shehan, email message to author, August 27, 2014; fn.19 in United States Senate, *Backpage.com's Knowing Facilitation of Online Sex Trafficking: Staff Report* (United States Senate, 2017), 5.

3. UN Office on Drugs and Crime (UNODC), "Traffickers Use of the Internet," in *Global Report on Trafficking in Persons* (New York: United Nations, 2020); Donna

M. Hughes, "Trafficking in Human Beings in the European Union: Gender, Sexual Exploitation, and Digital Communication Technologies," *SAGE Open* (2014): 5–6, https://doi.org/10.1177/2158244014553585.

4. Thomas Brewster, "Child Exploitation Complaints Rise 106% to Hit 2 Million in Just One Month: Is COVID-19 to Blame?" *Forbes*, www.forbes.com/sites/thomasbrewster/2020/04/24/child-exploitation-complaints-rise-106-to-hit-2-million[TYPE:Rebreak before hyphen]-in-just-one-month-is-covid-19-to-blame/?sh=661bcc7e4c9c; UN Human Rights Council (HRC), "Impact of Coronavirus Disease on Different Manifestations of Sale and Sexual Exploitation of Children: Report of the Special Rapporteur on the Sale and Sexual Exploitation of Children, including Child Prostitution, Child Pornography and Other Child Sexual Abuse Material, Mama Fatima Singhateh," A/HRC/46/31, January 22, 2021, para. 26 at 8.

5. HRC, "Impact of Coronavirus Disease," para. 24–29 at 7–8.

6. Kyleigh Feehs and Alyssa Currier Wheeler, *2020 Federal Human Trafficking Report* (Fairfax, VA: Human Trafficking Institute, 2020), 44–45.

7. Internet Watch Foundation, *Face the Facts: Annual Report 2020*, 41.

8. International Criminal Police Organization (Interpol) and ECPAT, *Towards a Global Indicator on Unidentified Victims in Child Sexual Exploitation Material: Technical Report* (Bangkok: ECPAT International, 2018), 47.

9. Sonia Livingstone et al., *Children's Online Activities, Risks and Safety: A Literature Review by the UKCCIS Evidence Group* (London: LSE Consulting, 2017), 5.

10. Livingstone et al., *Children's Online Activities*, 10–11.

11. UNCRC, "Guidelines Regarding the Implementation of the Optional Protocol to the Convention on the Rights of the Child on the Sale of Children, Child Prostitution and Child Pornography," CRC/C/156, September 10, 2019, para. 57 at 12 (hereafter referred to as OP-CRC-SC Guidelines).

12. UNICEF, *The Sale & Sexual Exploitation of Children: Digital Technology* (UNICEF Office of Research—Innocenti), 4.

13. UNGA, "Protocol to Prevent, Suppress and Punish Trafficking in Persons Especially Women and Children, Supplementing the United Nations Convention against Transnational Organized Crime," entered into force December 25, 2003, U.N.T.S. 2237 (hereafter referred to as the Palermo Protocol).

14. OP-CRC-SC Guidelines, para. 1 at 3.

15. OHCHR, *Human Rights and Human Trafficking: Fact Sheet no. 36* (New York: United Nations, 2014), 8.

Chapter 1

Slavery in the Twenty-First Century

The nature of slavery has varied in different times and places. The present chapter explores how the concept of slavery was defined in international law in the preceding century. A brief overview of the concept's evolution shows that even though the international community of states has condemned slavery, some of the core elements of its practice may be seen in dynamics that still persist in cyberspace. Indeed, I argue that activities around human trafficking connect to de facto slavery and should be condemned. Hence this chapter develops an understanding of slavery as a concept, institution, and exploitation process as it has been conceived in international law and as it operates in cyberspace today by examining the defining elements of the practice throughout history and how it has migrated from a real-world practice to digitally facilitated action in cyberspace. The chapter begins with a look at the historical practice and central themes of the abolition of traditional chattel slavery.

CHATTEL SLAVERY AND ITS ABOLITION: A BRIEF HISTORY

Historically, slavery has been defined by a relationship of ownership. In ancient Egypt, slaves were legally the property of their master. The majority of these slave populations were non-Egyptians acquired in war and subsequently forced to work in Sinaian and Nubian copper and gold mines, to serve nobles, or to fight in the Egyptian army.[1] Egyptian slaveholders had absolute rights over the lives of their slaves: they could grant them freedom or hold them in bondage indefinitely.

On a global scale throughout history, myriad factors have influenced the practice of slavery. Specific economic, political, and climate conditions of different regions played an important role in how specific slavery practices developed. Slavery arguably helped economies flourish. The literature has also identified it as an important source of labor that contributed to the emergence and consolidation of different colonies and cities worldwide.[2] A well-known example is plantation slavery, which existed in the United States, Brazil, other South American states, and the Caribbean. Characteristics of this form of slavery included forced labor, subjugation, and mistreatment of both male and female slaves. Slavery, from a historical perspective, did not discriminate based on sex. Although the use of male slaves was essential for certain types of work, in parts of Africa, female slaves were greater in number and more valuable.[3] In short, chattel slavery as an institution was not based on gender but instead focused on both sexes' internment and bondage to achieve slaveowners' desired ends.

Regarding the slave experience in the Americas, historians have detailed the ways in which American slaveholding societies grew around the institution of slavery. Generally the exploitation of valuable commodities such as gold and sugar depended on a slave class that could mine or harvest the resources for sale to an international market, and slaveholders, motivated to acquire these resources in order to gain societal wealth and power, used slaves to achieve their goal.[4] The economic efficacy of slavery is perhaps best seen in the development of the Mississippi River Valley, which produced more millionaires per capita than anywhere else in the United States.[5] In this manner, slaves became a significant part of the workforce in societies across the American South. Race-based slave practices in the Caribbean led to similar results in other parts of the Americas.

During the centuries of the global slave trade—from the sixteenth through the nineteenth century—ownership as the essential characteristic of the institution of chattel slavery gave slaveholders absolute rights and power over their slaves' lives. Slaveholders considered their slaves to be property, and this resulted in slaves being objects, not subjects, of the law. This absolute ownership—in retrospect, the debasement of slaves' fundamental human rights—has been an essential characteristic of slavery over time and illustrates changing notions of what it means to be human. For instance, during the Roman Empire, "a master could do what he liked with his slave, over whom he had the (theoretically) unrestricted power of life and death."[6] This faculty gave Roman slaveowners the legal power to use their slaves as they saw fit.

New World slavery was marked by a variety of exploitative practices derived from antiquity and by which slaves were considered legal possessions belonging to their master to be bought, sold, or inherited. Across the Americas and as late as the eighteenth century, slaves were commonly seen as less than human.[7] Interestingly, in some cases throughout history, slaveholders implemented systems of reward to motivate slaves' good behavior, sometimes even granting them freedom—although this freedom did not bestow on them the same rights as the majority population. For example, James, who was a slave in Sussex in 1795, was promised his freedom in four years in return for good behavior; however, any "misbehavior" on his part during that time would lead to him getting sold.[8] Importantly, this potential of freedom did not negate the inherent bondage associated with a slave's position but rather promoted the ends of the master.

The Era of Enlightenment and Revolution

Against this backdrop, it becomes important to analyze the conditions that led to the antislavery movement and the eventual end of chattel slavery. These conditions largely arose from the Enlightenment's moral philosophy and empirical science through which individual-based human rights philosophies gained general acceptance.

In the seventeenth century, a theory of rights was developed in part by the natural law philosopher Hugo Grotius, whose thought influenced the Enlightenment's political thought and moral theories and helped to plant the seeds of modern notions of human rights.[9] The notion of human dignity served as the basis for significant natural rights theories, particularly those of Jean-Jacques Rousseau and John Locke, and laid the ground for Immanuel Kant's ethical axioms.[10] The influential Enlightenment English philosopher John Locke asserted that all human beings are equal in dignity and in the natural rights they possess. Hence individual rights to life, liberty, and property emerged as an essential part of his theory.[11]

Jean-Jacques Rousseau, for his part, reflects the idea of dignity in a theoretical framework within republican ideals. Rousseau finds that citizens are members of a state community subordinate to the law as an expression of the general will where the state has the function of safeguarding freedom.[12] Consequently, this social contract governs the relationship between the state and its citizens. Rousseau's political treatise *The Social Contract* was notably influenced by democratic revolutions, nationalist values, and constitutionalist concepts with notions of autonomy and people's sovereignty.

The German philosopher Immanuel Kant contributed considerably to the concept of human rights, basing his moral theory on the inviolability of human dignity.[13] In 1785, Kant argued that one cannot treat human beings as means to other ends and that all persons are rational as ends in themselves.[14] In this way, Kantian philosophy expresses a view of respect of intrinsic freedom and equality as the basis of human treatment. Consequently, human beings have inherent value (i.e., dignity) and they have no price. Thus, human dignity refers to the status of all members of the human family with a clear connection to individual autonomy and reason as a basis for human rights.

Inspired by such Enlightenment ideals, the U.S. Declaration of Independence (1776) and France's Declaration of the Rights of Man and of the Citizen (1789) were both clear proclamations of respect for human dignity and the right to liberty. The Declaration of Independence points out that "all men are created equal" and affirms the existence of "unalienable Rights, that among these are Life, Liberty and the pursuit of Happiness."[15] However, the document refers exclusively to men since women, and certainly slaves and free blacks, would not be seen as equal for another century and a half. Nonetheless, these revolutionary era documents laid the groundwork for greater liberty and, eventually, equal rights for all adults.

The 1789 Declaration of the Rights of Man and of the Citizen embodied the principles of *liberté*, *égalité*, and *fraternité* as a goal. It thus upheld solidarity with others as a foundation for economic, social, and cultural rights (i.e., positive rights). It states that "men are born and remain free and equal in rights," declaring, therefore, that human equality and freedom are fundamental pillars of a democratic society.[16] Specifically, Articles 2 and 3 of the 1789 French declaration clearly state the ideals that the revolutionaries were fighting for: "The aim of every political association is the preservation of the natural and imprescriptible rights of Man. These rights are Liberty, Property, Safety and Resistance to Oppression."[17] The premise, then, that empowered the French to free themselves from the tyranny of a monarchical system of governance was one of civil liberties and related rights. Following this, "the principle of any Sovereignty lies primarily in the Nation. No corporate body, no individual may exercise any authority that does not expressly emanate from it."[18] This concatenation establishes a linkage between the ideas of inherent freedom and intrinsic human rights and the concept of citizenship.

In addition to the Declaration of Independence, the Founding Fathers postulated the importance of the values of liberty and equality in foundational documents such as the Constitution and the Bill of Rights. These revolutionary documents based on Enlightenment moral philosophy embodied modern values that still drive societies around the world toward the improvement of citizens' lives. Throughout the nineteenth and early twentieth centuries, these significant instruments served as the basis for bills of rights and exercised a normative influence on the constitutions of modern states. Nevertheless, slavery was still legal in all thirteen colonies following the ratification of the Declaration of Independence in 1776, and the Constitution in 1788 even included a Fugitive Slave Clause requiring runaway slaves to be returned to their masters.[19] Despite this legality, the Constitution placed limits on the practice of slavery. Article I, section 9, clause 1 of the Constitution effectively banned the importation of all slaves starting in 1808 and levied heavy taxes on slave trafficking from the date of ratification.[20] In this way, these documents, as initially drafted, can be seen as significant progress in the political philosophy and legal recognition of human rights even if they did not end the practice of slavery altogether.

Abolition

The inscription of the ideas of equal rights, antidiscrimination, and freedom for every man in these foundational documents opened the door to broader conceptions of the rights of individuals and eventually demonstrated the need for changes that would lead to greater protection for and guarantees of fundamental human rights, ensuring life and liberty for all individuals.

These movements demonstrated that a strong democracy is the best tool for protecting human rights in modern nations. They helped to further an understanding of citizens' rights based on universalist ideals. Eventually this view of human rights would help launch the antislavery movement in the United States, helping transform people's assumptions regarding the individuality and humanity of slaves and helping American slaves to become citizens and benefit from fundamental freedoms. Seventy years after the end of the revolutionary era in 1854, U.S. senator Abraham Lincoln said in one of his first public condemnations of the institution of slavery,

> But now new light breaks upon us. Now congress declares this ought never to have been; and the like of it, must never be again. The sacred right of self-government is grossly violated by it! . . . This declared indifference [toward the spread of slavery], but as I must think, covert real zeal for the spread of slavery, I cannot but hate. I hate it because of the monstrous injustice of slavery itself. I hate it because it deprives our republican example of its just influence in the world—enables the enemies of free institutions, with plausibility, to taunt us as hypocrites—causes the real friends of freedom to doubt our sincerity, and especially because it forces so many really good men amongst ourselves into an open war with the very fundamental principles of civil liberty—criticizing the Declaration of Independence, and insisting that there is no right principle of action but self-interest.[21]

As president, Abraham Lincoln, who described the institution of slavery as "evil" in its "design,"[22] officially abolished slavery in the United States with his Emancipation Proclamation—an executive order effective January 1, 1863. While only applicable to the eleven Confederate states and the portion of those states not in control of the Union, the Emancipation Proclamation was a milestone in the abolitionist movement. It gave slaves in the Confederacy legal status and the legal ability to join Northern military forces. It proclaimed "that all persons held as slaves" within the rebellious states "are, and henceforward shall be free."[23] Then in 1865, in the aftermath of the Civil War, the Thirteenth Amendment (Amendment XIII) to the Constitution was ratified, explicitly abolishing the institution of slavery.[24] The Fourteenth Amendment (Amendment XIV) made all former slaves into American citizens.[25] This ability of slaves to obtain citizenship status was a significant milestone in the field of human rights as it represented legal and national recognition that everyone is a human being and a citizen and, therefore, entitled to rights and freedoms without discrimination.

KEY INTERNATIONAL LEGAL INSTRUMENTS

The Universal Declaration of Human Rights

In 1948 the Universal Declaration of Human Rights (UDHR), which is regarded as the foundation of international human rights law, was adopted by the United Nations General Assembly (UNGA).[26] According to the UN,

> it represents the universal recognition that basic rights and fundamental freedoms are inherent to all human beings, inalienable and equally applicable to everyone, and that every one of us is born free and equal in dignity and rights. Whatever our nationality, place of residence, gender, national or ethnic origin, color, religion, language, or any other status, the international community on December 10, 1948, made a commitment to upholding dignity and justice for all of us.[27]

This formal and programmatic document is "a common standard of achievement for all peoples and all nations" that recognizes the universality of human dignity and the inalienable human rights of every human being. The UDHR as a UNGA resolution (A/RES/217 [III]) is by itself not legally binding but many of its provisions reflect customary international law.[28] This clear message on human rights protections extends to all human beings and thus to all children in every society worldwide. This living document makes explicit reference to children, particularly with mothers, and children's entitlement to "special care and assistance" and "social protection."[29]

In a single document, the UDHR encapsulates the ordinary people's highest aspiration and promotes the spirit of democracy and the rule of law. For example, Article 1 asserts that "all human beings are born free and equal in dignity and rights." Moreover, Article 4 establishes the principle that "no one shall be held in slavery or servitude; slavery and the slave trade shall be prohibited in all their forms."[30] The UDHR thus upholds the inviolability of the inherent dignity and intrinsic inalienability of human rights connected to protecting all individuals' personal integrity and freedom from acts of domination and degradation that directly attack their dignity.[31] At the same time, the UDHR's idea of the universality of human rights in connection with a provision that proclaims freedom from slavery is a direct reaffirmation of equal protection of the law. It recognizes previous, relevant, international instruments that prohibit all forms of slavery and, consequently, calls on governments to eliminate such practices as they are no longer tolerable in the world.[32]

The historical context of the creation of the UDHR clarifies its significance in the history of human rights. After World War II, the Allies created the United Nations because they had "called themselves the 'United Nations' during the war," and they decided to draw up an international bill of rights.[33] Subsequently the Economic and Social Council (ECOSOC) charged the Commission on Human Rights (CHR), chaired by Eleanor Roosevelt, with preparing a draft international bill of rights without specifying any particular terms of reference, nor did the UN charter set any specific direction for the draft. Considering the positions of representative nations at that time, drafting a declaration, a convention, and implementation measures was the preferred strategy.[34] The planned convention was divided into two covenants, known today as the International Covenant on Civil and Political Rights (ICCPR)[35] and the International Covenant on Economic, Social and Cultural Rights (ICESCR).[36] The draft declaration was the work of an eight-member committee established by the CHR and consisting of experts and distinguished scholars from countries worldwide.[37] During this legislative UN process, the drafting committee considered suggestions and proposals from various UN bodies and states. The committee subsequently produced a document that reflects many people's contributions, particularly the remarkable work of Canadian international lawyer John P. Humphrey and French law professor René Cassin.[38] The CHR received comments from UN members during the drafting process. Upon the document's completion, the ECOSOC and the General Assembly Third Committee reviewed it before presenting it to the UNGA. It passed on December 10, 1948.

The declaration identified a catalog of human rights and fundamental freedoms that was later codified in the ICCPR and ICESCR to make the instrument enforceable by member states.[39] Accordingly, the ICCPR focuses on rights that may express the need for immediate enforceability of action on behalf of the state (e.g., right to life, equality before the law, freedom of speech, assembly, and association). Additionally, the ICESCR focuses on rights that may have a progressive realization according to each state's maximum available resources (e.g., the right to work, social security, and education).[40] Together these two legally binding agreements, adopted in 1966 and entered into force in 1976, address most of the rights enshrined in the UDHR. Today both covenants and the UDHR together constitute the International Bill of Human Rights, which is the nucleus of international human rights law and provides comprehensive human rights protection.

Although the UDHR did not define the term "human dignity," it is based on the principle of the human person's inherent worth—as was evident during the drafting process in 1946 and 1948 and subsequent adoption in 1948.[41] Moreover, explicit invocations of human dignity are included in the ICCPR[42] and the ICESCR[43] and, therefore, maintain a commitment to equal rights for all individuals, including children.[44] The parameter of human dignity as the basis of all human rights recognizes that there are fundamental rights that are inalienable and universal; that is, they are intrinsic to all human beings.[45] These rights are embedded in natural rights thoughts, ethical traditions,[46] and eighteenth-century philosophies[47] as well as the development of international human rights law.[48] In this sense, Enlightenment thinking derived from natural law principles (i.e., *jus naturale*) consolidated the idea that human dignity is inviolable and recognized the intrinsic freedom and equality of human beings. In a fundamental sense, these precepts of natural law acknowledge that each person is worthy of respect as everyone is free and possesses the same basic rights. This idea served as an essential starting point in the shaping of the evolution of the contemporary understanding of human rights, including the UDHR.[49]

At the same time, the UDHR was a clear rejection of the atrocities committed during World War II. It thus assists in upholding each person's dignity and equality in the formulation of normative concepts and human rights standards. Today the UDHR is at the heart of UN activity and reflects the general recognition that the law must rest upon a respect for human rights.[50] The positive law of many Western countries has progressively recognized individual human rights listed in the UDHR.[51]

Eleanor Roosevelt referred to the UDHR as an international Magna Carta for all humanity.[52] The UDHR represents globally accepted standards in the community of nations for the benefit of all human beings. Since its inception it has been considered the foundational pillar of the contemporary human rights movement. Its adoption represented a crucial moment in the development of human rights and promoted respect for the human person's equal worth. Hence, human dignity became the foundational principle in the new international legal order created after World War II.[53] The UDHR is a living instrument that serves as a standard of reference for every human rights document and related treaty.[54] Today this monumental declaration is influential in establishing the concept of rights instantiated at the domestic level.

International Covenant on Civil and Political Rights

The prohibition of slavery or servitude in Article 4 of the UDHR is adopted in the ICCPR in Article 8(1) and (2). The provisions declare that "no one shall be held in slavery; slavery and the slave trade in all their forms shall be prohibited," and "no one shall be held in servitude." States parties have the legal obligation to protect all individuals, without distinction, against slavery and servitude practices. Although this legally binding international human rights treaty did not define the terms "slavery" and "servitude," the interpretation of a treaty is "in accordance with the ordinary meaning to be given to the terms of the treaty in their context and in the light of its object and purpose" according to Article 31 of the Vienna Convention on the Law of Treaties (VCLT), which sets the basic rules of interpretation of treaties between states.[55] The meaning of these terms may thus be taken as defined in legal instruments such as the definition of slavery established in the 1926 Slavery Convention and the concept of "institutions and practices similar to slavery" established in the 1956 Supplementary Slavery Convention, which refers to servile status.[56] Moreover, according to the treaty's *travaux prépara-toires* (preparatory works), the drafters drew a distinction between slavery and servitude as two fundamentally different concepts. For this reason the drafters addressed these ideas in two different paragraphs.[57] The drafters pointed out that while slavery implies the destruction of a human being's juridical personality, servitude covers "all conceivable forms of dominance and degradation of human beings by human beings."[58] Furthermore, they rejected a French suggestion to substitute "trade in human beings" for "slave trade" based on the reasoning that an international ban on slavery and slave trade should be narrowly interpreted.[59] At the same time, the Human Rights Committee (HRCttee; i.e., the monitoring body for the implementation of the ICCPR and its optional protocols by states parties) in General Comment no. 28 is of the opinion that states parties are required under Article 8 to provide information to the HRCttee on "measures taken to eliminate trafficking of women and children within the country or across borders and forced prostitu-tion."[60] In this regard, for example, the HRCttee expressed concerns on the need for the state to ensure positive measures to prevent and combat such practices in particular against children concerning Articles 8 and 24 in its concluding observations of Portugal in 2020, stating that

> while noting the efforts made by the state Party to curb trafficking in persons, the Committee remains concerned by the low level of reporting about such crimes, as well as the low rate of prosecutions and convictions. It is concerned about the lack of an adequate identification mechanism for victims of trafficking in persons in the asylum procedures, including with respect to children.[61]

The need for states to ensure positive measures to curb human trafficking, protect children against all forms of exploitation, and strengthen the overall child protection system relate to some ICCPR provisions. Such practices may violate and impair other fundamental human rights (e.g., Article 3 on equal enjoyment of the rights of all citizens in compliance with the covenant, Article 6 on the right to life, Article 7 on the right not to be subjected to torture or ill treatment, and Article 24 on protection for minors).[62]

Children's Rights

The Babylonian Codex Hammurabi (Code of Hammurabi), which dates to approximately 1780 BCE, represents a historical reference for children's position in the law. This early codification established fundamental rules for the Babylonian people and for the welfare of all classes of society, including women, children, slaves, and the king.[63] In this regard, the Code of Hammurabi refers to subjects related to protecting children and parents' responsibilities toward them.[64]

Moreover, one can see the vulnerability of children in abuse and exploitation situations in Joseph's story, in the biblical book of Genesis. Joseph was sold at the age of seventeen[65] by his brothers to the Ishmaelites[66] for twenty pieces of silver.[67] They took him to Egypt and later sold him to Potiphar, one of Pharaoh's officials who was the guard's captain,[68] and ultimately into servitude (between approximately 2000 and 1800 BCE).[69] Subsequently, in the Roman family law context, the father, the person who provided for the *patria potestas*, exercised absolute power (i.e., *jus vitae necisque*) over the child.[70] Moreover, according to Justinianus laws, an infant, referring to a person under seven years of age, was one *qui fari non potest*, meaning that the law did not allow the child to speak as they were not yet old enough.[71] These provisions demonstrate that in certain historical periods, children were not subjects of rights.

The 1924 Geneva Declaration on the Rights of the Child and the 1959 UN Declaration on the Rights of the Child

In 1924 the League of Nations (LoN)—a precursor to the UN—adopted the Geneva Declaration on the Rights of the Child (i.e., the Declaration of Geneva). In adopting this instrument, the LoN recognized that "mankind owes children the best that it has to give." This moral statement was aligned with a time when many children were still suffering from the aftermath of World War I in Europe and it still applies today.[72] The declaration was historic since it was the first instrument to recognize specific rights of children in the international context. It stated that all people owe children the right to means "for their development; special help in times of need; priority for relief; economic freedom and protection from exploitation; and an upbringing that instills social consciousness and duty."[73] Then in 1959, the UNGA adopted the Declaration on the Rights of the Child, explicitly referring to the UDHR and the dignity and worth of the human person but focusing on child welfare.[74] The 1959 declaration established the principle that "the best interests of the child shall be the paramount consideration" in enacting laws concerning children.[75] In addition, it proclaimed children's rights to education, adequate nutrition, play and recreation, social services, and a supportive environment.[76] Consequently, the 1959 declaration promoted each child's enjoyment of rights and protection against all forms of neglect, cruelty, and exploitation, and it made an explicit reference to the word "traffic."[77] Although this declaration was nonbinding on states, it represented a clear consensus among them on the core principles of children's rights.

A Specified Core Human Rights Instrument for Children: The Convention on the Rights of the Child

The ICCPR[78] and ICESCR[79] reference children, and children are thus beneficiaries of the rights in such instruments. Nonetheless, the adoption of the 1989 UNCRC—which entered into force September 2, 1990—marks a milestone in the concept of the child as a rights holder.[80] In a specific, international legally binding convention, the UNCRC mandates to states parties the full protection of all children without distinction of any kind within their jurisdictions.[81] Therefore, the UNCRC strongly influenced governments—often indebted to notions of traditional Roman law—to promote and safeguard the rights and human dignity of children by explicitly recognizing them as autonomous holders of fundamental rights and freedoms rather than as vulnerable beings in need of protection at their parents' discretion.

This new instrument's landmark contribution was investing children with inalienable and indivisible rights founded on the dignity and worth of the child's human person.[82] More specifically, it forbid violence, abuse, and all forms of exploitation, including economic and sexual exploitation.[83] For example, Article 34 of the UNCRC sets forth states parties' obligation to integrate all appropriate measures into their domestic legal systems to prevent children from being induced or coerced to engage in unlawful sexual activity.[84] In addition, the UNCRC includes, in particular, states parties' legal obligation to take measures to protect children from use in prostitution and other unlawful sexual practices and in pornographic performances and materials.[85] Read in conjunction with Article 35, this establishes a clear mandate to states parties to develop and enforce measures to protect children against sexual exploitation and prohibit the sale or trafficking of children for any aim or in any practice.[86]

The convention does not explicitly define the term "child exploitation." However, the Committee on the Rights of the Child (CRC; a body that monitors states parties' implementation of the UNCRC and its optional protocols) in its authoritative opinions regarding the content of the provisions therein affirms that sexual abuse and exploitation include the inducement or coercion of a child into unlawful or psychologically harmful sexual practices, the use of a child to engage in commercial sexual activity, use of a child in abuse-related audio or visual images, and sexual slavery, trafficking, sale for sexual purposes, and early or forced marriage.[87] States' obligations also align with Article 19 of the UNCRC, which mandates that states parties take action to protect children from "all forms of physical or mental violence, injury or abuse, neglect or negligent treatment, maltreatment or exploitation, including sexual abuse."[88] Therefore, states are obliged to prevent all forms of violence including emerging sexual practices associated with psychological harm in cyberspace.

The UNCRC is also essential in its provision of a definition of "child." According to Article 1, "a child means every human being below the age of 18 years unless under the law applicable to the child, majority is attained earlier."[89] Therefore, childhood ends when a person reaches eighteen years of age unless the age of majority in relevant domestic legislation is different. Under the state law applicable to the child, once a child reaches the age of majority, he or she can freely consent to sexual activity or marriage.[90] In this respect, the CRC has set clear recommendations for states on an age threshold when referring to children (i.e., under eighteen years), thus ensuring that all children up to that age enjoy all the rights that the convention enshrines. This definition is also consistent with the term "child" referred to in other international legal instruments, including the 1956 Supplementary Slavery Convention, the ILO Worst Forms of Child Labour Convention 1999 (No. 182), and the Palermo Protocol. Together they provide the basis for a holistic response to trafficking minors. States parties to these binding agreements have a legal obligation to ensure appropriate measures for protecting child victims of trafficking and exploitation, including sexual exploitation, regardless of whether the victims have reached the age of majority in their domestic legal systems.[91]

Pursuant to the UNCRC, states parties must fully respect and act by the principle of the child's best interests. The convention relies on this premise throughout for realizing children's rights in all actions concerning them.[92] More specifically, when a state party's national legislation establishes a legal age of consent for sexual activity of children under eighteen, it is still required to apply the general principles of the convention: the right to nondiscrimination of any kind toward children (Article 2), the best interests of the child (Article 3[1]), evolving capacities (Article 5), the right to life, survival, and development (Article 6), and the right to be heard (Article 12). These are ultimately essential for each child's growth and well-being. Therefore, the state's duty to ensure the child's best interests is of particular relevance in protecting children in all settings, including cyberspace.[93] This mandate requires that states parties apply these provisions to all children, implying that all trafficked children have the right to receive complete protection to cover all their needs. Therefore, states cannot treat child victims as criminals for exploitative acts committed against themselves. They are entitled to the right to protection to ensure their immediate and long-term safety and well-being.[94] States should ensure that national policies and legislation that may impact children's rights, including those regarding cyberspace, make the principle of the child's best interests a primary consideration.

In summary, children enjoy special protection under international law. The UNCRC recognizes children as holders of rights and provides a comprehensive framework for protecting such rights and as well with reference to trafficking and sexual exploitation. Almost all countries have ratified the UNCRC, which has 196 current states parties.[95] It thus represents a global consensus and a clear international commitment to harmonizing national laws and policies toward the full realization of every child's right. Ultimately worldwide implementation of the children's rights outlined in the UNCRC requires each nation's effective incorporation at domestic levels to advance its provisions from theory to realizing every child's rights in practice.

Optional Protocol to the Convention on the Rights of the Child on the Sale of Children, Child Prostitution, and Child Pornography

Normative developments in the protection of children's rights occurred in 2000 with the adoption of two optional protocols to the UNCRC by the UNGA—one regarding the sale of children, child prostitution, and child pornography,[96] and the other regarding the involvement of children in armed conflict.[97] They entered into force in 2002 and strengthened the UNCRC with a common and more specific obligation for nations to respond to these increasingly common violations of children's rights and dignity. For present purposes, the UNCRC Optional Protocol on the Sale of Children, Child Prostitution, and Child Pornography is particularly relevant as it focuses on the prohibition and criminalization of such offenses.[98] Therefore, the UNCRC Optional Protocol covers crimes beyond the sphere of trafficking in children. Although this treaty only addresses the word "trafficking" in its preamble,[99] the CRC has recognized that although the "sale of children" and "trafficking of children" are not the same, they may overlap.[100] "Sale of children" is any act or transaction whereby any person or group transfers a minor to another for payment or any other compensation.[101] "Sale of children" implies at least one party who offers or delivers a child and another who accepts or receives that child in a transaction where there may be a financial or another kind of benefit. The committee notes that while the sale of children requires some form of commercial exchange, children can become victims of trafficking by deception or force and without a form of commercial transaction necessarily taking place. In addition, trafficking in children involves exploitation while the sale of children does not have an exploitative nature per se.[102] Hence in the context of the sale of children for sexual exploitation, the 176 current states parties to the Optional Protocol must establish a legal basis at the national level for prohibiting the acts of "offering" or "delivering" a child for sexual exploitation and of "accepting," by whatever means, a child for such purposes.[103] In this respect, the committee has expressed concern for the child's vulnerability to being sold and trafficked for prostitution and sexual exploitation. The committee has also stressed that states must strengthen measures to address the root causes of the offenses that the OP-CRC-SC covers and to reduce consumer demand for sexual acts with children.[104]

Moreover, the CRC has emphasized that under the OP-CRC-SC, states parties should not penalize children younger than eighteen for sexual offenses committed against them as they cannot consent to exploitative or abusive sexual acts.[105] The committee, therefore, calls on states to review existing national legislation (and adjust it if needed) and to investigate, prosecute, and sanction all perpetrators of such offenses, including prosecuting perpetrators who sexually exploit or buy and sell children as a commodity via digital environments.[106] In light of this, the CRC explicitly recognizes the evolving nature of the offenses covered by the OP-CRC-SC, taking into account technological advancements that enable new means of violating the child's rights. The committee recommends that states ensure their legal and policy responses are adaptable to rapidly changing realities, including legislative measures of protection, to ensure child victims have access to redress, safe counseling, and mechanisms to report incidents.[107]

INTERNATIONAL PROHIBITIONS

This section examines key instruments of international law and court cases to trace the evolution of the legal definition of slavery. It explores how current cybertrafficking practices with the aim of exploitation that threaten human dignity represent a contemporary manifestation of slavery. The appropriate context for understanding that manifestation is the history of legally protected human rights.

The Universal Character of the Prohibition of Slavery

In customary international law, states' practices and their consent evidence that the prohibition of slavery is an obligation *erga omnes*. Therefore, all states must follow this norm, and all states have a legal interest in its protection.[108] Furthermore, this rule is a peremptory norm of general international law (i.e., *jus cogens*). The peremptory nature of this fundamental right, or *jus cogens*, means that it is a norm

> accepted and recognized by the international community of states as a whole as a norm from which no derogation is permitted and which can be modified only by a subsequent norm of general international law having the same character.[109]

Hence belonging to this category, this human-rights norm enjoys the highest international law status. Therefore, this rule prevails over any other ordinary treaty provision or regular customary norm. Although there is not a consensus regarding the definition of the customary norms that qualify as *jus cogens*, generally accepted peremptory norms of international law that bring into existence an obligation *erga omnes* are as follows:[110]

> The prohibition of aggression, the prohibition of genocide, the prohibition of crimes against humanity, the basic rules of international humanitarian law, the prohibition of racial discrimination and apartheid, the prohibition of slavery, and the prohibition of torture, and the right of self-determination.[111]

In this way, the prohibition of slavery has a universal character. It serves as both a human rights protection and a state's obligation to take positive measures to enforce such a ban. States must respect this norm at all times: both in normal times and in times of public emergency.

For example, the nonderogable nature of this human rights norm is ensured in treaty form in the ICCPR so states cannot derogate this right even during a state of emergency.[112] The ICCPR permits states parties to exercise their power for derogation of certain rights enshrined in the convention temporarily and exceptionally in emergencies. Specifically, Article 4 allows governments to take measures for derogation "in time of public emergency which threatens the life of the nation." According to the article, states can do so to the extent strictly required by the exigencies of the situation and provided that such measures do not involve discrimination solely on the grounds of race, color, sex, language, religion, or social origin.[113] In this sense, according to the principle of legality and the rule of law, a government of any state party that declares a state of emergency has special temporary powers that allow for the unilateral enactment of a derogative measure of a formally contracted obligation under the covenant. The HRCttee in its authoritative commentaries regarding Article 4 notes that when a state proclaims a state of emergency it has the option of restricting certain covenant rights strictly necessary to remove the event and restore stability (i.e., a proportionality principle).

However in Article 4, paragraph 2, the convention explicitly excepts certain rights from such derogations even in times of emergency including the right of persons to be free from slavery, the slave trade, and servitude.[114] A state party cannot lawfully restrict these provisions under any circumstances. States parties must ensure the protection of personal freedom from both slavery and servitude as compatible with the object and purpose of the treaty and other human rights obligations of states under international law.[115]

A Brief Introduction to Multilateral Legal Agreements

1904 International Agreement for the Suppression of the White Slave Traffic

This international agreement adopted in 1904 was an early response in connection to the criminalization of trafficking acts that was intended to condemn the "criminal traffic" of women and girls procured for immoral purposes abroad.[116] Specifically, it mandates the contracting states to keep watch in places such as railway stations and ports of embarkation and instructs authorities to attain all information possible to lead to discovery of criminal human trafficking.[117] The agreement used the term "white slavery" to refer to the recruitment of females across borders for exploitation in prostitution. Its preamble illustrates this point in that representatives of states parties expressed a desire to secure adequate protection against criminal trafficking for women and girls subject to deception or control.

1910 International Convention for the Suppression of the White Slave Traffic

In 1910 this early agreement regarding white slavery obliged states to punish "whoever, in order to gratify the passions of another person, has procured, enticed, or led away, even with her consent, a woman or girl under age, for immoral purposes," so that the consent of a woman or underaged girl (referring to women and girls under twenty completed years of age) victim seems to be irrelevant in such acts. Moreover, concerning women over twenty completed years of age, there is a requirement of prohibited means of "fraud, violence, threats, abuse of authority, or any other method of compulsion" to procure, entice, or lead away that woman for immoral purposes. In both provisions, perpetrators could be liable even if they committed the acts abroad.[118] However the drafters considered this criterion to be a minimum standard for protection. They consequently gave states the option to punish other actions such as the procurement of women or girls even if the victim consented as such individuals suffered from being "in effect delivered over to an immoral life."[119] These normative provisions bear a resemblance to the legal definition of trafficking in persons established in the Palermo Protocol.[120]

1921 International Convention for the Suppression of the Traffic in Women and Children

To advance the efforts of previous legal agreements (i.e., in 1904 and 1910), the LoN concluded and adopted an international agreement in 1921. The 1921 convention encouraged states to ratify the previous instruments if they were not already a party. However, it recognized "the traffic in children of both sexes" in Article 2. In addition, Article 5 elevated the age limit for protection to "21 completed years of age."[121] Although the 1921 convention did not define the term "traffic," it was mainly concerned with the movement of women and children abroad for exploitation in prostitution. Article 7 requires states to take measures relating to "the protection of women and children traveling on emigrant ships, not only at the points of departure and arrival but also during the journey." Additionally this normative provision obliges states to post notices in railway stations and ports warning women and children of the danger of trafficking and providing information on places where they might find accommodation and assistance.

1926 Slavery Convention

Freedom from chattel slavery was among the first rights to receive recognition under public international law, with slavery and the slave trade outlawed beginning in the early nineteenth century.[122] The 1926 Slavery Convention, however, under the auspices of the LoN, articulated a legal definition of slavery: "the status or condition of a person over whom any or all of the powers attaching to the right of ownership are exercised."[123] Therefore, the exercise of one or more powers of ownership is a fundamental part of the definition of slavery. Although the Slavery Convention did not define the "powers attached to the right of ownership," it seems that the drafters intended to refer to the attributes of the authority of the master over the slave—the concept of the *dominica potestas* in Roman law.[124] According to a 1953 report by the UN secretary-general (UNSG), characteristics of the various powers attaching to the right of ownership over a person are

1. The individual . . . may be made the object of a purchase.
2. The master may use the individual . . . and in particular his capacity to work, in an absolute manner.
3. The products of labor of the individual . . . become the property of the master without any compensation commensurate to the value of the labor.
4. The ownership of the individual . . . can be transferred to another person.

5. The servile status is permanent, that is to say, it cannot be terminated by the will of the individual subject to it.
6. The . . . status is transmitted *ipso facto* to descendants of the individual having such status.[125]

Therefore, considering these elements and the definition of slavery as a "status or condition," the parameters of slavery extend beyond the legal right to ownership (i.e., slavery de jure [status]). Slavery also encompasses situations in which an individual exercises one or more powers attaching to the right of ownership over another person (i.e., slavery de facto [condition]). Consequently the attributes of the original concept of slavery remain applicable today.[126]

The 1926 definition of slavery is also replicated in international criminal law in the 1998 Rome Statute of the International Criminal Court (ICC), which identifies enslavement as a crime against humanity "when committed as part of a widespread or systematic attack directed against any civilian population, with knowledge of the attack" (Art. 7[1]c). The ICC defines enslavement in the same terms as the 1926 Slavery Convention: "in the course of trafficking in persons, in particular women and children" (Art. 7[2]c). The reference to the 1926 definition of slavery in this provision may illustrate that the traditional concept of slavery has evolved to include de facto situations where an individual directly attacks the essence of another person's human dignity.[127]

1933 International Convention for the Suppression of the Traffic in Women of Full Age

Under the auspices of the LoN, this 1933 convention aimed to "secure more completely the suppression of the traffic in women and children."[128] Per Article 1 of this convention, states could punish "attempted offences, and, within the legal limits, acts preparatory to the offences in question." Furthermore, the term "country" broadly included the colonies and protectorates of states parties as well as territories where they exercised a mandate.[129] This interpretation of the term may indicate states' recognition that female prostitution was widespread across borders and required international regulation, including cross-border cooperation. Moreover, this agreement expanded the principle of the irrelevancy of consent of women and girls of full age.[130]

1949 Convention for the Suppression of the Traffic in Persons and on the Exploitation of the Prostitution of Others

This convention affirms in its preamble that "prostitution and the accompanying evil of the traffic in persons . . . are incompatible with the dignity and worth of the human person." It also notes that trafficking is a danger to "the welfare of the individual, the family and the community." Under these premises and taking into account previous international legal instruments, this agreement obliges states parties to punish an individual who

1. Procures, entices or leads away, for purposes of prostitution, another person, even with the consent of that person.
2. Exploits the prostitution of another person, even with the consent of that person.[131]

These normative provisions pertain to both women and men and confirm the irrelevance of the victim's consent to such practices. Additionally, these legislative measures deal with aspects related to the process of trafficking (e.g., procurement, enticement, or leading away) and the purpose of the offense (e.g., trafficking for prostitution). The innovative approach of the 1949 convention is evident in Article 2, which mandates that states parties punish any person who

1. Keeps or manages or knowingly finances or takes part in the financing of a brothel.
2. Knowingly lets or rents a building or other place or any part thereof for the purpose of the prostitution of others.[132]

Thus, the 1949 convention extends its scope to brothels[133] and seems to adopt an abolitionist approach to prostitution.[134] However, Article 16 mandates that states parties take measures "for the prevention of prostitution and for the rehabilitation and social adjustment of the victims of prostitution."[135] Therefore, it appears to seek a consensus between states in favor of outlawing prostitution and those in favor of regulating it for the sake of broad ratification of the treaty. However, as of today, this treaty only has eighty-two states parties, indicating its potentially problematic nature.[136] Moreover, the adoption of a new treaty[137] on the same subject matter of trafficking may be relevant to imply states' consent on the applicability of that subsequent instrument.[138]

1956 Supplementary Convention on the Abolition of Slavery, the Slave Trade, and Institutions and Practices Similar to Slavery

This treaty, known as the 1956 Supplementary Slavery Convention, extended the application of the law to institutions and practices held to be *similar to slavery*,[139] specifically debt bondage, serfdom, specific types of servile marriage, and the exploitation of children.[140] Thus, states parties of the 1956 Supplementary Slavery Convention are mandated to abolish these institutions or practices whether or not an ownership power is exercised as established in the definition of slavery from the 1926 Slavery Convention. The 1956 Supplementary Slavery Convention adopted the same definition of slavery as the 1926 Slavery Convention but added the new concept of "a person of servile status." The convention goes beyond previous legal constructions by also defining the term "slave":

> "Slavery" means, as defined in the Slavery Convention of 1926, the status or condition of a person over whom any or all of the powers attaching to the right of ownership are exercised, and "slave" means a person in such condition or status.[141]

Furthermore, Article 7(b) defines "a person of servile status" as "a person in the condition or status resulting from any of the institutions or practices mentioned in Article 1 of this Convention."[142] According to this article, a person can be a victim of slavery (i.e., a slave) or a victim of any of the institutions and practices referred to and become "slave-like" (a person of servile status).[143] These are generally seen as two separate concepts; servitude is more general than slavery, which is "the worst form of bondage"[144] whereby the victim is treated as an object of another person. Servitude covers, for instance, the obligation of the serf to provide labor services and subject to exploitation with the impossibility of changing their condition.[145] It is not possible for any person to contract themselves into any form of bondage (either slavery or servitude).[146]

Protocol to Prevent, Suppress, and Punish Trafficking in Persons, Especially Women and Children, Supplementing the UN Convention against Transnational Organized Crime

This instrument, known as the Palermo Protocol, was adopted by the UNGA in 2000 as part of the UN Convention against Transnational Organized Crime (UNTOC). The protocol entered into force December 25, 2003. As of June 2021 it has been ratified by 178 states.[147] The Palermo Protocol is the international cornerstone that addresses the problem of human trafficking.

States parties must incorporate the treaty provisions into national legislation to effectively prevent and penalize trafficking offenses and protect and assist victims.[148] The Palermo Protocol also promotes cooperation among countries in a comprehensive criminal justice response to human trafficking while building a framework for international action.[149] Indeed, the connection between trafficking in persons and slavery is confirmed in the widely accepted definition of "trafficking" from the Palermo Protocol of 2000, which makes reference to the term "slavery."[150] (This is discussed in detail in chapter 2.)

HUMAN TRAFFICKING AS MODERN-DAY SLAVERY AS ESTABLISHED IN KEY CASES

International Criminal Law: International Criminal Tribunal for the Former Yugoslavia (*Prosecutor v. Kunarac, Vukovic, and Kovac*)

The legal line of interpretation where there is a clear link between trafficking and slavery and where there is not necessarily a "right of ownership" but "presence of one or more of the powers attached to such a right" over a person was recognized by the International Criminal Tribunal for the former Yugoslavia (ICTY) in a precedent-setting case in 2001. Dealing with atrocities in former Yugoslavia, the trial chamber set a jurisprudential precedent in *Prosecutor v. Kunarac, Vukovic, and Kovac* (2001; *Kunarac et al.* henceforth), a case of great importance as it established, inter alia, a conviction of enslavement as a crime against humanity for sexual exploitation.[151] The trial chamber defined this evolved traditional concept of slavery, often referred to as "chattel slavery," as including various contemporary forms of slavery where perpetrators do not hold victims as slaves in the traditional sense. However, victims are considered slaves if subjected to the exercise of any or all of the powers attached to such a right (i.e., ownership).

In this case, Dragoljub Kunarac, a Bosnian Serb commander of a reconnaissance unit, and two other Serb soldiers were held responsible for and convicted of the torture, rape, and enslavement of Bosnian Muslim women and girls in the area of Foča.[152] In a significant development of case law, the trial chamber outlined specific factors (i.e., indicia) that one must consider for determining whether a particular phenomenon constitutes enslavement. They include

> the control of someone's movement, control of physical environment, psychological control, measures taken to prevent or deter escape, force, threat of force or coercion, duration, assertion of exclusivity, subjection to cruel treatment and abuse, control of sexuality, and forced labor.[153]

The trial chamber clarified that the *mere ability* to enforce any of these factors is insufficient as the actual occurrence of any of these actions is necessary to determine whether someone experienced enslavement.[154] Hence the trial chamber interpreted the classic paradigm of slavery (linked to the right of legal ownership) to include a variety of contemporary forms of slavery encompassing subtle forms of coercion where an individual exercises one or more powers attached to the right of ownership. Furthermore, under this broader definition, a victim's consent is rendered impossible or irrelevant due to the influence of factors such as "the threat or use of force or coercion, the fear of violence, deception or false promises, the abuse of power, the victim's position of vulnerability, detention or captivity, or psychological oppression."[155] The judgment recognized that not all powers attaching to the right of ownership need be exercised; any single one is sufficient for committing the crime.

Key to my argument in this book is that under this evolved meaning of the concept of slavery in international law, elements of control and ownership are nuanced. These conditions leave room for current human trafficking situations where traffickers hold victims under their absolute and effective control through means such as force, fraud, deception, or coercion for exploitation. Thus, this interpretation of slavery establishes the grounds to properly designate human trafficking as modern-day slavery.[156] Consider some of the details of *Kunarac et al.* where the trial chamber found the following facts to be proven beyond reasonable doubt:

> The Trial Chamber . . . accepts that the witnesses were not free to go where they wanted to, even if, as [Witness] FWS-191 admitted, they were given the keys to the house at some point. . . . The girls, as described by FWS-191, had nowhere to go, and had no place to hide from Dragoljub Kunarac and [the soldier with the pseudonym] DP 6, even if they had attempted to leave the house. . . . Kunarac and DP 6 . . . were fully aware of this fact. (para. 740)

> The Trial Chamber is satisfied that FWS-191 and [Witness] FWS-186 were denied any control over their lives by Dragoljub Kunarac and DP 6 during their stay there. They had to obey all orders, they had to do household chores, and they had no realistic option whatsoever to flee the house in [the village of] Trnova or to escape their assailants. They were subjected to other mistreatments, such as Kunarac inviting a soldier into the house so that he could rape FWS191 for 100 Deutschmark if he so wished. On another occasion, Kunarac tried to rape FWS-191 while in his hospital bed, in front of other soldiers. The two women were treated as the personal property of Kunarac and DP 6. The Trial Chamber is satisfied that Kunarac established these living conditions for the victims in concert with DP 6. Both men personally committed the act of enslavement.[157] (para. 742)

Among other forms of mistreatment, women victims were held in coercive detention, subjected to conditions of forced labor, including cooking and cleaning, and raped. The trial chamber concluded that enslavement as a crime against humanity in customary international law involves the "exercise of any or all of the powers attaching to the right of ownership over a person."[158] Furthermore, the "*actus reus* [i.e., the material element] of the violation is the exercise of any or all of the powers attaching to the right of ownership over a person" while "the *mens rea* [i.e., the mental element] of the violation consists in the intentional exercise of such powers."[159] The trial chamber recognized that contemporary practices of slavery had made their way throughout the world, exercising one or more powers attached to ownership over their victims (i.e., modern slaves) and enshrining elements of exploitation and evidence of perpetrators' absolute control over them.

The accused appealed, inter alia, because the victims "had freedom of movement within and outside the apartment and could therefore have escaped or attempted to change their situation" and "the victims were not forced to do household chores but undertook them willingly."[160] However the court confirmed *Kunarac et al.* on appeal. The appeals chamber pronounced and endorsed the trial chamber's chief thesis, asserting that

> the traditional concept of slavery, as defined in the 1926 Slavery Convention and often referred to as "chattel slavery," has evolved to encompass various contemporary forms of slavery, which are also based on the exercise of any or all of the powers attaching to the right of ownership.[161]

Contemporary forms of slavery were described by the appeals chamber as follows: "In all cases, as a result of the exercise of any or all of the powers attaching to the right of ownership, there is some destruction of the juridical personality."[162] The appeals chamber confirmed that it was not possible to determine in advance all cases that would meet this expanded redefinition as it would depend on the operation of the factors or *indicia* of slavery identified by the trial chamber.[163] Therefore, it was not necessary that victims be in persistent physical confinement from the outside world to be considered subject to a contemporary form of slavery as these situations were assessed on the basis of various indicia of slavery. All cases, though, involved the exercise by the perpetrator of any or all of the powers attaching to the right of ownership over someone thus adhering to the core definitional elements of the 1926 Slavery Convention.

Regional Human Rights Law: European Court of Human Rights (*Rantsev v. Cyprus and Russia* and *Siliadin v. France*)

This evolved interpretation of enslavement defined by the ICTY found confirmation in human rights law by the European Court of Human Rights (ECtHR) in *Rantsev v. Cyprus and Russia* (2010). This significant case dealt with trafficking in persons for the purpose of exploitation by prostitution. As an antecedent of this landmark judgment, the applicant, a Russian national, brought a complaint against the Republic of Cyprus and Russia in the ECtHR for the death of his twenty-year-old daughter Oxana Rantsev.[164] The ECtHR ruled with regard to member states' positive obligations to combat the crime of human trafficking in general and in individual cases arising under Article 4 of the convention.[165] Notably the ECtHR highlighted that in the context of trafficking in human beings, criminal investigations and prosecutions constituted only one aspect of member states' general duties to combat the phenomenon. The court explained that member states also must implement operational measures to protect victims or potential victims in situations where "the state authorities [are] aware, or ought to [be] aware, of circumstances giving rise to a credible suspicion that an identified individual [has] been, or [is] at real and immediate risk of being, trafficked or exploited"[166] as in the *Rantsev* case.

With regard to states' duties to effectively investigate potential trafficking situations, the ECtHR observed that this obligation "must be independent from those implicated in the events. It must also be capable of leading to the identification and punishment of individuals responsible, an obligation not of result but of means." Implicit in this is the requirement of promptness and reasonable expedition in all cases but especially urgent in those cases "where the possibility of removing the individual from the harmful situation is available."[167] Accordingly the ECtHR held the Republic of Cyprus accountable for its failure to provide Ms. Rantsev practical and effective protection against trafficking in general, to protect her with specific measures, and to investigate whether she had been a victim of trafficking. Additionally the court found the Republic of Cyprus further accountable for failing to conduct an effective investigation into her death.

On the other hand, the court determined the Russian Federation to be responsible for its failure to provide an investigation into the recruitment phase of the suspected trafficking of Ms. Rantsev to Cyprus, which in the words of the court, "allow[ed] an important part of the trafficking chain to act with impunity."[168] Consequently the ECtHR held both Russia and Cyprus responsible for failing to conduct an effective investigation into what had occurred. The court reiterated its stance concerning the duty of state authorities to thoroughly and effectively investigate allegations of trafficking from recruitment to exploitation. This was in harmony with the preamble of the Palermo Protocol, which expressly requires of states the adoption of a comprehensive international approach in the countries of origin, transit, and destination.

This ECtHR decision in the field of human rights is particularly significant as the court followed an international trend of considering slavery according to the evolved definition rather than in the traditional sense of the concept. Specifically, the ICTY's legal interpretation allowed the ECtHR to recognize that "trafficking in human beings, by its very nature and aim of exploitation, is based on the exercise of powers attaching to the right of ownership."[169] Thus, the court interpreted the provision of Article 4, in light of the object and purpose therein, going beyond its ordinary meaning. Following this line of reasoning, the court highlighted that

> [human trafficking] treats human beings as commodities to be bought and sold and put to forced labor, often for little or no payment. . . . It implies close surveillance of the activities of victims, whose movements are often circumscribed. It involves the use of violence and threats against victims.[170]

Although slavery has been strongly condemned by various international instruments, the ECtHR notes that human trafficking is the "modern form of the old worldwide slave trade."[171] Therefore, based on the assumption of human trafficking as a de facto form of slavery, the ECtHR articulated member states' positive obligations in regards to trafficking. Within the meaning of Article 3(a) of the Palermo Protocol and Article 4(a) of the Council of Europe (CoE) Convention on Action against Trafficking in Human Beings (Anti-Trafficking Convention), these fall within the scope of Article 4 of the European Convention on Human Rights (ECHR), which deals with the prohibition of slavery and forced labor.[172] This assertion of the ECtHR clarified key obligations of states with regard to trafficking.

In light of this connection of trafficking to slavery, it is worth noting that the *Rantsev* judgment was not the first case where the court pronounced on the "powers attaching to the rights of ownership" over someone in light of Article 4 of the ECHR. One can see this international jurisprudence in the case of *Siliadin v. France* (2005), a case that dealt exclusively with forced or compulsory labor in a situation of domestic servitude involving a minor. In their judgment, the court held that

> although the applicant was . . . clearly deprived of her personal autonomy, the evidence does not suggest that she was held in slavery in the proper sense, in other words, that Mr. and Mrs. B. exercised a genuine right of legal ownership over her, thus reducing her to the status of an "object."[173]

The ECtHR referred to the traditional definition of slavery in Article 1 of the 1926 Slavery Convention and unanimously ruled that although the applicant was not a victim of slavery in its traditional sense, Mr. and Mrs. B. held her in servitude within the meaning of Article 4 of the convention. In this regard, the ECtHR noted that servitude is "a particularly serious form of denial of freedom" and that it includes "the obligation to perform certain services for others." Additionally the ECtHR affirmed that for the purposes of the ECHR, "'servitude' means an obligation to provide one's services that is imposed by the use of coercion, and is to be linked with the concept of 'slavery.'"[174] In these terms, in order to address issues of states' responsibility under the

1956 Supplementary Convention, the ECtHR called upon each of the states parties to "take all practicable and necessary legislative and other measures to bring about the complete abolition or abandonment of [those] institutions and practices."[175] Accordingly the court established specific positive obligations on the part of member states to put in place appropriate criminal law provisions to effectively prevent, criminalize, and prosecute any act aimed at keeping a person in such situations under Article 4 of the ECHR.[176] Indeed, as the ECtHR described in both the *Rantsev* and *Siliadin* cases, contemporary slavery and slave-like practices are incompatible with human dignity, thereby threatening the human person's fundamental freedoms and the basic values of the democratic societies enshrined in the ECHR.[177]

CONCLUSION

As this review of international law instruments and their deployment in several watershed cases has illustrated, the international community recognizes a redefinition of the concept of slavery as encompassing practices that require an exercise of any or all powers attached to the right of ownership over a person. This broader definition represents an international trend that contemplates this interpretation in light of present-day conditions for the effective protection of the rights and fundamental liberties of those who are "under the regime of modern slavery." Furthermore, this interpretation is also held by the ECtHR, evidencing that the ECHR serves as a living document in harmony with relevant rules and principles of international law that firmly assesses violations of the fundamental values of democratic societies as the ones enshrined in Article 4 therein.

Historical practices involving the absolute authority of masters over slaves, which reflect masters' property rights over slaves and confer a de jure slave status, share characteristics with modern slavery practices including the exercise of the attributes of the right of ownership, subjecting humans to the condition of slavery de facto. The following list highlights several examples of this overlap.

1. In the past, property rights over a person involving the exercise of a legal right of ownership could manifest as a person's ability to buy, sell, transfer, or inherit another person.[178] Today situations in which "there is evidence that a person has been bought and sold" for exploitation are an indicator that trafficking may have taken place.[179] They also constitute a relevant factor in determining the existence of the exercise of one or more powers of the right of ownership over someone and thus may reveal slavery in modern times.

2. In the past individuals exercised absolute control over the person they legally owned. Consequently this status deprived the slave of their fundamental freedoms. Today the exercise of the attributes of property can relate to controlling someone with the aim of their exploitation "by using, managing, taking advantage of, transferring, or disposing of the person concerned." These conditions significantly restrict or deny individual liberty as established by the Inter-American Court of Human Rights in its 2016 judgment of the *Hacienda Brasil Verde Workers v. Brazil*.[180] In this case the Inter-American Court referred to exploitative situations in which "control tantamount to possession" over a person may indicate slavery.[181] The Inter-American Court found the workers to be victims of trafficking and subjected to this control, which reduced their personal autonomy and represented a direct attack on their integrity and human dignity.[182]

3. In the past an individual could possess and use a slave. Today an individual exercises elements of control and exploitation over another person, which can involve use of "tattoos or other marks indicating 'ownership' by [the victims'] exploiters" that may indicate a possible trafficking situation.[183] Traffickers force trafficking victims to comply with all their demands and orders as victims do not enjoy their natural freedoms.

4. Both historically and in the present, evidence shows that recruitment methods of children who become de facto slaves include the selling of children by parents, caregivers, or family members or the trade of children to pay debts.[184] In many situations, parents or family members may be the first contact person of a child victim with a recruiter. A recruiter usually deceives parents into relinquishing their child under the pretense that the child will have a better life and more opportunities; instead, the child faces exploitation.

5. Today, trafficked girls can be exposed to early pregnancies so that the child usually has the same fate as the trafficked mother. These circumstances echo the fate of those born in similar situations in the past where children born to a slave woman were slaves themselves, belonging to the woman's master regardless of whether the master himself were the father.[185] In general, chattel slaves were considered property that was also inheritable by another person. Today the status of a modern slave refers to indicia of ownership by their exploiters.

While the list of comparisons between past and present slavery can continue, the bottom line is that many human beings in history have been seen and treated as commodities. At present, trafficked children and adults belong de facto to their traffickers. This condition means that although modern slaves are not legal objects belonging to masters—as they retain their legal personality—they are de facto enslaved for the purpose of exploitation, which usually results in profit for traffickers. Furthermore, perpetrators do not distinguish between human beings: children, women, and men are all victimized.

Certainly the legal understanding of what constitutes slavery has evolved and is commonly associated with trafficking in persons. Human trafficking is potentially linked to the legal prohibition of slavery and to notions of property—practices that continue every day around the world. Human trafficking situations deny the inner attributes of victims' humanness.

Undoubtedly slavery and practices analogous to slavery threaten human dignity and the fundamental freedoms of human beings and are therefore incompatible with a democratic society. In 2000, the European Union (EU) codified the idea that "human dignity is inviolable, and it must be respected and protected in every human being."[186] Nevertheless a new wave of exploitation is becoming prevalent that infringes on human dignity and the fundamental pillars of modern democracies and the rule of law, affecting nations worldwide.[187]

Consequently, considering the international trend toward recognizing human trafficking as a form of de facto slavery, the question arises regarding how to apply this evolved concept of slavery to situations in cyberspace. More specifically in cyberspace, can a child be commoditized to the point that he or she is no longer treated and seen as a real person? In this sense, how do practices of online child sexual exploitation amount to trafficking and modern slavery? The following chapter considers these questions.

NOTES

1. Paul Challen, "Everyday Life," in *Life in Ancient Egypt* (New York: Crabtree Publishing, 2005), 14.

2. Robert L. Paquette and Mark M. Smith, *The Oxford Handbook of Slavery in the Americas* (Oxford: Oxford University Press, 2016).

3. Sean Stilwell, *Slavery and Slaving in African History* (Cambridge: Cambridge University Press, 2014), 5.

4. Ira Berlin, *Many Thousands Gone: The First Two Centuries of Slavery in North America* (Cambridge, MA: Harvard University Press, 1998), 9.

5. Walter Johnson, *River of Dark Dreams: Slavery and Empire in the Cotton Kingdom* (Cambridge, MA: Harvard University Press, 2013), 5.

6. Paul J. du Plessis, *Borkowski's Textbook on Roman Law*, 4th ed. (Oxford: Oxford University Press, 2010), 92–93.

7. Stephen B. Thomas and Erica Casper, "The Burdens of Race and History on Black People's Health 400 Years after Jamestown," *American Journal of Public Health* 109, no. 10 (2019): 1346–1347, https://doi.org/10.2105/AJPH.2019.305290.

8. William H. Williams, *Slavery and Freedom in Delaware, 1639–1865* (Lanham, MD: Rowman & Littlefield, 1996).

9. Michael Haas, "Typologies," in *Improving Human Rights* (Westport, CT: Praeger, 1994), 2.

10. Siegfried Wiessner, "Re-Enchanting the World: Indigenous Peoples' Rights as Essential Parts of a Holistic Human Rights Regime," *UCLA Journal of International Law and Foreign Affairs* 15, no. 239 (2012): 259.

11. Patrick Hayden, "John Locke: The Second Treatise of Government," in *The Philosophy of Human Rights* (St. Paul: Paragon House, 2001), 71–79.

12. Jean-Jacques Rousseau, *The Basic Political Writings*, 2nd ed., trans. Donald A. Cress (Indianapolis, IN: Hackett, 2011).

13. Immanuel Kant, *Grounding for the Metaphysics of Morals:* With *On a Supposed Right to Lie Because of Philanthropic Concerns*, 3rd ed., trans. James W. Ellington (Indianapolis, IN: Hackett, 1993).

14. Ibid.

15. Second Continental Congress, "Declaration of Independence," 1776.

16. National Constituent Assembly of France, "Declaration of the Rights of Man and the Citizen," approved on August 26, 1789.

17. National Constituent Assembly of France, "Declaration of the Rights of Man," art. 2.

18. Ibid., art. 3.

19. U.S. Constitution Art. IV, § 2, cl. 3: "No Person held to Service or Labor in one State, under the Laws thereof, escaping into another, shall, in Consequence of any Law or Regulation therein, be discharged from such Service or Labor, but shall be delivered up on Claim of the Party to whom such Service or Labor may be due."

20. U.S. Constitution Art. I, § 9, cl. 1: "The Migration or Importation of such Persons as any of the States now existing shall think proper to admit, shall not be prohibited by the Congress prior to the Year one thousand eight hundred and eight, but a Tax or duty may be imposed on such Importation, not exceeding 10 dollars for each Person."

21. Abraham Lincoln, "Peoria Speech, October 16, 1854," National Park Service, www.nps.gov/liho/learn/historyculture/peoriaspeech.htm#:~:text=In%20this%20 speech%20Abraham%20Lincoln,speech%20Lincoln%20criticized%20popular%20 sovereignty.&text=Lincoln%20argued%20that%20the%20slaves,consequently%20 possessed%20certain%20natural%20rights.

22. Abraham Lincoln, "Seventh Debate: Alton, Illinois," National Park Service, www.nps.gov/liho/learn/historyculture/debate7.htm.

23. National Archives and Records Administration, "The Emancipation Proclamation," www.archives.gov/exhibits/featured-documents/emancipation-proclamation.

24. U.S. Constitution Amend. XIII, §1: "Neither slavery nor involuntary servitude, except as a punishment for crime whereof the party shall have been duly convicted, shall exist within the United States, or any place subject to their jurisdiction. Section 2: Congress shall have power to enforce this article by appropriate legislation."

25. U.S. Constitution Amend. XIV: "All persons born or naturalized in the United States and subject to the jurisdiction thereof, are citizens of the United States and of the State wherein they reside."

26. UNGA, Resolution 217 A (III), Universal Declaration of Human Rights, (December 10, 1948; hereafter referred to as UDHR).

27. United Nations (UN), "The Foundation of International Human Rights Law," www.un.org/en/sections/universal-declaration/foundation-international-human-rights-law/index.html.

28. UN, "Statute of the International Court of Justice," adopted June 26, 1945, T.S. 993, art. 38(1)(c).

29. UDHR, art. 25.

30. Ibid., art. 1, 4.

31. Ibid. Article 7 expressly states, "All are equal before the law and are entitled without any discrimination to equal protection of the law."

32. See Slavery Convention, entered into force March 9, 1927, U.N.T.S. 2861; ECOSOC, "Supplementary Convention on the Abolition of Slavery, the Slave Trade, and Institutions and Practices Similar to Slavery," entered into force April 30, 1957, U.N.T.S. 3822 (hereafter referred to as Supplementary Slavery Convention); "Forced Labour Convention, 1930 (no. 29)," entered into force May 1, 1932, C29.

33. John P. Humphrey, "The UN Charter and the Universal Declaration of Human Rights," in *The International Protection of Human Rights*, ed. Evan Luard (New York: Frederick A. Praeger, 1967), 47.

34. Ibid., 47; Dag Hammarskjöld Library, "Drafting of the Universal Declaration of Human Rights," http://research.un.org/en/undhr/draftingcommittee.

35. UNGA "International Covenant on Civil and Political Rights," entered into force March, 23, 1966. U.N.T.S. 999 (hereafter referred to as ICCPR).

36. UNGA, "International Covenant on Economic, Social and Cultural Rights," entered into force January 3, 1976, U.N.T.S. 993 (hereafter referred to as ICESCR).

37. Ashild Samnøy, "The Origins of the Universal Declaration of Human Rights," in *The Universal Declaration of Human Rights: A Common Standard of Achievement*, ed. Gudmundur Alfredsson and Asbjørn Eide (Leiden: Martinus Nijhoff, 1999), 6–8.

38. Carol Devine, Carol Rae Hansen, Ralph Wilde, Daan Bronkhorst, Frederic A. Moritz, Baptiste Rolle, and Rebecca Sherman, *Human Rights: The Essential Reference*, ed. Carol Devine and Hilary Poole (Phoenix, AZ: Oryx Press, 1999), 61.

39. For example, a reflection on the inclusion of economic, social, and cultural rights in the UDHR, art. 28, states, "Everyone is entitled to a social and international order in which the rights and freedoms set forth in this Declaration can be fully realized."

40. See the difference between ICCPR, "Where not already provided for by existing legislative or other measures, each State Party to the present Covenant undertakes to take the necessary steps, in accordance with its constitutional processes and with the provisions of the present Covenant, to adopt such laws or other measures as may be necessary to give effect to the rights recognized in the present Covenant," and ICESCR, art. 2(1), "Each State Party to the present Covenant undertakes to take steps, individually and through international assistance and co-operation, especially

economic and technical, to the maximum of its available resources, with a view to achieving progressively the full realization of the rights recognized in the present Covenant by all appropriate means, including particularly the adoption of legislative measures."

41. UDHR, preamble, starts by proclaiming that "recognition of the inherent dignity and of the equal and inalienable rights of all members of the human family is the foundation of freedom, justice and peace in the world." Furthermore, this universal instrument expressly corroborates "faith in fundamental human rights, in the dignity and worth of the human person and in the equal rights of men and women" that is in conformity with UN, "Charter of the United Nations," signed June 26, 1945, ch. XIV, art. 1.

42. ICCPR, preamble, art. 10.

43. ICESCR, preamble, art. 13.

44. ICCPR, art. 24; ICESCR, art. 10, 13.

45. The meaning of human dignity has not always been identified in connection with the inherent value of the human person. It comes from the Latin word *dignitas*, and in ancient Rome the term was usually associated with a social concept: the elevated social status of senators relative to common men or women, and slaves. See Paolo G. Carozza, "Human Dignity," in *The Oxford Handbook of International Human Rights Law*, ed. Dinah Shelton (Oxford: Oxford University Press, 2013), 349.

46. For example, the philosopher Peng-chun Chang, vice chair of the CHR, explained that aspects of Confucian doctrine align with a common understanding of human dignity in the UDHR (see "Drafting of the Universal Declaration of Human Rights").

47. Allan Rosas and Martin Scheinin, "Categories and Beneficiaries of Human Rights," in *An Introduction to the International Protection of Human Rights*, ed. Raija Hanski and Markku Suksi (Turku: Institute for Human Rights, Âbo Akademi University, 1999), 49.

48. Marcus Düwell, Jens Braarvig, Roger Brownsword, and Dietmar Mieth, "Why a Handbook on Human Dignity?" in *The Cambridge Handbook of Human Dignity: Interdisciplinary Perspectives*, ed. Marcus Düwell, Jens Braarvig, Roger Brownsword, and Dietmar Mieth (Cambridge: Cambridge University Press, 2014).

49. Walter Kälin and Jörg Künzli, *The Law of International Human Rights Protection*, 2nd ed. (Oxford: Oxford University Press, 2019), 5.

50. David Kretzmer and Eckart Klein, eds., *The Concept of Human Dignity in Human Rights Discourse* (Dordrecht: Springer Netherlands, 2002).

51. Roza Pati, "Rights and Their Limits: The Constitution for Europe in International and Comparative Legal Perspective," *Berkeley Journal of International Law* 23, no. 1 (2005): 223–229.

52. United for Human Rights, "A Brief History of Human Rights," www.humanrights.com/what-are-human-rights/brief-history/the-united-nations.html.

53. UN, "Charter of the United Nations," preamble.

54. See OHCHR, "The Core International Human Rights Instruments and Their Monitoring Bodies," www.ohchr.org/EN/ProfessionalInterest/Pages/CoreInstruments.aspx.

55. The VCLT provides basic rules for the interpretation of treaties, see UN, "Vienna Convention on the Law of Treaties," signed May 23, 1969, U.N.T.S. 1155 (hereafter referred to as VCLT, art. 31, 1).

56. Marc Bossuyt, *Guide to the* Travaux Préparatoires *of the International Covenant on Civil and Political Rights* (New York: Springer, 1987), 164; VLCT, art. 31, 32.

57. UNSG, "Draft International Covenants on Human Rights: Annotation Prepared by the Secretary-General," A/2929, July 1, 1955.

58. UNSG, "Draft International Covenants on Human Rights," para. 18, at 92; Manfred Nowak, *UN Covenant on Civil and Political Rights* (Leipzig: N. P. Engel, 2005), 199.

59. UNSG, "Draft International Covenants on Human Rights," para. 17, at 92; Nowak, *U.N. Covenant*, 199.

60. HRCttee, "CCPR General Comment no. 28: art. 3 (The Equality of Rights between Men and Women)," CCPR/C/21/Rev.1/Add.10, March 29, 2000, para. 12, at 3.

61. HRCttee, "Concluding Observations on the Fifth Periodic Report of Portugal," CCPR/C/PRT/CO/5, April 28, 2020, para. 32, at 7.

62. HRCttee, "Concluding Observations in the Absence of the Initial Report of Dominica: Human Right Committee," CCPR/C/DMA/COAR/1, April 24, 2020, para. 33, at 6; HRCttee, "Concluding Observations on the Third Periodic Report of the Central African Republic," CCPR/C/CAF/CO/3, April 30, 2020, para. 29, at 7.

63. Paul G. Lauren, ed., *The Evolution of International Human Rights: Visions Seen*, 3rd ed. (Philadelphia: University of Pennsylvania Press, 2011). King Hammurabi established the code, proclaiming, "Some laws are so fundamental that they apply to everyone—even the king."

64. Rule 168, for example, affirmed that "if a man wishes to put his son out of his house" but "the son be guilty of no great fault, for which he can be rightfully put out, the father shall not put him out," while rule 169 provides that if a son be found guilty of a grave fault "which should rightfully deprive him of the filial relationship, the father shall forgive him the first time; but if he be guilty of a grave fault a second time the father may deprive his son of all filial relation." See Avalon Project, "The Code of Hammurabi," Rule 168, https://avalon.law.yale.edu/ancient/hamframe.asp.

65. Gen. 37:2.

66. Gen. 37:27.

67. Gen. 37:28.

68. Gen. 37:36.

69. Gen. 39. See generally Noël B. Busch-Armendariz, Maura Nsonwu, and Laurie C. Heffron, *Human Trafficking: Applying Research, Theory and Case Studies* (New York: Sage Publications, 2018), 43.

70. Christopher D. Stone, *Should Trees Have Standing? Toward Legal Rights for Natural Objects*, 3rd ed. (Oxford: Oxford University Press, 2010), I. In the context of a father's rights over his child, "*jus vitae necisque*—the power of life and death—over his children . . . he had the power of uncontrolled corporal chastisement; he can modify their personal condition at pleasure; he can give a wife to his son; he can give his daughter in marriage; he can divorce his children of either sex; he can transfer

them to another family by adoption; and he can sell them. The child was less than a person: an object, a thing."

71. Jaap E. Doek, "The Human Rights of Children: An Introduction," in *International Human Rights of Children*, ed. Ursula Kilkelly and Ton Liefaard (New York: Springer, 2019), 4. The author makes reference to Justinianus 533.

72. UNSG, "Geneva Declaration of the Rights of the Child of 1924," E/CN.4/512, February 19, 1951.

73. UNICEF, "History of Child Rights," www.unicef.org/child-rights-convention/history-child-rights.

74. UNGA, Resolution 1386 XIV, "Declaration of the Rights of the Child," A/RES/1386(XIV) (November 20, 1959).

75. UNGA, Resolution 1386 XIV, "Declaration of the Rights of the Child," principle 2, stating, "In the enactment of laws . . . the best interests of the child shall be the paramount consideration."

76. Ibid., principles 4, 6, 7.

77. Ibid. Principle 9 states that the child "shall not be the subject of traffic, in any form."

78. ICCPR, art. 2, 1.

79. ICESCR, art. 3.

80. UNGA, "Convention on the Rights of the Child," entered into force September 2, 1990, U.N.T.S. 1577 (hereafter referred to as UNCRC).

81. UNGA, "Convention on the Rights of the Child," art. 2(1).

82. The 1989 UNCRC makes reference to the inherent dignity and worth of the human person of the child in the preamble and arts. 23, 28, 37, 39, and 40.

83. UNCRC, art. 19, refers to "all forms of physical or mental violence, injury or abuse, neglect or negligent treatment, maltreatment or exploitation, including sexual abuse," art. 32 refers to "economic exploitation," including child labor, art. 33 pertains to protecting children from "the illicit use of narcotic drugs and psychotropic substances," art. 34 is about "all forms of sexual exploitation and sexual abuse," art. 35 is on "the abduction of, the sale of or traffic in children for any purpose or in any form," and art. 36 protects the child against "all other forms of exploitation."

84. Ibid., art. 34(a).

85. Ibid., art. 34(b), (c).

86. Ibid., art. 35.

87. CRC, "General Comment no. 13 (2011): The Right of the Child to Freedom from All Forms of Violence," CRC/C/GC/13, April 18, 2011, para. 25, at 10.

88. UNCRC, art. 19(1).

89. Ibid., art. 1.

90. During the drafting of the UNCRC, a submission by the delegations of France and the Netherlands proposed to cover all forms of exploitation, particularly sexual exploitation of the child, as well as against all degrading treatment and all acts prejudicial to the moral, spiritual, mental, or physical inegrity of the child. If this attempt were successful, the word "unlawful" would be removed from para. (a) [art. 34] and as such, all sexual activity with a person under eighteen years old would have to be

prevented. See CHR, "Report of the Working Group on a Draft Convention on the Rights of the Child," E/CN.4/1987/25, March 9, 1987.

91. The 1956 Supplementary Slavery Convention, art. 1(d); ILO, "Worst Forms of Child Labour Convention, 1999 (No. 182)," entered into force November 19, 2000, C182, art. 2; Palermo Protocol, art. 3(d).

92. The principle of best interests, for example, appears in arts. 9, 18, 20, and 21.

93. UNCRC, art. 3(1); CRC, "Draft General Comment no. 25 (202x): Children's Rights in Relation to the Digital Environment," CRC/C/GC/, August 13, 2020.

94. UNCRC, art. 37, 40.

95. OHCHR, "Status of Ratification Interactive Dashboard: Convention on the Rights of the Child," http://indicators.ohchr.org.

96. UNGA, "Optional Protocol to the Convention on the Rights of the Child on the Sale of Children, Child Prostitution and Child Pornography," entered into force January 18, 2002, U.N.T.S 2171 (hereafter referred to as OP-CRC-SC).

97. UNGA, "Optional Protocol to the Convention on the Rights of the Child on the Involvement of Children in Armed Conflict," entered into force February 12, 2002, U.N.T.S. 2173.

98. OP-CRC-SC, art. 2(a), (b), (c).

99. Ibid., preamble.

100. OP-CRC-SC Guidelines, para. 15, at 5.

101. OP-CRC-SC, art. 2(a).

102. OP-CRC-SC Guidelines, para. 15, at 5.

103. OP-CRC-SC, art. 3(1). For the status of ratification of the Optional Protocol, see UN Treaty Collection, "Status of Treaties," https://treaties.un.org/pages/ViewDetails.aspx?src=TREATY&mtdsg_no=IV-11-d&chapter=4&clang=_en.

104. OP-CRC-SC, preamble, art. 10(3).

105. OP-CRC-SC Guidelines, para. 72, at 14.

106. Ibid., para. 19, at 5.

107. For example, CRC, "Concluding Observations on the Combined 5th and 6th Periodic Reports of El Salvador: Committee on the Rights of the Child," CRC/C/SLV/CO/5–6, November 29, 2018, para. 53, at 14.

108. *Barcelona Traction, Light and Power Company, Limited* (*Belgium v. Spain*), Second Phase, ICJ 32 (February 5, 1970), para. 33–34, at 33.

109. VLCT, art. 53 (*jus cogens*).

110. It is important to note that under international law, *jus cogens* rules imply *erga omnes* obligations to states. However, not all *erga omnes* obligations meet the status of *jus cogens*.

111. UNGA, "Chapter V: Peremptory Norms of General International Law (*Jus Cogens*)," in *Report of the International Law Commission: Seventy-First Session* (New York: United Nations, 2019), 147.

112. ICCPR, art. 4(2).

113. ICCPR, art. 4(1).

114. Ibid., art. 4(2).

115. HRCttee, "CCPR General Comment no. 29, Article 4: Derogations during a State of Emergency," CCPR/C/21/Rev.1/Add.11, August 31, 2001, para. 11, at 4.

116. UNGA, "International Agreement for the Suppression of the White Slave Traffic," signed May 18, 1904, U.N.T.S. 92, art. 1.

117. Ibid., art. 2.

118. "International Convention for the Suppression of the White Slave Traffic," signed May 4, 1910, GR. Brit. T.S. 20, as amended by the "Protocol Amending the International Agreement for the Suppression of the White Slave Traffic, and Amending the International Convention for the Suppression of the White Slave Traffic, May 4, 1949, 2 U.S.T. 1999, 30 U.N.T.S. 23," entered into force June 21, 1951, U.N.T.S. 23, art. 1–2.

119. "Protocol Amending the International Agreement for the Suppression of the White Slave Traffic, and Amending the International Convention for the Suppression of the White Slave Traffic, May 4, 1949, 2 U.S.T. 1999, 30 U.N.T.S. 23" (C).

120. Roza Pati, "States' Positive Obligations with Respect to Human Trafficking: The European Court of Human Rights Breaks New Ground in *Rantsev v. Cyprus and Russia*," *Boston University International Law Journal* 29, no. 5 (Spring 2011): 106.

121. LoN, "International Convention for the Suppression of the Traffic in Women and Children," signed September 30, 1921, U.N.T.S. 9.

122. Some of these legal agreements against slavery and the slave trade include the Peace Treaties of Paris (1814–1815), the Treaty for the Suppression of the African Slave Trade signed in London in 1841, and the Treaty between the United States and Great Britain for the Suppression of the Slave Trade, also known as the Lyons-Seward Treaty of 1862.

123. "Slavery Convention," art. 1(1).

124. ECOSOC, "Slavery, the Slave Trade, and Other Forms of Servitude," E/2357, January 27, 1953, 27.

125. Ibid., 48.

126. LoN Assembly Sixth Committee, *Slavery Convention: Report Presented to the Assembly by the Sixth Committee* (Geneva: Imp. Kundig, 1926), 2; LoN, "Draft Convention on Slavery, Replies of Governments, Reply from the Government of the Union of South Africa," A.10(a).1926.VI, July 22, 1926, 5. The Union of South Africa commented that "a person is a slave if any other person can, by law or enforceable custom, claim such property in him as would be claimed if he were an inanimate object; and thus the natural freedom of will possessed by a person to offer or render his labor or to control the fruits thereof or the consideration therefrom is taken from him" at 5. See also Jean Allain, "The Definition of Slavery in International Law," *Howard Law Journal* 52, no. 2 (2009), 15–18.

127. Roza Pati, "Trafficking in Humans: A New Haven Perspective," *Asia Pacific Law Review* 20, no. 2 (Fall 2012): 150.

128. LoN, "International Convention for the Suppression of the Traffic in Women of Full Age," entered into force August 24, 1934, L.N.T.S. 150, preamble.

129. LoN, "International Convention for the Suppression of the Traffic in Women of Full Age," art. 1.

130. Ibid.

131. UNGA, Convention for the Suppression of the Traffic in Persons and on the Exploitation of the Prostitution of Others, A/RES/317, December 2, 1949, art. 1(1), (2).

132. UNGA, "Convention for the Suppression of the Traffic in Persons and on the Exploitation of the Prostitution of Others," art. 2(1), (2).

133. Ibid., art. 3–4.

134. Ibid., art. 6.

135. Ibid., art. 16.

136. United Nations Treaty Collection, "Status of Ratification: Convention for the Suppression of the Traffic in Persons and of the Exploitation of the Prostitution of Others," https://treaties.un.org/Pages/ViewDetails. aspx?src=IND&mtdsg_no=VII-11-a&chapter=7&clang=_en.

137. Palermo Protocol, art. 3.

138. Anne T. Gallagher, *The International Law of Human Trafficking* (Cambridge: Cambridge University Press, 2012), 63–64.

139. Supplementary Slavery Convention, art. 1, as follows: "Each of the states Parties to this Convention shall take all practicable and necessary legislative and other measures to bring about progressively and as soon as possible the complete abolition or abandonment of the following institutions and practices, where they still exist and whether or not they are covered by the definition of slavery contained in article 1 of the Slavery Convention signed at Geneva on September 25, 1926."

140. Ibid., art. 1(a), (b), (c), (d).

141. Ibid., art. 7(a).

142. Ibid., art. 7(b).

143. Anne T. Gallagher, "Using International Human Rights Law to Better Protect Victims of Trafficking: The Prohibitions on Slavery, Servitude, Forced Labor and Debt Bondage," in *The Theory and Practice of International Criminal Law: Essays in Honour of M. Cherif Bassiouni*, ed. L. N. Sadat and M. P. Scarf (Leiden: Martinus Nijhoff, 2008), 7.

144. UNSG, "Draft International Covenants on Human Rights," para. 18, at 92.

145. *Siliadin v. France*, 2005-ECtHR (October 26, 2005), no. 73316/01, paras. 122–124, at 33.

146. UNSG, "Draft International Covenants on Human Rights," para. 18, at 92.

147. United Nations Treaty Collection, "Status of Ratification: Protocol to Prevent, Suppress and Punish Trafficking in Persons, Especially Women and Children, Supplementing the United Nations Convention against Transnational Organized Crime," https://treaties.un.org/pages/ViewDetails. aspx?src=TREATY&mtdsg_no=XVIII-12-a&chapter=18&c.

148. Palermo Protocol, art. 2(a), (b).

149. Ibid., art. 2(c).

150. Ibid., art. 3(a).

151. *Prosecutor v. Dragoljub Kunarac et al.*, 2001-ICTY Trial Chamber II Judgment, para. 539–541, at 192 (February 22, 2001), IT-96–23/1-T.

152. Ibid., para. 2–3, at 10.

153. Ibid., para. 543, at 194.

154. Ibid.

155. Ibid., para. 542, at 193.

156. Roza Pati, "Trafficking in Human Beings: The Convergence of Criminal Law and Human Rights," in *The SAGE Handbook of Human Trafficking and Modern Day Slavery*, ed. Jennifer B. Clark and Sasha Poucki (London: Sage Publications, 2019), 286.

157. *Prosecutor v. Dragoljub Kunarac et al.*, para. 740, at 239 and para. 742, at 240.

158. Ibid., para. 539, at 192.

159. Ibid., para. 540, at 192.

160. *Prosecutor v. Dragoljub Kunarac, Radomir Kovac and Zoran Vukovic* (Appeal Judgment), 2002-ICTY Appeals Chamber, para.108, at 33 (June 12, 2002), IT-96–23 & IT-96–23/1-A.

161. *Prosecutor v. Dragoljub Kunarac, Radomir Kovac and Zoran Vukovic* (Appeal Judgment), para. 117, at 35–36.

162. Ibid.

163. Ibid., para. 119, at 36.

164. *Rantsev v. Cyprus and Russia*, 2010-ECtHR (January 7, 2010), no. 25965/04, 2.

165. Ibid., para. 285, at 69–70.

166. Ibid., para. 286, at 70.

167. Ibid., para. 288, at 70–71.

168. Ibid., para. 307, at 76.

169. Ibid., para. 281, at 68.

170. Ibid., para. 281, at 68.

171. Ibid., para. 281, at 68.

172. Ibid., para. 282, at 69.

173. *Siliadin v. France*, para. 122, at 33.

174. Ibid., para. 123–124, at 33.

175. Ibid., para. 125, at 31.

176. Ibid., para. 148–149, at 37.

177. *Rantsev v. Cyprus and Russia*, para. 282, at 69. The ECtHR specifically mentions that "there can be no doubt that trafficking threatens the human dignity and fundamental freedoms of its victims and cannot be considered compatible with a democratic society and the values expounded in the Convention." In addition, the ECtHR considers "together with art. 2 and 3, art. 4 of the Convention enshrines one of the basic values of the democratic societies making up the Council of Europe." See *Siliadin v. France*, para. 82, at 25.

178. ECOSOC, "Slavery, the Slave Trade, and Other Forms of Servitude," 48. See characteristics 1, 4, 6.

179. UNODC, *Anti-Human Trafficking Manual for Criminal Justice Practitioners: Indicators of Trafficking in Persons (Module 2)*, (New York: United Nations, 2009), 11.

180. *Workers of the Hacienda Brasil Verde Workers v. Brazil* (Preliminary Objections, Merits, Reparations and Costs), I/A Court HR (October 20, 2016), Ser. C no. 318.

181. Jean Allain, "Bellagio-Harvard Guidelines on the Legal Parameters of Slavery," in *The Law and Slavery* (Leiden: Brill/Nijhoff, 2015), guideline 2, at 556.

182. *Workers of the Hacienda Brasil*, 5.

183. UNODC, *Anti-Human Trafficking Manual*, 11.

184. See UNODC, *Anti-Human Trafficking Manual for Criminal Justice Practitioners: Control Methods in Trafficking in Persons (Module 4)* (New York: United Nations, 2009), 9; and CRC, "General Comment no. 6: Treatment of Unaccompanied and Separated Children Outside Their Country of Origin," CRC/GC/2005/6, September 1, 2005, para. 2, at 4.

185. Jennifer L. Morgan, "*Partus Sequitur Ventrem*: Law, Race, and Reproduction in Colonial Slavery," *Small Axe* 22, no. 1 (2018): 1–17, https://doi.org/10.1215/07990537-4378888.

186. This idea is incorporated in EU, "Charter of Fundamental Rights of the European Union," 2012/C 326/02, December 7, 2000, Title 1, art. 1.

187. ILO, *Global Estimates of Modern Slavery: Forced Labour and Forced Marriage* (Geneva: International Labour Organization, 2017), 9.

Chapter 2

Online Sex Trafficking

Indicia of Slavery on the Internet

Most of the time we think slavery no longer exists. This is because we are thinking of it in the sense of chattel slavery and forced labor. However we still find situations in which some people subjugate others for exploitative practices through means such as physical, economic, emotional, or psychological coercion that reduce their human status to that of an object and implicitly dehumanize them by limiting their rights. Illicit contemporary practices connected to slavery—human trafficking—not only continue but since the 1990s have been aided by factors such as increased globalization, information and communication technologies, and the easy movement of people and goods around the world.

The exercise over a victim of one or more powers attached to ownership has resulted in human trafficking acts being regarded as a form of slavery as demonstrated in the precedent-setting cases in international human rights and criminal law discussed in chapter 1. The present chapter explores the possibility—and indeed the importance—of applying to cybertrafficking situations the precedent of the *Kunarac et al.* case and the definition set forth in the Palermo Protocol, which makes it a crime to traffic people "for the purpose of exploitation."[1] The trial chamber followed the line of the 1926 Slavery Convention, which defined slavery as a situation in which one or more elements of power attaching to ownership are exercised by one person over another and established the foundation for applying the prohibition of slavery to human trafficking.[2] Significantly, the trial chamber thus depicted human trafficking as a form of modern-day slavery. In this chapter, I explore the question of whether under this evolved legal concept of slavery certain conditions present in the exploitation that occurs in cyberspace can be likened to exercising powers of ownership. To answer these questions we need to consider how these attributes can be and are exercised on the Internet. We are referring to powers that, as in the past, represent *dominus* over a person

39

"owned"[3] and today—under this evolved legal concept of slavery—encompass conditions in which the exercise of the attributes of property is present. The question with significant legal ramifications is whether such acts, even if they do not include the physical proximity of the trafficker to the child, demonstrate the exercise of ownership powers in cyberspace and provide evidence of a contemporary form of slavery. To answer this, we consider normative elements of trafficking set forth in the Palermo Protocol.

THE PALERMO PROTOCOL

In 2000 the UNGA argued for the necessity of combatting human trafficking at the international level. As stated in the preamble to the Palermo Protocol,

> effective action to prevent and combat trafficking in persons, especially women and children, requires a comprehensive international approach in the countries of origin, transit and destination that includes measures to prevent such trafficking, to punish the traffickers and to protect the victims of such trafficking, including by protecting their internationally recognized human rights . . . [and] taking into account the fact that, despite the existence of a variety of international instruments containing rules and practical measures to combat the exploitation of persons, especially women and children, there is no universal instrument that addresses all aspects of trafficking in persons. . . . In the absence of such an instrument, persons who are vulnerable to trafficking will not be sufficiently protected.

The Palermo Protocol sets out the following definition of human trafficking:

> "Trafficking in persons" shall mean the recruitment, transportation, transfer, harbouring or receipt of persons, by means of the threat or use of force or other forms of coercion, of abduction, of fraud, of deception, of the abuse of power or of a position of vulnerability or of the giving or receiving of payments or benefits to achieve the consent of a person having control over another person, for the purpose of exploitation. Exploitation shall include, at a minimum, the exploitation of the prostitution of others or other forms of sexual exploitation, forced labour or services, slavery or practices similar to slavery, servitude or the removal of organs; (b) The consent of a victim of trafficking in persons to the intended exploitation set forth in subparagraph (a) of this article shall be irrelevant where any of the means set forth in subparagraph (a) have been used; (c) The recruitment, transportation, transfer, harbouring or receipt of a child for the purpose of exploitation shall be considered "trafficking in persons" even if this does not involve any of the means set forth in subparagraph (a) of this article; (d) "Child" shall mean any person under eighteen years of age.[4]

Therefore, the Palermo Protocol establishes exploitation as the ultimate end of trafficking and defines exploitation to include "at a minimum, the exploitation of the prostitution of others or other forms of sexual exploitation, forced labor or services, slavery or practices similar to slavery, servitude or the removal of organs."[5] Additionally it establishes that the victim's consent is to be considered irrelevant in cases where any of the means set out in the definition are used.[6] The significance of this is that the consent of the victim is irrelevant in these situations of trafficking: "Once it is established that deception, coercion, force or other prohibited means were used, consent is irrelevant and cannot be used as a defence."[7] This stipulation recognizes that once the personal freedom of a person is taken away by the use of prohibited means—namely, force, threats, coercion, abuse of authority, or other forms of compulsion—consent is not possible.

With specific regard to situations involving children (i.e., any person under eighteen years of age), the Palermo Protocol offers strong protections by stating that to establish an offense as child trafficking, claimants are required to demonstrate only an *act* (e.g., recruitment, transportation, transfer, harboring, or receipt of a child) intended for the specific *purpose* of exploitation. Simply put, once a minor is subjected to some act for the purpose of their exploitation, the situation is considered one of trafficking regardless of the *means*.[8] Hence the means element of the definition of human trafficking is an essential consideration only in cases involving adults, not children. This special protection recognizes children as a group particularly vulnerable to exploitation. Due to their age, the sexual exploitation of children is a trafficking-related practice prohibited under international human rights law.[9]

HOW THE PALERMO PROTOCOL DEFINITION APPLIES IN CYBERSPACE

Now that we have seen how the internationally accepted definition of human trafficking was established, we must consider how this instrument applies in the context of cybertrafficking. The operation of the key elements that constitute the crime of human trafficking—those included in the categories of *act*, *means*, and *purpose* and the absence (or legal irrelevance) of consent—are identified and explored in the digital context. For example, what would the *act* element of a online sex trafficking offense be? A contextual analysis provides insight into the potential constitutive acts and their significance and into the trafficking process itself in cyberspace.

An Act (What Is Done)

In accordance with the Palermo Protocol, the crime of trafficking in children occurs when there is an *act*—the recruitment, transportation, transfer, harboring, or receipt of a child—committed for the *purpose* of exploitation.[10] In other words, there must be an act (*actus reus*) carried out with the intention of exploiting a child (*dolus specialis*) for it to be considered trafficking even if the end result of exploitation does not necessarily take place.[11] It follows that there is no need to demonstrate the involvement of any *means*.[12] The question is how these practices that constitute the *act* element—recruitment, transportation, transfer, harboring, or receipt of a child—can be translated into the online context. Although there is no guidance in the *travaux préparatoires* of the Palermo Protocol on the intention of the drafters on this question, a 2009 study on trafficking in organs by the CoE and UN attempted to provide such guidance. In the context of a more general discussion, this study explored the potential breadth of activities that could be considered neutral actions that when undertaken through certain means or with the intent of exploiting a person take on a different character and become criminally relevant.

Understood in a broad sense, "recruitment" refers to "any activity leading from the commitment or engagement of another individual to his or her exploitation" regardless of "means, and therefore also includ[ing] the use of modern information technologies."[13] This implies that "recruitment is regarded as trafficking in human beings . . . regardless of how the recruitment is performed—whether through personal contact or contact through third persons, newspapers, advertisements or the Internet."[14] "Transportation" is similarly means independent, referring to the "act of transporting a person from one place to another."[15] "Transfer" refers to "any kind of handing over or transmission of a person to another person . . . where control over individuals . . . may be handed over to other people. As the term and the scope of the offence are broad, the explicit or implied offering of a person for transfer is sufficient; the offer does not have to be accepted for the offence of trafficking in human beings to be constituted if the other elements are also present."[16]

"Harboring" refers to "accommodating or housing persons in whatever way, whether during their journey to their final destination or at the place of the exploitation" while "*receipt* of persons is not limited to receiving them at the place where the exploitation takes place either but also means meeting victims at agreed places on their journey to give them further information on where to go or what to do."[17] In the context of cybercrime, it is vital to derive interpretations of these terms that underscore the variety, ambiguity, and fluidity of activities that take place before the actual exploitation activities and that fulfill the *act* element of the Palermo Protocol definition. The range of specified acts means that trafficking refers to the process (e.g., recruitment into situations of exploitation) as well as aspects of the result (e.g., buying or maintenance of a child in a situation of exploitation).[18] This interpretation of the scope of terms in the concept of trafficking has the potential to bring a variety of exploiters within the definition of the crime including online recruiters, brokers, buyers, and controllers who have the intent to foster the exploitation of a child. Indeed, Article 5 of the Palermo Protocol mandates states parties to criminalize any group or individual that intentionally exploits a minor and anyone who attempts to or directs other persons to commit a trafficking offense or participates in one.[19] States parties to the Palermo Protocol are obliged to enforce this broader approach of criminalization that includes both preparatory acts and unsuccessful attempts to commit forms of trafficking that are punishable under their domestic laws.[20] In addition this central mandatory provision can be extended to hold legally liable any legal persons, such as private sector actors, involved in the initiation or sustenance of exploitation, which may include criminal, civil, or administrative sanctions, and such liability would be without prejudice to the criminal responsibility of the natural persons who have committed the offense.[21]

In an Internet context, cybercriminals are able to lure, recruit, advertise, offer, procure, or provide children; to trade images; or to organize, communicate, or expand their networks all with the intent of exploiting a minor or selling their "services." Moreover, based on objective factual circumstances in each case, offenders can be accused of a crime for acts involved in preparing the commission of a trafficking offense in cyberspace without an act of exploitation having been committed against a minor. In other words, the acts of cyberoffenders can be a real manifestation of their firm intention to sexually exploit a minor. For example, in the case of consumers of child sexual abuse materials (CSAM), these individuals knowingly obtain access to such images, an intention that is evidenced by their returning to any site where these materials can be found, thus demonstrating intent to enter such a site, and in situations where a payment is made for a download or service.[22]

Situations of trafficking occur when a minor is brought into a situation of exploitation—for example, when the child is recruited or made an object of purchase—or when "ownership" of the child is transferred to another person. This includes cases in which a child is kept in a situation of exploitation as a victim. Therefore, girls and boys can be considered victims of online sex trafficking when they are subject to such forms of control and possession where the intent to exploit exists.[23] Although such a situation may not be accompanied by physical harm, cognizance must be taken of the severity of the psychological pressure or control over the child, which may be accompanied by deception and threats, including threats to their family; limitations on their freedom; or the undermining of their rights and integrity to the point where they are treated and seen as an object as opposed to a human being.

In this sense, the *actus reus* or material act(s) of the offense is accompanied by intent to exploit the child (*mens rea*). This requirement of the element of intention speaks to the state of mind of the offender who acts for the purpose of exploitation.

As we have seen, the consent of children to their involvement in a sexual exploitative act is legally irrelevant since no person under the age of eighteen years can give legal consent to sexual exploitation, including exploitation via CSAM. This notion is an essential postulate to understand when defining the crime of child trafficking.[24] Accordingly and as in the real world, in cyberspace children cannot give meaningful consent to their own sexual exploitation.[25] Under this construction, "online sex trafficking of children" is an umbrella term that includes both act and intention—that is, any prohibited form of process or dealing for the purpose of exploitation. Consequently "online sex trafficking of children" refers to exploitative situations where an abuser demeans a child such that they treat and see that child as an object of sexual gratification or as a commercial commodity.

In this context the child victim cannot consent and their exploitation falls under the third element of the legal definition of trafficking. In the discussion above, we saw links to the definition of trafficking in the Palermo Protocol, which does not require the presence of physical confinement, physical force, or transportation for these online exploitative situations to be considered crimes of trafficking. However in cyberspace, the ability to exploit a child virtually—without physical interaction—allows traffickers to find many other ways to commit these offenses against child victims while also avoiding detection.

The Internet makes it possible for children to engage in exploitative sexual activity online, such as pornographic performances on webcams and chat platforms, without the physical presence of the criminal involved in their trafficking and exploitation who nonetheless causes severe harm and trauma to the child victim. When the trafficking victim is under eighteen years of age, it is unnecessary to establish a means to declare the trafficking a criminal act. Nevertheless, since some means behaviors can also be used in the Internet context and are capable of leading a minor into a situation of sexual exploitation, the next part analyzes certain components of this aspect that are likely to occur in Internet situations involving children.

The Means (How It Is Done)

The absence of improper means does not mitigate crimes against children as international law affords special protection to children due to their age and other vulnerabilities.[26] This is a key difference from cases involving adult trafficking victims, which require evidence of means that nullify consent. Nevertheless, although the means are only significant in adult trafficking cases, this reference is important as some such means are used to establish the *actus reus* of child trafficking online. Furthermore, the intention of the perpetrator can be established in various ways and may manifest as one of the listed means for the ultimate purpose of exploitation, specifically,

> threat or use of force or other forms of coercion, of abduction, of fraud, of deception, of the abuse of power or of a position of vulnerability or of the giving or receiving of payments or benefits to achieve the consent of a person having control over another person.[27]

Offenders use direct and indirect methods such as fraud, deception, and coercion to lure, intimidate, blackmail, or place or maintain a minor in a situation of exploitation, including the making of pornographic materials. Hence these means are control mechanisms that vary. Some overlap and some do not require an explicit explanation (e.g., the threat or use of force). Traffickers may use them to control victims in a number of ways according to the victims' vulnerabilities and needs, the type of exploitation, the stage of the trafficking process, and the victims' location. Traffickers need not be in physical proximity to their victims but can control them from a distance. Thus, some components of the *means* element can potentially be translated to an Internet trafficking context.

For example, among other elements, coercion can facilitate traffickers' control over victims, including in cyberspace, with the firm intention to exploit a child. Coercion is essential to the idea of online sex trafficking as a variety of both direct and indirect forms can be employed by cybertraffickers to subject a child to a situation of exploitation such as threats, deception, and psychological pressure. As in the real world, in the dynamics of trafficking in cyberspace, the psychological control tactics of traffickers create situations in which the victim submits to abuse due to fear of the consequences of not doing so. Psychological coercion can be a subtle but formidable means of exercising effective control over a person online. Consequently, psychological compulsion can be as significant as, or even more powerful than, physical violence and as such it is considered a valid means of inducing someone to exploitation in both the Palermo Protocol and the U.S. Trafficking Victims Protection Act.[28]

There are circumstances in which cybertraffickers ensure long-term exploitation of children without the need to meet the child offline or exercise physical force against them. This postulate is in line with General Comment no. 13 of the CRC, which expressly states that the sexual victimization, abuse, and exploitation of children need not be "accompanied by physical force or restraint" to "nonetheless [be] psychologically intrusive, exploitive and traumatic."[29] Therefore, inducing or coercing a child in cyberspace to perform any sexual act is a form of abuse and exploitation and is illegal. The General Comment no. 13 describes violence against children in broad terms as encompassing all forms of harm against them—physical or mental—and may therefore include forms of abuse, neglect, exploitation, and psychological maltreatment.[30]

Moreover, fraud and deception are closely connected with this issue as they are less-direct forms of control and also represent *means* elements that online traffickers often use to get children to an intended point of exploitation. These elements frequently relate to emotional control within relationships. For example, exploiters may lead victims to believe they are engaged in a boyfriend-girlfriend relationship and then use this belief to coerce the victims to engage in activities that can then be used to coerce further exploitation (such as through the threat of blackmail). Trafficking can arise from situations in which children initially form such a relationship willingly but are subsequently deceived and manipulated into positions in which the trafficker can exercise control over them. Accordingly these means can be effected in several ways online and can be connected to the nature of the rewards promised by the trafficker (e.g., love, work, or studies abroad). Means may also involve the exchange of money or gifts online.

The abuse of power or of a position of vulnerability (APOV) is an additional means through which minors can be brought into a online sex trafficking situation. Although the Palermo Protocol does not define the term "abuse of power," evidence suggests it was originally conceived of as "abuse of authority" such as "the power that male family members might have over female family members in some legal systems and the power that parents might have over their children."[31] When translated to the online context, such a formulation demonstrates that this form of control can be especially relevant in the case of family-based relationships, guardians, and caregivers—for example, in situations where parents have the power to make decisions on behalf of the child (e.g., parents "selling" children for livestreaming forms of abuse at a distance via cellphone or a computer with webcam in the Philippines, as identified by the 2017 U.S. Department of State Trafficking in Persons [TIP] Report).[32] Mail-order bride cases can represent a similar situation in which a girl may trust her parents or other relative with authority and is offered as a bride online with their consent. The parents or relative may have the illusion that this will give the girl a better life and opportunities to succeed, but ultimately these authority figures are potentially involved in child trafficking.

APOV refers to any situation in which the person being abused cannot seek redress for the abuse. The vulnerability can be of any kind: physical, psychological, economic, social, or legal (e.g., illegal residence in a country). In general the vulnerability of the child in question must be of such a nature that they have virtually no choice but to accept being exploited. Vulnerability can be psychological, emotional, family-related, or related to social or economic conditions.[33] Exploitative situations online clearly demonstrate that an individual is taking advantage of a child's lack of power. In such cases, the UNODC issue paper on APOV and the guidance note on this subject recognize the age of a child as a preexisting vulnerability that can be abused by offenders in order to engage in a trafficking offense.[34] More specifically, age—like "illness, gender and poverty"[35]—is considered a preexisting vulnerability that is therefore intrinsic to the victim rather than being created by the traffickers as in the case of factors such as "isolation, dependency and, sometimes, irregular legal status."[36] In any case, offenders can abuse both types of vulnerability factors to manipulate a child and do so also from a distance. In short, children are "inherently vulnerable to trafficking."[37]

An interpretative note in the *travaux préparatoires* of the Palermo Protocol defines "abuse of a position of vulnerability" as "any situation in which the person involved has no real and acceptable alternative but to submit to the abuse involved,"[38] which is a feature present in most if not all cases of trafficking.[39] Thus, the APOV usually appears together with other means of trafficking and some of them may overlap. In fact, it seems the drafters included APOV within the means element of the trafficking definition in order to ensure that the protocol covered all the means offenders might use to place a person in an exploitive situation and keep them there.[40] In practice, APOV may appear as a subsidiary means to substantiate other means of trafficking. For example, APOV can help demonstrate that children are easier to manipulate on the Internet through the abuse of their vulnerability.[41] In such situations, traffickers can use APOV alongside other means—for example, threats and other forms of coercion, including physiological manipulation—to accomplish their exploitative goals with the targeted minor. As with offline instances, trafficking in cyberspace is certainly a crime with a specific intent—the purpose of exploitation—with offenders abusing the position of vulnerability of minors.

In regard to the *means* element of "the giving or receiving of payments or benefits to achieve the consent of a person having control over another person," neither the *travaux préparatoires* nor the interpretative documents such as the legislative guide or the 2009 UNODC Model Trafficking Law offer clear guidance. This aspect appears to refer to situations when in the course of trafficking, payment or other benefits are promised or granted to a person with authority over the child to induce them to act contrary to the child's interests, human rights, and human integrity.[42] This can include situations of "ownership" over a child, particularly girls, whereby parents or guardians misuse their power by agreeing to offer their daughters to a bidder online or in marriage when the intention of the husband is the sexual exploitation of the child.

In general, since there is no need to establish any means in child trafficking offenses, one might assume that establishing cases of child trafficking would be simple. However given the nature of the Internet and the broad definition of what can be considered cybertrafficking of children, defining offenses related to the process and to the identified end result of exploitation may pose additional challenges. The matter is further complicated by the fact that children may not always identify themselves as victims or report offenses or indeed even be aware of the possibility of their being virtually objectified. In cyberspace, the use of means such as coercion, fraud, deception, and APOV demonstrates that trafficking can occur without the use of any physical violence.[43]

Exploitative Purpose (Why It Is Done)

Cyberactivity related to trafficking connects to the purpose of exploitation. The reference in the Palermo Protocol's definition of "for the purpose of" exploitation necessitates a *mens rea* requirement, or the *intent* of the offender to commit the material act (action) against a child for the purpose of the specific result of exploitation (*dolus specialis*). Therefore, the mental element of trafficking is required in order to find a perpetrator guilty of the criminal act. As stated earlier, a situation of online sex trafficking can arise when a trafficker intentionally performs any of the stipulated acts regardless of whether the final result is achieved (sexual exploitation). On a practical level, this would facilitate the prosecution of suspected online traffickers involved as recruiters and brokers (i.e., those at the beginning of the trafficking chain) who have knowledge of the ultimate purpose of the act committed against the child as well as online buyers (i.e., those at the end of the chain) who knowingly benefit from receiving or buying the exploitative use of a child.

What, though, constitutes "exploitation"? Although there is no international legal definition of the term "exploitation" in a human trafficking context, the Palermo Protocol provides a nonexhaustive list of examples where the purpose of exploitation can be found for the crime of human trafficking. Specifically, the protocol mentions "at a minimum, the exploitation of the prostitution of others or other forms of sexual exploitation, forced labor or services, slavery or practices similar to slavery, servitude or the removal of organs."[44] The phrase "at a minimum" leaves open the definition and therefore the possibility for states parties of the protocol to extend the ultimate purposes of trafficking to include other exploitative practices in their national laws.[45] Thus, the Palermo Protocol was designed to address a broad spectrum of forms of exploitation that refers to "the act of taking unjust advantage of another for one's own benefit" as defined by the International Organization for Migration in its glossary on migration.[46] The nonexhaustive list of examples in the Palermo Protocol assists in determining what constitutes exploitation on a case-by-case basis.

Significant for our purposes is the inclusion of "practices similar to slavery" in the understanding of what amounts to exploitation. With this the Palermo Protocol incorporates the exploitation of children referenced in the 1956 Supplementary Slavery Convention as part of the legal definition:

> Any institution or practice whereby a child or young person under the age of 18 years, is delivered by either or both of his natural parents or by his guardian to another person, whether for reward or not, with a view to the exploitation of the child or young person or of his labour.[47]

This provision on the intention to use a child for the purposes of exploitation refers to a child victim as a slave-like person (see "Key International Legal Instruments" in chapter 1). Slavery and practices analogous to slavery are the ultimate purpose of trafficking. In practice, exploitative uses of children may vary with regard to the degree of control and whether or not ownership is exercised over the child.[48]

The UNODC sees a potential relationship between the servile status of a child and the characteristics of various powers attached to the right of ownership. For instance, the UNODC affirms with respect to illicit adoption practices that "can be prosecuted under the umbrella of trafficking crimes" that "the act may be transporting or receiving a child and the purpose may be slavery or sexual exploitation."[49] This recognition means that exploited children subject to a practice similar to slavery can be considered in a situation of ownership that reduces them to objects. This position is in line with a 2018 report by the special rapporteur on contemporary forms of slavery, Urmila Bhoola, who noted that the sale of children for exploitation purposes as a practice similar to slavery (1956 Supplementary Slavery Convention) is a contemporary form of slavery: although there is no legal right to ownership over a child, it constitutes slavery in the context of the exercise of powers tantamount to ownership, reducing the child to a commodity.[50] Accordingly the perpetrator can exercise the material element of trafficking over a child (e.g., they may purchase a child, transfer ownership of the child to another person, or place the child in a situation the child cannot terminate even if they wish to do so) with the intention of reducing the child's status as a human being to one of slavery.

In general terms, the UN recognizes that the term "sexual exploitation" is for "sexual purposes" with motives including "but not limited to profiting monetarily, socially or politically."[51] This broad definitional approach to motives was clearly established in the Palermo Protocol as it recognizes that some individuals may have motives other than profit while still committing trafficking offenses for sexual exploitation purposes. For example, according to the *travaux préparatoires* of the protocol, during the drafting process some delegations proposed a profit element to describe criminal acts that constitute trafficking in persons for sexual exploitation purposes. However the drafters did not accept the proposal because it was argued that an explicit reference to profit would be an unnecessarily restrictive condition.[52] In the context of cyberspace and from a trafficker's standpoint, it is possible to obtain economic benefit (commercial sexual exploitation) as well as personal gratification (noncommercial exploitation) in the same act, blurring any distinction between these forms of abuse.[53] This can be demonstrated in situations where an offender might sell a child's live online sex shows, thereby obtaining financial gain, in addition to distributing the same material in online communities to gain entry or access to more materials for no commercial gain.

Just as the broad definitions of exploitation and motives for it are of value in cases of cybertrafficking, so too, I argue, is the legal irrelevance of child victims' consent. Child sex trafficking in cyberspace involves children who cannot and would not consent to an act of sexual exploitation against them that is committed or facilitated via computer technology or the Internet. In other words, a person exploits the vulnerability of a child online. Therefore, any form of consent or seemingly voluntary conduct is irrelevant with respect to protecting children under the age of eighteen years from forms of sexual exploitation. There is no exception to this rule. The special rapporteur of the UN CHR on the sale of children, child prostitution, and child pornography, Ofelia Calcetas-Santos, highlighted this position when explaining that the act of engaging or offering the services of a child is committed by the other party rather than by the child.[54] Hence offenders exploit the innocence and vulnerabilities of children in persuading them to engage in sexually exploitative activities in cyberspace.

Defining Exploitation and Purpose in Other International Instruments and Materials

Sexual exploitation denotes the use of a child for sexual purposes and covers any commercial sexual activity including child prostitution and CSAM.[55] More explicitly, the OP-CRC-SC obliges states parties to fully cover under their criminal law the prohibition of acts and activities in the context of the sale of children. They are obliged to include the type of practices in which the child is a victim of a transaction for sexual exploitation. These acts include offering, delivering, or accepting a child for the offender's benefit—that is, either the use of a child for profit or to satisfy sexual desires with a view to the child's sexual exploitation.[56] States parties of the OP-CRC-SC are required to establish a legal basis at the national level for the prohibition of these acts and criminalization of individuals who buy, trade, or sell sexual acts with a child. These offenses are criminal acts regardless of whether their commission occurs domestically or transnationally, individually or in a group setting, online or offline.

Sexual exploitation of children in cyberspace encompasses a commercial transaction or any other form of consideration (an element of exchange) making the child available for sexual purposes. UNICEF explains that in circumstances of sexual exploitation, a second party benefits—through profit or quid pro quo—from sexual activity involving the child. In these terms, purchasing or selling a minor's services online for monetary or other compensation may demonstrate that due to this treatment the child is essentially a commodity for sexual purposes. In addition to forms of prostitution or pornography, this may include situations such as those involving child brides, as discussed above. This provides evidence of an expanded and evolved concept of the commercial sexual exploitation of children (CSEC) to embrace situations that may go beyond the sexual exploitative use of children as a commodity for profit and that encompass situations in which the offenders may accrue economic or other personal gain.[57]

Similarly the Stockholm Declaration and Agenda for Action (the Stockholm Declaration) adopted at the First World Congress against Commercial Sexual Exploitation of Children in 1996 recognizes that CSEC is a form of abuse through which children are treated and viewed as commodities. The Stockholm Declaration describes CSEC as

> sexual abuse by the adult and remuneration in cash or kind to the child or a third person or persons. The child is treated as a sexual object and as a commercial object [which] constitutes a form of coercion and violence against children, and amounts to forced labour and a contemporary form of slavery.[58]

These are situations in which a child is used for sexual purposes in exchange for cash, goods, favors, affection, or protection that is given to the child or to an intermediary who benefits from the child's sexual exploitation (e.g., given or received online payments). Furthermore, in an online environment there are certain cases in which a child may be persuaded to engage in a sexually exploitative activity to receive an object of exchange—mostly to fulfill some essential need. The element of exchange in online exploitative practices against children may not always be tangible. While it may be cash or material items, it can also take the form of love, protection, or any other intangible good. Either way, the exploiter comes to see the child or treat them as a sexual object or commodity on the Internet. Although there is no appropriation of the legal personality of a child—as in examples of slavery in the past—there is still an appropriation of the very humanity of the child inherent in his or her commodification.

The broader CSEC approach is also reflected in the 2001 Yokohama Global Commitment in the Second World Congress against Commercial Sexual Exploitation of Children, where representatives and leaders from around the world declared their commitment to promote cooperation and combine efforts "to eliminate all forms of sexual exploitation and sexual abuse of children worldwide" without emphasizing a commercial aspect. Rather, they enforced a broader approach in the context of sexual exploitation, recognizing the variety of motives that exploiters may have (in addition to the merely monetary).[59] In both the Yokohama Commitment and the Rio Declaration, participants affirmed their commitment to ending child trafficking, including the use of the Internet and new technologies for actions related to child pornography and child grooming that could lead to online and offline forms of abuse.[60] Overall, they condemned CSEC as a fundamental violation of children's rights and dignity through which children are treated and seen as mere commodities.

Moreover, Article 3 of the ILO Worst Forms of Child Labour Convention 1999 (No. 182) specifically refers to "the use, procuring or offering of a child for prostitution, for the production of pornography or for pornographic performances" and any "work which, by its nature or the circumstances in which it is carried out, is likely to harm the health, safety or morals of children"[61] as the worst forms of child labor. This convention mandates states parties to prohibit and eliminate these practices at the national level without delay and to provide child victims with direct assistance, rehabilitation, and social reintegration.[62] In addition, in 2008 the ILO articulated an expanded approach to defining the use of children in commercial sexual exploitation, inclusive of forms linked to the Internet, as follows:

- the use of children in sexual activities remunerated in cash or kind to the child (personal gratification purposes)
- trafficking in children in the sex industry (financial gain)
- child sex tourism (for financial or personal gratification purposes or both)
- the production, distribution, and viewing of child pornography (for obtaining an economic benefit or personal gratification or both)
- the use of children to perform sex shows (for economic gain or personal gratification or both)[63]

These are offenses that relate to the sale and sexual exploitation of a child, facilitated by exploiters' control and ownership over the child victim, that can, furthermore, be facilitated through the Internet. These include situations in which a third party benefits from the exploitation of the child as well as when an offer is made to the child to induce them to agree to perform a sexual activity online with an element of remuneration or exchange involved.

CYBERSPACE CONTEXT IN LINKING CHILD SEXUAL EXPLOITATION AND TRAFFICKING LAWS

As is clear from the above, the Palermo Protocol is a legally binding instrument of utmost importance as it provides a legal framework with respect to trafficking in persons, including trafficking in children. The protocol defines what conduct is to be identified as trafficking in national law, thereby offering guidance on the obligations of states parties to respond to trafficking in accordance with the protocol's international normative standards. In this regard, it is important to note that at the time the protocol was adopted in 2000, the nature and extent of the problem of trafficking did not have the linkage to cyberspace that it may have today.[64] The reality today is that offenders commit acts against children with the intent to exploit them on the Internet, thus posing new challenges to states, particularly with regard to the child protection framework.[65] Child exploitation in cyberspace complicates the interpretation of the Palermo Protocol specifically because the protocol was not specific to cyberspace. The conceptual framework of the international legal definition of child trafficking from the Palermo Protocol analyzed above may elucidate the legal aspects and practical considerations in relation to these cyberpractices when a child is subjected to an *act* element with the intent of sexual exploitation of that child (*purpose*) committed or facilitated via cyberspace. "Online sex trafficking" of children can be defined as

> the use of computer systems, networks, and computer data to engage in the recruitment, solicitation, offering, advertisement, transportation, sale, transfer, harboring, or receipt of a child for the purpose of sexual exploitation regardless of the child's consent. Sexual exploitation shall include, at a minimum, the sexual exploitation of children in prostitution or other forms of sexual exploitation, sexual services, slavery or practices similar to slavery, or sexual servitude.
>
> It shall be considered online sex trafficking of children with or without the use of means of the threat or the use of coercion, fraud, deception, the abuse of power or a position of vulnerability, or the giving or receiving of payments or benefits to achieve the consent of a person having control over a child for the purpose of sexual exploitation.[66]

Accordingly online sex trafficking exists in situations where a child has been the victim of an *act* that has the purpose of sexually exploiting that child. This understanding is also in line with EU Anti-Trafficking Directive 2011/36/EU, which in Article 2(1) provides binding legislation to member states that an "exchange or transfer of control over those persons" amounts to an act of trafficking and that trafficking therefore does not always require the transportation or movement of the person concerned.[67] In such cases, the act committed online is aimed at exploiting a child.

Through misuse of the Internet, perpetrators target children and take advantage of their vulnerabilities with the goal of inducing them into slavery or sexual exploitation and ensnare them in the trafficking chain. It has been clearly demonstrated that elements of trafficking in the Palermo Protocol's definition, including the *actus reus* of the violation and the exploitation element, can be captured in both the real world and in cyberspace.

I have argued that there may be a direct link between online sex trafficking and modern slavery. Because there is the exercise of one or more powers attached to the right of ownership, online exploitative acts over a child may be considered a form of slavery. Child victims are not capable of giving their consent, and perpetrators' actions may represent the commodification of the child in order to exploit the child sexually. After analyzing the core definitional elements of trafficking for the understanding of acts and activities that represent online sex trafficking, it is important to examine in detail technology-mediated child exploitation as cybercrimes possibly linked to online sex trafficking. However before examining these cases, in chapter 3 I closely examine the legal foundation of the *information society*, recognizing the potential that Internet technology provides to greatly improve our lives.

Today—particularly in relation to children and young people—the Internet has become a medium through which all can express their views freely and think critically according to their age and maturity. I argue that the openness and freedom the Internet enables also enables crime, including online child sexual exploitation and abuse. Due to the mass connectivity of the Internet, traffickers can multiply their activities online speedily and automatically, reaching a huge number of children and a global market.

NOTES

1. Palermo Protocol, art. 3(a).

2. *Prosecutor v. Dragoljub Kunarac et al.*, 2001-ICTY Trial Chamber II Judgement, para. 540, at 192; (February 22, 2001), IT-96–23-T & IT-96–23/1-PT; Roza Pati, "Trafficking in Human Beings: The Convergence of Criminal Law and Human Rights," in *The SAGE Handbook of Human Trafficking and Modern Day Slavery*, ed. Jennifer B. Clark and Sasha Poucki (London: Sage Publications, 2019), 286.

3. According to UNSG, "Slavery, the Slave Trade, and Other Forms of Servitude," E/2357, January 27, 1953, 48, it might be considered that the drafters when referring to "powers attaching to the right of ownership" had in mind the absolute authority of the masters over slaves in Roman law.

4. Palermo Protocol, art. 3(a), (b), (c), (d).

5. Ibid., art. 3(a).

6. Ibid., art. 3(b).

7. UNODC, *Legislative Guides for the Implementation of the UN Convention against Transnational Organized Crime and the Protocols Thereto* (New York: United Nations, 2004), 270.

8. Palermo Protocol, art. 3(c).

9. See OHCHR, *Human Rights and Human Trafficking: Fact Sheet no. 36*, https://www.ohchr.org/documents/publications/fs36_en.pdf.

10. Palermo Protocol, art. 3(c).

11. UNODC, *Anti-Human Trafficking Manual for Criminal Justice Practitioners: Definition of Trafficking in Persons and Smuggling of Migrants (Module 1)* (New York: United Nations, 2009), 4–6.

12. Palermo Protocol, art. 3(c).

13. CoE, *Trafficking in Organs, Tissues and Cells and Trafficking in Human Beings for the Purpose of the Removal of Organs*, https://rm.coe.int/16805ad1bb.

14. Ibid.

15. Ibid.

16. Ibid.

17. Ibid.

18. OHCHR, *Human Rights and Human Trafficking*.

19. Palermo Protocol, art. 5(s).

20. UNODC, Travaux Préparatoires *of the Negotiations for the Elaboration of the United Nations Convention against Transnational Organized Crime and the Protocols Thereto* (New York: United Nations, 2006), 361, 364.

21. The Organized Crime Convention's provision on the liability of legal persons should be taken into consideration when formulating criminal offenses under the Palermo Protocol. See UNGA, "United Nations Convention against Transnational Organized Crime," entered into force September 29, 2003, U.N.T.S. 2225, art. 10 (hereafter referred to as UNTOC); UN Center for International Crime Prevention, *Part Two: Legislative Guide for the Implementation of the Protocol to Prevent, Suppress and Punish Trafficking in Persons, Especially Women and Children, Supplementing the United Nations Convention against Transnational Organized Crime* (New York: United Nations, 2004), 15, mentioning that "Protocol offences shall also be regarded as offences established in accordance with the Convention."

22. A position that is in line with postulates in "Directive 2011/93/EU of the European Parliament and of the Council of 13 December 2011 on Combating the Sexual Abuse and Sexual Exploitation of Children and Child Pornography, and Replacing Council Framework Decision 2004/68/JHA," Official Journal of the European Union 335 (2011), sec. 18. (hereafter Directive 2011/93/EU)..

23. Jean Allain, "Bellagio-Harvard Guidelines on the Legal Parameters of Slavery," in *The Law and Slavery* (Leiden: Brill/Nijhoff, 2015), guideline 2, at 556.

24. UNODC, *Issue Paper: The Role of "Consent" in the Trafficking in Persons Protocol* (Vienna: United Nations, 2014), 5–8.

25. UNODC, *Study on the Effects of New Information Technologies on the Abuse and Exploitation of Children* (New York: United Nations, 2015).

26. UNODC, *Anti-Human Trafficking Manual*, 5; Palermo Protocol, art. 3(c).

27. Palermo Protocol, art. 3(a).

28. Victims of Trafficking and Violence Protection Act of 2000, H.R. 3244, 106th Cong. (2000), reauthorized in 2003 (H.R. 2620), 2005 (H.R. 972), 2008 (S. 3061), and 2013 (as Public Law 113–4 under the Title XII of Reauthorization of the Violence against Women Act); 18 USC § 77, sec. 1591; Noël B. Busch-Armendariz, Maura Nsonwu, and Laurie C. Heffron, *Human Trafficking: Applying Research, Theory and Case Studies* (London: Sage Publications, 2018), 27.

29. CRC, "General Comment no. 13 (2011): The Right of the Child to Freedom From All Forms of Violence," CRC/C/GC/13, April 18, 2011, para. 25, at 10.

30. Ibid., para. 4, at 4; para. 25, at 10.

31. UNODC, *Travaux Préparatoires*, 343, note 20.

32. U.S. Department of State, *TIP Report* (2017), 32.

33. For example, guidance on the concept of APOV in CoE, "Explanatory Report to the Council of Europe Convention on Action against Trafficking in Human Beings," May 16, 2005, Counsel of Europe T.S. 197, para. 83, at 15.

34. UNODC, *Abuse of a Position of Vulnerability and Other "Means" within the Definition of Trafficking in Persons: Issue Paper* (New York: United Nations, 2013), 3. See generally UNODC, *Guidance Note on 'Abuse of a Position of Vulnerability' as a Means of Trafficking in Persons in Article 3 of the Protocol to Prevent, Suppress and Punish Trafficking in Persons, Especially Women and Children, Supplementing the United Nations Convention against Transnational Organized Crime* (2012), 2.

35. UNODC, *Abuse of a Position of Vulnerability*, 3.

36. Ibid., 3.

37. Ibid., 13.

38. UNODC, *Travaux Préparatoires*, Interpretative Note C(a) on art. 3, 347.

39. UNODC, *Abuse of a Position of Vulnerability*, 3.

40. Ibid., 18.

41. Ibid., 73.

42. UNODC, *Model Law against Trafficking in Persons*, V.09–81990 (E), (UNODC, 2009), 25.

43. Ibid., 24.

44. Palermo Protocol, art. 3(a).

45. UNODC, *Anti-Human Trafficking Manual*, 5–6.

46. International Organization for Migration, *no. 34 Glossary on Migration*, 2nd ed., (Geneva: International Organization for Migration, 2019), 68.

47. Supplementary Slavery Convention, art. 1(d).

48. UNODC, *Travaux Préparatoires*, Interpretative note C (d) on art. 3, 347: "Where illegal adoption amounts to a practice similar to slavery as defined in art.

1, para. (d) of the Supplementary Convention on the Abolition of Slavery, the Slave Trade, and Institutions and Practices Similar to Slavery, it will also fall within the scope of the protocol."

49. UNODC, *Anti-Human Trafficking Manual*, 7.

50. HRC, "Report of the Special Rapporteur on Contemporary Forms of Slavery, Including Its Causes and Consequences, Urmila Bhoola," A/73/139, July 10, 2018, para. 13, at 6.

51. UN Secretariat, "Secretary-General's Bulletin: Special Measures for Protection from Sexual Exploitation and Sexual Abuse," ST/SGB/2003/13, October 9, 2003, 1.

52. UNODC, *The Concept of "Exploitation" in the Trafficking in Persons Protocol: Issue Paper* (Vienna: United Nations, 2015), 26.

53. UNODC, *Study on the Effects of New Information Technologies*, 7.

54. CHR, "Report of the Special Rapporteur on the Sale of Children, Child Prostitution and Child Pornography, Ofelia Calcetas-Santos," E/CN.4/1996/100, January 17, 1996, para. 7, at 3.

55. UNCRC, art. 34(b), (c).

56. OP-CRC-SC, art. 3(1)(a)(i)(a.).

57. Subgroup against the Sexual Exploitation of Children NGO Group for the UNCRC, *Semantics or Substance? Towards a Shared Understanding of Terminology Referring to the Sexual Abuse and Exploitation of Children* (2005), 57–58.

58. ECPAT International, *Declaration and Agenda for Action: First World Congress against Commercial Sexual Exploitation of Children* (ECPAT, 1996), para. 5, at 1.

59. Second World Congress against Commercial Sexual Exploitation of Children, "Yokohama Global Commitment 2001," adopted December 20, 2001.

60. World Congress III against Sexual Exploitation of Children and Adolescents, The Rio de Janeiro Declaration and Call for Action to Prevent and Stop Sexual Exploitation of Children and Adolescents (UNICEF, 2008), 12; Second World Congress against Commercial Sexual Exploitation of Children, "Yokohama Global Commitment 2001."

61. ILO, "Worst Forms of Child Labour Convention, 1999 (No. 182)," art. 3(b), (d).

62. Ibid., art. 7(2)(b).

63. ILO and International Programme on the Elimination of Child Labour, *Commercial Sexual Exploitation of Children and Adolescents: The ILO's Response* (Geneva: International Labour Organization, 2008), 1.

64. See V. Greiman and C. Bain, "The Emergence of Cyber Activity as a Gateway to Human Trafficking," *Journal of Information Warfare* 12, no. 2 (2013): 41–49. See generally Sabine Witting, "'Cyber' Trafficking? An Interpretation of the Palermo Protocol in the Digital Era," Völkerrechtsblog, https://voelkerrechtsblog.org/de/cyber-trafficking-an-interpretation-of-the-palermo-protocol-in-the-digital-era/.

65. The CRC encourages states parties to introduce new provisions in their penal law to ensure that they can adequately address sexual offenses against children committed or facilitated through ICT. See OP-CRC-SC Guidelines, para. 44, at 10.

66. Author's definition of online sex trafficking of children.

67. CoE, "Directive 2011/36/EU of the European Parliament and of the Council of 5 April 2011 on Preventing and Combating Trafficking in Human Beings and Protecting Its Victims, and Replacing Council Framework Decision 2002/629/JHA," OJ L. 101/1–101/11, April 15, 2011, art. 2(1).

Chapter 3

Human Rights in Cyberspace

The Internet offers a new social space in which online actors, from governments to individuals, can interact with one another. Personal computing technology has revolutionized information sharing and social interaction.[1] These advances have implications for human rights, as UN special rapporteur Frank La Rue underscored in a report to the UNGA. This is due to the unique and transformative nature of the Internet, which enables individuals to exercise their right to freedom of opinion and expression and to realize a range of other human rights, including the right to education.[2] Indeed, the Internet has become one of the most powerful tools of the twenty-first century, with the potential to promote economic development and human progress in a global society.

The UN has argued that the Internet is a human development tool[3] that can promote the seventeen sustainable development goals (SDGs) of the 2030 Agenda for Sustainable Development.[4] The Internet has impacted human behavior and is now part of virtually every aspect of modern human life. Technological advances in computing over the past few decades, particularly the Internet, have facilitated the transfer and exchange of information, connected individuals online across the globe through powerful and efficient processes, and played a major role in globalization as well as the expansion of personal freedoms around the world. The present chapter explores the evolution of human rights promotion on the Internet, particularly with regard to the establishment of an information society for all, with reference to the UDHR, delineating global Internet governance standards. However, while cyberspace offers immense potential for human and societal development, it also can enable the misuse of technology for criminal purposes, including online trafficking.

THE RELATIONSHIP BETWEEN HUMAN
RIGHTS AND THE INTERNET

The development and spread of ICTs have the potential to enable individuals to access information and knowledge, thereby promoting human progress and reducing inequalities.[5] In 2003 at the World Summit on the Information Society (WSIS) in Geneva, world leaders declared a "common desire and commitment to build a people-centered, inclusive and development-oriented Information Society" in which each individual can access, create, use, and share information and knowledge to achieve their full potential and improve their quality of life.[6] This common vision of the information society is based on the purposes and principles of the UN charter and the full respect and defense of the UDHR. In essence, this vision recognizes that human beings are at the center of what the UN calls the information society and that technology plays a key role in their service by facilitating the promotion of social and economic development and improving quality of life for all.[7]

Moreover, the shared vision that technology can promote a more equitable and sustainable world also includes children, as evidenced by the declaration of principles. Section A, paragraph 11 of "Our Common Vision of the Information Society" states the WSIS commitment to ensuring that the development and operation of ICTs, and the applications and services associated with them, respect the rights of children as well as their protection and well-being.[8] This statement demonstrates that children can also benefit from the opportunities provided by ICTs.

More than 11,000 participants from 175 countries who attended the WSIS and related events endorsed the first phase of the WSIS, namely, the Geneva phase.[9] The declaration of principles is akin to a road map for the information society.[10] Section B, titled "An Information Society for All: Key Principles,"[11] makes a number of key affirmations. For example, section B2 ("Information and Communication Infrastructure: An Essential Foundation for an Inclusive Information Society") asserts,

> Connectivity is a central enabling agent in building the Information Society. Universal, ubiquitous, equitable and affordable access to ICT infrastructure and services, constitutes one of the challenges of the Information Society and should be an objective of all stakeholders involved in building it. Connectivity also involves access to energy and postal services, which should be assured in conformity with the domestic legislation of each country.[12]

Section B10, titled "Ethical Dimensions of the Information Society," contains the following passage:

All actors in the Information Society should take appropriate actions and preventive measures, as determined by law, against abusive uses of ICTs, such as
. . . all forms of child abuse, including paedophilia and child pornography, and
trafficking in, and exploitation of, human beings.[13]

Ensuring access to information appears to be a precondition for achieving the
vision of the inclusive information society presented by the declaration of
principles. Therefore, the information society calls for the free flow of information to all humanity. On the other hand, however, such openness presents
threats against which vulnerable populations (such as children) need to be
protected.

In addition to the declaration of principles, the other most important document in the Geneva phase of the WSIS, the plan of action, presents a clear
commitment to translating the declaration of principles into practice by
meeting concrete targets elaborated during the second phase of the WSIS in
Tunis in 2005.[14] Hence, the first phase of the WSIS created a framework for
building a global and inclusive information society on the basis of using ICTs
as tools with the potential to improve people's social, economic, and cultural
lives and to contribute to the goals enshrined in the millennium declaration.[15]
The WSIS's Geneva phase raised awareness of the importance of ICTs in
shaping the future and led to the WSIS's second phase, which focused "on
the highly political issues of Internet governance and financing to bridge the
digital divide as well as on defining the implementation and follow-up process to pave the way ahead"[16] to the realization of the Internet Governance
Forum (IGF).

The idea of translating human rights to Internet governance was raised
and widely endorsed at the Tunis Summit in 2005.[17] Notably, one of the
outcome documents adopted during the second phase of the WSIS, the Tunis
Commitment, highlighted the importance of the UN charter. The Tunis
Commitment cites the UN charter as its foundation. Therein, states reaffirmed
their support for the declaration of principles and the plan of action adopted
at the first phase of the summit in Geneva in 2003.[18] In addition, the Tunis
Commitment confirmed that the UN charter principles are the foundation
for universal access to and sharing of information. The information society
offers equal access to information and empowers all people to achieve their
full potential and benefit from all of the value that ICTs bring to humanity.
Thus, the Tunis Commitment reflected progress toward ensuring that everyone has access to the Internet, in line with the UDHR and the declaration of
principles. The document is particularly relevant for children as it acknowledges the need to protect children and their rights in the context of ICTs.
It emphasizes that children's best interests are a primary consideration and
those interests should guide Internet governance standards. Paragraph 24 of

the Tunis Commitment also recognizes the role of ICTs in the protection of children and the enhancement of their development.[19]

In the same spirit, the Tunis Agenda for Information Society—the second product of the Tunis phase of the WSIS—was derived from the declaration of principles and references the UDHR's evolution into a road map for Internet governance. In paragraphs 29 and 30, it recognizes that the Internet's management should be multilateral, transparent, and democratic with the full involvement of all stakeholders.[20] The Tunis Agenda now delineates global Internet governance standards by supporting the right of all to enjoy the benefits of access to technology and information, which requires foundational principles aligned with those established in the UDHR.[21] Furthermore, the Tunis Agenda catalyzed the formation of the IGF, through the formal request of the UN secretary-general, "to convene, by the second quarter of 2006, a meeting of the new forum for multistakeholder policy dialogue—called the Internet Governance Forum."[22]

Accordingly, WSIS outcomes reflected a solid international commitment to the protection of children online. The formative and pioneering work that took place during the WSIS period incorporated guidance from the UDHR and therefore upheld the idea that human dignity must be respected and protected in all settings, including cyberspace.[23] The successor of the WSIS, materialized in 2006 in the form of the IGF, now offers a multistakeholder dialogue on public policy issues related to Internet governance.[24]

In 2010, the mandate of the IGF, which was established in paragraphs 72–78 of the Tunis Agenda, was renewed for five years (2011–2015); with UNGA Resolution 70/125 in 2015, it received an extension for another ten years (2016–2025).[25] Part of the IGF's significant impact (particularly with regard to child online protection), the IGF Dynamic Coalition on Child Online Safety, provides an open, multistakeholder platform to address fundamental issues that affect children in online environments.

Additionally, the secretary-general of the International Telecommunication Union (ITU) launched the Global Cybersecurity Agenda (GCA) in 2007 as a framework for international cooperation among relevant partners to improve confidence and security in the information society.[26] Thus, the development of countries' cybersecurity capabilities can include responding to threats such as cybercrime. The GCA has launched the Child Online Protection Initiative (COP) as a part of ongoing efforts to improve online child safety around the world and to specifically address child exploitation in cyberspace.[27] COP seeks to create an international collaborative network and represents a multistakeholder effort among ITU members to encourage the development of tools and resources to mitigate risks.

Thus, the integration of cybercrime awareness within a broader cybersecurity program requires the improvement of legislation that protects Internet users. This consideration is an integral part of making the Internet safer, including for children, who should be able to use technology with confidence. Moreover, the ITU's Council Working Group on Child Online Protection is a platform for member states to raise awareness of child online safety issues and exchange views regarding the advancement of COP. It provides support in the implementation of road maps for COP and coordinates among stakeholders.[28] The importance of strengthening international cooperation to combat cybercrime, including the use of new information technologies to abuse and exploit children, has also been addressed in the UN Commission on Crime Prevention and Criminal Justice (CCPCJ) Resolutions 22/7[29] and 22/8.[30]

UNIVERSAL ACCESS TO THE INTERNET

The Internet is both a cause and a result of globalization and development. The UN special rapporteur on the promotion and protection of the right to freedom of opinion and expression, David Kaye, underscores in his 2015 annual report to the HRC,

> [The Internet] magnifies the voice and multiplies the information within reach of everyone who has access to it. Within a brief period, it has become the central global public forum. As such, an open and secure Internet should be counted among the leading prerequisites for the enjoyment of the freedom of expression today.[31]

In addition to the Internet's significant value for freedom of opinion and expression, Special Rapporteur Kaye highlighted that it also enables individuals to exercise the full range of other rights. These rights include "privacy, religious belief, association and peaceful assembly, education, culture and freedom from discrimination."[32] In fact, the HRC, the UNGA, and states have affirmed that "the same rights that people have offline must also be protected online."[33] Hence, human rights and fundamental freedoms apply equally online. States are required to ensure that individuals can freely exercise their rights online, such as the freedom of expression. The beneficial and empowering role of the Internet applies to children as well as adults as children are also human beings with rights highlighted by the UNCRC.[34] This interpretation aligns with sentiments expressed by Kaye's predecessor La Rue, who noted the beneficial and empowering role of the Internet in the lives of children and young people. La Rue also noted the significance of the Internet as a means "for children to exercise their right to freedom of expression [that] can serve as a tool to help children claim their other rights, including the right to education, freedom of association and full participation in social, cultural and political life."[35] This recognition encompasses the principle of children's "evolving capacities," which is enshrined in Article 5 of the UNCRC and implies that children are entitled to access to the Internet and to protection from harm. Indeed, parents and caregivers have a duty to guide children while taking into account their gradual process of maturation.[36] As such, the principle of the best interests of the child is at the forefront of all actions and decision-making processes that affect children's lives and applies equally in cyberspace. In light of this principle, the child's family assumes the primary responsibility for facilitating the child's development, hearing the child's opinions, and taking the child's views seriously. Children must learn the necessary skills to become active participants in society, including knowledge of their freedom of expression (UNCRC, Article 12, para. 1).[37] In the same spirit, the primary consideration of the best interests of the child also implies that the state assumes a positive obligation to respect children's right to access information and to protect them when legitimate concerns for their safety and well-being arise online.[38]

Globally the importance of technology for sustainable development in the Post-2015 Agenda (2015–2030) has a relationship with SDG 17, which recognizes partnerships with civil society as a critical action to achieve rapid, universal, and affordable access to the Internet for all.[39] Regarding the engagement of Internet users on digital platforms, La Rue noted that individuals are "no longer passive recipients, but also active publishers of information," which has also contributed "to the discovery of the truth and progress of society as a whole."[40] The Internet continues to enable access to information that might otherwise be unavailable. Thus, the Internet represents an important facilitator of the right to freedom of opinion and expression and other human rights.[41] Although access to the Internet has not yet received universal recognition as a human right, countries have employed various domestic law and policy approaches, and some have promoted Internet access as a right. Some notable examples are listed below:

- Estonia's parliament passed legislation in 2000 that declared Internet access to be a basic human right.
- France's constitutional council effectively declared Internet access a fundamental right in 2009.
- Costa Rica's constitutional court reached a similar decision in 2010.
- Finland passed a decree in 2009 that required a minimum speed of one megabyte per second for all broadband Internet connections.[42]

In addition, Article 5A(2) of the constitution of Greece affirms that the right to information society participation is universal: "Facilitation of access to electronically transmitted information, as well as of the production, exchange and diffusion thereof, constitutes an obligation of the State."[43] This stance aligns with a decision by the high court of the state of Kerala in India, which ruled in 2019 that the right to Internet access had become part of the right to education and the right to privacy under Article 21 of the constitution of India.[44] In Spain, as of January 1, 2020, Telefónica de España S.A.U. (Movistar) is required to guarantee broadband Internet access at a speed of at least one megabyte per second at affordable prices to users throughout the country.[45]

Although this positive obligation of states to promote the enjoyment of rights and the necessary means for people to exercise their rights online should be a priority, states cannot achieve this aim instantly. For example, in many developing countries, access to essential commodities such as electricity is difficult; therefore, states' efforts to facilitate Internet access should align with their infrastructure or technological possibilities.[46] Efforts toward digital progress can help bridge the digital divide between individuals with effective access to digital and information technologies and those with very limited or no access in order to facilitate economic development and the enjoyment of a range of human rights. Access to the Internet can reduce some inequalities, creating opportunities that did not previously exist.

CONCLUSION

Broad efforts since the late 1990s have laid the groundwork for viewing the Internet as a powerful technology with considerable potential to promote human progress, development, and enjoyment of the rights that the UDHR delineates. Since the first phase of the WSIS concluded in 2003, the Internet has continued to play a key part in society. Today the Internet can play an essential role in promoting civil, political, economic, social, and cultural development. Thus, ensuring that everyone has access to the Internet should be a priority for all states.[47] While Internet access is growing rapidly around the world[48] (including among children),[49] criminals such as human traffickers also have increased opportunities to access, lure, and manipulate new populations of child victims for sexual exploitation. The Internet provides further grounds for offenders to commit offenses in which children are at greater risk of experiencing exploitative treatment or being bought and sold as commodities—especially given the ongoing COVID-19 pandemic.[50] In addition, data from 2019 indicated that approximately 1.8 million adult men with a sexual interest in children became new Internet users.[51] In light of these findings, the next chapter details Internet-facilitated child sex trafficking offenses in which children are exploited or treated like merchandise rather than human beings.

NOTES

1. Daniel J. Solove and Paul Schwartz, "Introduction," in *Privacy Information and Technology*, 3rd ed. (New York: Aspen, 2011).

2. HRC, "Report of the Special Rapporteur on the Promotion and Protection of the Right to Freedom of Opinion and Expression, Frank La Rue," A/HRC/17/27, May 16, 2011, para. 22, at 7.

3. For example, HRC, Resolution 20/8, "The Promotion, Protection and Enjoyment of Human Rights on the Internet," A/HRC/RES/20/8 (July 16, 2012), para. 2, at 2; HRC, Resolution 26/13, "The Promotion, Protection and Enjoyment of Human Rights on the Internet," A/HRC/RES/26/13 (July 14, 2014), para. 2, at 2; HRC, Resolution 32/13, "The Promotion, Protection and Enjoyment of Human Rights on the Internet," A/HRC/RES/32/13 (July 18, 2016), para. 2, at 3.

4. HRC, Resolution 32/13, para. 2, at 3. See UNGA, Resolution 70/1, "Transforming Our World: The 2030 Agenda for Sustainable Development," A/RES/70/1 (October 21, 2015), para. 16(10), at 26.

5. HRC, "Report of the Special Rapporteur on the Promotion and Protection of the Right to Freedom of Opinion and Expression, Frank La Rue," A/HRC/17/27, para. 85, at 22.

6. WSIS, "Declaration of Principles: Building the Information Society, a Global Challenge in the New Millennium," WSIS-03/GENEVA/DOC/4-E, December 12, 2003, sec. A, para. 1.

7. ITU, "What Is the Information Society?" www.itu.int/net/wsis/basic/faqs.asp.

8. WSIS, "Declaration of Principles," sec. A, para. 11.

9. WSIS, "Basic Information: About WSIS," ITU, www.itu.int/net/wsis/basic/about.html.

10. WSIS, *The Geneva Declaration of Principles and Plan of Action* (Geneva: World Summit on the Information Society Secretariat, 2013), 1.

11. WSIS, "Declaration of Principles," sec. B.

12. Ibid., sec. B8, 21.

13. Ibid., sec. B10, 59.

14. WSIS, "Plan of Action," WSIS-03/GENEVA/DOC/5-E, December 12, 2003.

15. UNGA, Resolution 55/2, United Nations Millennium Declaration, A/RES/55/2 (September 8, 2000); WSIS, "Declaration of Principles."

16. WSIS, "Tunis Phase of the World Summit on the Information Society (WSIS)," Tunis, November 16–18, 2005, DM-05/1205, July 7, 2005.

17. IGF and Internet Rights and Principles Dynamic Coalition, *The Charter of Human Rights and Principles for the Internet*, 4th ed. (2014), 5.

18. WSIS, "Tunis Commitment," WSIS-05/TUNIS/DOC/7-E, November 18, 2005.

19. Ibid., para. 24.

20. WSIS, "Tunis Agenda for the Information Society," WSIS-05/TUNIS/DOC/6(Rev. 1)-E, November 18, 2005, para. 29–30.

21. WSIS, "Tunis Agenda for the Information Society," para. 35–42. https://www.itu.int/net/wsis/basic/faqs_answer.asp?lang=en&faq_id=70.

22. WSIS, "Tunis Agenda for the Information Society," para. 72.

23. WSIS, "Declaration of Principles." See generally David P. Fidler, "Cyberspace and Human Rights," in *Research Handbook on International Law and Cyberspace*, ed. Nicholas Tsagourias and Russell Buchan (Camberley, UK: Edward Elgar, 2015), 94.

24. IGF, "About IGF FAQs," www.intgovforum.org/multilingual/content/about-igf-faqs.

25. UNGA, Resolution 70/125, A/RES/70/125 (February 1, 2016), para. 63, at 12.

26. ITU, "Global Cybersecurity Agenda," www.itu.int/en/action/cybersecurity/Pages/gca.aspx.

27. ITU, "Child Online Protection," www.itu.int/en/cop/Pages/default.aspx.

28. ITU, "Council Working Group on Child Online Protection," www.itu.int/en/council/cwg-cop/Pages/default.aspx.

29. CCPCJ, "Strengthening International Cooperation to Combat Cybercrime," RES 22/7 (April 26, 2013).

30. CCPCJ, "Promoting Technical Assistance and Capacity-Building to Strengthen National Measures and International Cooperation against Cybercrime," RES 22/8 (April 26, 2013).

31. HRC, "Report of the Special Rapporteur on the Promotion and Protection of the Right to Freedom of Opinion and Expression, David Kaye," A/HRC/29/32, May 22, 2015, para. 11, at 5.

32. HRC, "Report of the Special Rapporteur on the Promotion and Protection of the Right to Freedom of Opinion and Expression, David Kaye," A/HRC/32/38, May 11, 2016, para. 8, at 5. See also HRC, "Report of the Special Rapporteur on the Promotion and Protection of the Right to Freedom of Opinion and Expression, David Kaye," A/HRC/35/22, March 30, 2017, para. 76, at 20.

33. HRC, Resolution 20/8, para. 1, at 2; HRC, Resolution 26/13, para. 1, at 2; HRC, Resolution 32/13, para. 1, at 3. See also UNGA, Resolution 68/167, "The Right to Privacy in the Digital Age," A/RES/68/167 (January 21, 2014), para. 3, at 2.

34. HRC, "Report of the Special Rapporteur on the Promotion and Protection of the Right to Freedom of Opinion and Expression, Frank La Rue," A/69/335, August 21, 2014, para. 2, at 3.

35. HRC, "Report of the Special Rapporteur on the Promotion and Protection of the Right to Freedom of Opinion and Expression, Frank La Rue," A/69/335, para. 65, at 16.

36. Ibid., para. 13, at 5.

37. CRC, "Report on the Forty-Third Session," CRC/C/43/3, July 16, 2007, para. 911–1002, at 191–210, especially para. 1002, at 210. See generally CRC, "General Comment no. 12: The Right of the Child to Be Heard," CRC/C/GC/12, July 20, 2009, para. 2, at 5: "The CRC has identified Article 12 as one of the four general principles of the Convention . . . which highlights the fact that this article establishes not only a right in itself, but should also be considered in the interpretation and implementation of all other rights."

38. HRCttee, "General Comment no. 34, Article 19: Freedoms of Opinion and Expression," CCPR/C/GC/34, September 12, 2011, para. 19, 21, at 5.

39. UN, "SDG Goal 17 targets 17.6–17.8, Sustainable Development Goals, Goal 17: Revitalize the Global Partnership for Sustainable Development," www.un.org/sustainabledevelopment/globalpartnerships/.

40. HRC, "Report of the Special Rapporteur on the Promotion and Protection of the Right to Freedom of Opinion and Expression, Frank La Rue," A/HRC/17/27, para. 19, at 6–7.

41. Ibid., para. 22, at 7.

42. Ibid., para. 65, at 18.

43. Kostas Mavrias and Epaminondas Spiliotopoulos, eds., *Constitution of Greece*, trans. Xenophon Paparrigopoulos and Stavroula Vassilouni (Athens: Hellenic Parliament Publications Department, 2008), art. 5a(2).

44. *Shirin R.K. v. State of Kerala*, The High Court of Kerala at Ernakulam (September 19, 2019), W.P(C).No.19716/2019-L.

45. Gobierno de España: Ministerio de Asuntos Económicos Y Transformación Digital, "Connection to the Network, with Broadband Capacity to 1Mbps, + Fixed Telephone Service," https://avancedigital.gob.es/en-us/Servicios/InformeUniversal/Paginas/ConexServTelefyBA.aspx.

46. HRC, "Report of the Special Rapporteur on the Promotion and Protection of the Right to Freedom of Opinion and Expression, Frank La Rue," A/HRC/17/27.

47. Ibid., para. 85, at 22.

48. Simon Kemp, "Digital 2021: Global Overview Report," DataReportal, https://datareportal.com/reports/digital-2021-global-overview-report.

49. UNICEF, *The State of the World's Children 2017: Children in a Digital World* (New York: UNICEF, 2017), 1.

50. UNODC, "Traffickers Use of the Internet: Digital Hunting Fields," in *Global Report on Trafficking in Persons 2020* (New York: United Nations, 2020).

51. WeProtect Global Alliance (WPGA), *Global Threat Assessment 2019* (London: Crown Copyright, 2019), 10–11.

Chapter 4

Cyberspace, Nexus of Child Sexual Slavery

In our globalized world, children are increasingly using the Internet and mobile technology at younger ages. The Internet can be an extraordinary tool for children to realize their rights such as freedom of expression and education as all aspects of the International Bill of Human Rights apply to the online environment. However the Internet may also expose children to a variety of risks, including practices meant to exploit them. The present chapter explores specific practices likely linked to the online sex trafficking of children. It contextualizes activities in which perpetrators exploit children. Such situations can be considered slavery if one or more of the powers attached to the right of ownership is exercised over the child. I argue that online sex trafficking is a direct threat to any child that also causes direct harm to society. To prevent the proliferation of these crimes, policymakers must understand the unique dynamics of trafficking in cyberspace including new modalities that are still emerging and the possibility of other forms that may emerge at any given time and become trends.

CYBERCRIME AGAINST CHILDREN

The Internet has created a new kind of region or space that requires governance—cyberspace—located in no specific geographic location but accessible to anyone, anywhere in the world merely via access to the Internet. Because "the Internet is so vast and complex that it defies real-world definitions based on territory," it has effectively "blurred the line between cyberspace and real space."[1] Cyberspace can be considered an electronic and operational domain of information and technology infrastructures, including the Internet, that facilitates online communications and exchanges, complete with new opportunities, challenges, risks, and threats.

Furthermore, the globally networked nature of modern communications poses challenges to the detection and prosecution of criminal offenders. The term "cybercrime" has been internationally recognized and adopted by the UN and the CoE Convention on Cybercrime.[2] Although there is no universally accepted definition, cybercrime, rather than being one single activity, encompasses a range of illicit activities carried out in cyberspace. Specifically, cybercrime involves the following:

- The use of computers, computer networks, or other ICTs to assist traditional offenses that occur in the offline world. This type of Internet-related crime can also be considered "cyber-enabled crime" because the Internet can facilitate the occurrence of terrestrial crime by increasing scale or reach.[3] For instance, the Internet can be used to commit fraud and theft, purchase drugs, launder money, and gain access to sensitive company records or restricted information to facilitate extortion in the offline world.[4]

- The use of the Internet or an ICT infrastructure as the target and means of attack. In this sense, cybercrimes can have the nature of "cyber-dependent offenses." The Internet has created a new environment within which novel forms of crimes are committed. These acts include the creation and dissemination of viruses or other malware, ransomware, distributed denial-of-service attacks, forms of online violence and vandalism, and bot networks.[5]

- The use or help of computer systems, including the Internet, to commit cyber-related crimes against children related to sexual abuse and exploitation.[6] Cybercriminals use computer networks with global reach for child abuse and exploitation purposes. Significantly, a range of illicit exploitation activities that are perpetrated using computer systems or computer data cause personal harm to children and include both computer-related acts (e.g., computer-related solicitation or the grooming of children) and computer-content–related acts (e.g., computer-related production, distribution, or possession of child pornography). In addition, computer-related acts with the intention of trafficking in persons may fit within the broad category of computer-related cybercrime acts.[7] In this way, the act committed with the use or help of a computer system leads to the crime of trafficking offline. Primarily driven by the demand for minors in the sex industry and the promise of profits, traffickers have abused Internet channels to boost the child sex market. Internet-related crimes to sexually exploit children are an affront to their dignity because these crimes inherently threaten their humanity. The types of offending behaviors through which children are treated as exploitable sex objects can be seen as Internet violence because they cause psychological harm or facilitate physical harm.[8]

- The use of computer systems to store relevant information in computers (e.g., records of messages sent and received, CSAM, a customer database, and information about operations by cities) may entail the incidental use of a computer. This activity relates to *computer-supported crimes*, and such information may constitute digital evidence of a crime.[9]

The focus of this book is the novelty of social interactions in online environments combined with the "placelessness" of cyberspace. The latter trait makes possible new forms of criminality and illegal acts—particularly the trafficking of children for commercial and noncommercial sexual exploitation—and creates the need for a legal instrument applied internationally to cyberspace. In the age of the Internet, close proximity between perpetrator and victim is no longer necessary for crimes to occur. Criminals now have the option of committing offenses in the virtual world. Thus, the Internet—as the connection between the virtual world and the real world—acts as an instrument for child sex trafficking.

In short, the relatively unregulated environment of the digitally interconnected world can foster digital crime and create new opportunities for offenders. Various crimes become possible because perpetrators take advantage of the diffuse, diverse, and geographically borderless nature of cyberspace as well as its many forms of concealment. Online offenders conceal their identity and activities by taking advantage of encryption technologies that make detection and tracing of evidence difficult. In fact, the risk of being detected in online environments is lower than in the real world, which is a benefit for offenders.[10] This is largely due to the lack of a centralized global governing or regulating body that oversees the Internet in combination with different laws and levels of control in different countries. Indeed, child sex trafficking perpetrators have become creative and resourceful in exploiting contemporary means such as the borderless realm of cyberspace to facilitate the commission of crimes. In some cases, perpetrators target child victims from countries with weak or nonexistent laws or enforcement related to this cybercrime, making these places safe havens as there may be no legal consequences (e.g., investigation and prosecution) of their criminal behavior. Exploitation cases demonstrate how traffickers innovate and use the Internet and digital technology to work in flexible ways, expanding their operations across borders. Internet-based applications have eased the process of targeting and contacting victims, the arrangement of transferring money, and the coordination between different criminal groups. Moreover, the use of degrees of anonymity and encrypted messaging facilitates the creation and dissemination of exploitative child sexual images and videos.

Child sexual exploitation via the Internet continues to increase. According to European Union Agency for Law Enforcement Cooperation (Europol) data, referrals from the United States regarding eighteen member states increased from 44,000 in 2017 to 190,000 in 2018. By June 2019, referrals for that calendar year had already reached 170,000. In addition, a similar increasing trend was seen in the referrals from Canada, which (regarding all EU member states) increased from 6,000 in 2018 to approximately 24,000 in 2019.[11] The U.S. Department of State has brought attention to this and in its 2017 TIP Report identified online sexual exploitation of children as an alarming trafficking trend.[12] The report explicitly discusses how, in this process of online trafficking, offenders induce minors through psychological manipulation and coercion for sexual exploitation. The report identified the modalities of livestreaming of child sexual abuse and "sextortion" as growing trends and emphasized that any child can be a victim of online exploitation even at a very young age. In addition, this recognition of the close link between the sexual exploitation of children on the Internet and human trafficking was reflected in the President's 2019 Interagency Task Force Report on U.S. Government Efforts to Combat Trafficking in Persons.[13]

The UK government in 2019 identified online harms—including both content and activities—that can be linked to modern slavery.[14] International concern about this kind of crime is articulated by the WeProtect Global Alliance (WPGA), which includes ninety-seven governments, forty-one global technology companies, and forty-four leading international and nongovernmental organizations (NGOs). In its 2018 Global Threat Assessment Report, the WPGA states, "cybersex trafficking has emerged as a new and brutal form of modern-day slavery."[15] With the ease of information sharing and exchange on the Internet, cybertraffickers see children as sexual commodities that can be found and purchased online. This kind of victimization can be facilitated via camera or webcam from anywhere in the world. Therefore, offenders can gather a large number of sex buyers, other criminals, and potential child victims. Furthermore, with the continual development of Internet technology and the growing sophistication of online criminal activity, cybertrafficking is an evolving crime.

As I argued in the first two chapters of this book, slavery continues to exist today in forms of exploitation that involve the exercise of any power associated with the right of ownership over another person. In the borderless realm of cyberspace, it is possible to subject a child to slavery or sexual exploitation even without physical proximity playing a role. This chapter presents practices likely to be defined as online sex trafficking because they are committed against children by cybertraffickers with the intent of sexually exploiting them, thus violating their basic rights. These practices include situations in which children are considered sexual commodities and induced to perform sexual activities or are transferred to another person (e.g., offered, bought, sold) for value received. Because the scale and extent of this online phenomenon continues to grow along with the evolution of new technologies, there is a need to examine emerging trends and established realities associated with child sexual exploitation as a form of cybercrime that likely reflects one or more powers corresponding to ownership. To this end, this chapter considers three primary types of cybercrime perpetrated against children and characterized by sexual exploitation:

1. Internet-facilitated noncontact exploitation
   a. Commodified sexual "relationships"
   b. Online CSAM
   c. Online sexual coercion and extortion against children, or "sextortion"
   d. Livestreaming of child sexual abuse and exploitation
   e. "Sexting," an area of concern
2. Internet-facilitated contact exploitation
3. Internet-facilitated noncommercial sexual exploitation of children
   a. Mail-order brides and child marriages for sexual exploitation
   b. Illegal child adoption for the purpose of exploitation

INTERNET-FACILITATED NONCONTACT EXPLOITATION

Under the evolved definition of slavery discussed in chapter 1, the exercise of complete control over a child in the context of the exercise of attributes normally attached to the right of ownership would be considered slavery.[16] Ownership situations include any exercise of control over children that significantly deprives them of their personal freedom. With this type of offense in cyberspace, a child can be sexually exploited without an in-person or physical encounter with the offender. Child sexual activity is usually offered in exchange for anything of value to the child or the other party. Exploitative acts include the production, distribution, or possession of CSAM because a depicted child (existing or nonexistent) is used in a process to sexually exploit children.[17] These offenses are described in the sections below.

Commodified Sexual Relationships

This online practice is a relatively new form of cybercrime that can relate to the sexual exploitation of children in prostitution.[18] According to the OP-CRC-SC, "child prostitution means the use of a child in sexual activities for remuneration or any other form of consideration."[19] In accordance with

Article 3(1)(b) of the OP-CRC-SC, states must criminalize the acts of "offering, obtaining, procuring, or providing a child for child prostitution." Even where the child's participation is ostensibly voluntary, the preceding analysis of international legal instruments (in particular the Palermo Protocol) shows that the consent of any child—that is, a person under the age of eighteen years—is legally irrelevant to considerations of exploitation or slavery. In cyberspace, children can be coaxed into transactional sex in exchange for money, goods, or benefits, or the promise of such.

Criminals abuse a position of power and children's vulnerabilities to encourage, coerce, and control a "consensual" sexual act. This practice may include making children watch sexual abuse or sexual activities even if they do not participate in the sexual acts.[20] Although this offense may cause psychological harm and damage to the personality of the child, states parties to the Lanzarote Convention may decide not to criminalize such acts if the minor is above the age of sexual consent under national legislation.[21]

Commodified relationships are a form of cyberpredation that occurs in real-time through a camera or webcam. Their use of the Internet makes their linkage to trafficking highly plausible because under such exploitative business models, online offenders can sexually exploit a child for their own sexual gratification and may also generate profit by recording, distributing, and selling explicit sexual materials (e.g., images and videos) via the web without the child's knowledge.

Online Child Sexual Abuse Material

CSAM, or child pornography, is a form of child sexual exploitation that includes the production and dissemination of sexually explicit material of underage persons. The OP-CRC-SC defines child pornography as "any representation, by whatever means, of a child engaged in real or simulated explicit sexual activities or any representation of the sexual parts of a child for primarily sexual purposes."[22] This is a broad definition as the phrase "any representation" may include nonvisual depictions such as in writing and audio files.[23] At the same time, this mandatory provision obliges states parties to take all necessary measures to prohibit forms of offenses related to child pornography "by whatever means," hence covering forms of material available offline or online.[24] Moreover, the reference to "simulated explicit sexual activities" includes any material that depicts or otherwise represents a child involved in sexually explicit conduct.[25] Real or simulated explicit sexual activities include, at a minimum, "sexual intercourse and intentional sexual touching involving a child, independent of the sex of all involved persons, and any lascivious exhibition of the genitals or the pubic area of a child."[26] Accordingly there is no requirement to establish physical contact between the offender and the child victim in relation to an act in a form of sexual activity.[27] Sexual activities can be committed through other forms of contact such as visual connection and may constitute serious harm to the sexual integrity of children and cause them severe trauma.

Furthermore, the OP-CRC-SC mandates states parties to criminalize the production, distribution, sale, or possession of child pornography.[28] The CRC has strongly recommended that states parties, when interpreting and implementing the OP-CRC-SC, take a protective approach to child sexual exploitation. Thus, the committee has urged states parties to criminalize at the national level the simple possession of such materials in a computer system or on a computer data storage medium.[29] However, advances in ICT technologies now mean material need not be downloaded and can instead be engaged with online, posing challenges to notions of what constitutes possession of such material.[30] These situations demonstrate new challenges for states and evidence the urgent need to adopt legislation and practices to protect children from emerging forms of sexual exploitation.

A 2017 survey of international survivors found that the majority of child victims were younger children, with 56 percent suffering the abuse before the age of four and 87 percent before the age of twelve.[31] Additionally, a 2019 report on CSAM found that 91 percent of the victims were girls while 7 percent were boys, and 92 percent of all victims were younger than thirteen.[32] A 2018 report on online CSAM found that men represented 92 percent of known offenders and provided further insight into the nature of such exploitation.[33] This report identified a correlation between the child's age and the severity of the abuse wherein younger children suffered more severe abuse; additionally, boys were depicted in the most egregious content.[34] This correlation demonstrates the seriousness of the crime, which is likely to feature minors at increasingly earlier ages, including babies and toddlers in the most severe images. As a consequence, CSAM poses greater challenges for judiciary and law enforcement agencies as self-reporting is limited given the young age of victims, many of whom are preverbal or maintain a dependency on predators that restrains them from disclosing the victimization.

Defining Child Pornography in the Council of Europe Convention on Cybercrime

The Convention on Cybercrime was adopted by the CoE and entered into force on January 7, 2004. Since then it has been open for ratification by member states and nonmember states of the CoE.[35] Currently, the convention has sixty-five states parties, including twenty-one nonmembers of the CoE,[36] reflecting a broad international acceptance. This international treaty, also known as the Budapest Convention on Cybercrime or the Budapest

Convention, is a cornerstone in combating cybercrime and is primarily focused on computer systems and data.[37] In this way, the Budapest Convention on Cybercrime is a regional instrument that has made significant achievements internationally in establishing a consensus on states' obligations regarding crimes committed via the Internet and other computer networks. The aim of the convention is to identify, for domestic criminal substantive law, elements of offenses committed via the Internet and other computer networks by establishing a common minimum standard for those significant crimes. Part of this standard is the safeguard of the principle of proportionality, as stated in Article 15, which requires states parties to ensure an adequate balance between the interest of law enforcement and the protection of fundamental human rights including the right to freedom of expression and rights related to the respect for privacy.[38]

The Convention on Cybercrime provides a common criminal policy to prevent computer-related offenses and includes provisions addressing the criminalization of child pornography. In conformity with an explanatory report accompanying the convention, and taking into account that cyber-criminal behaviors are not restricted by geographic limitations or national boundaries, the drafters of the convention recognized the importance of implementing technical measures to protect computer systems concurrent with legal measures to prevent and discourage online criminal behavior out of respect for human rights in the information society.[39] In that context, with the aim of addressing cybercrime against children, the Cybercrime Convention's preamble affirms that the convention was prepared on the basis of the 1989 UNCRC and the 1999 ILO's Worst Forms of Child Labour Convention.[40] Hence the convention recognizes human rights standards to promote and increase the well-being of children and Internet users in the Internet age. This premise helps explain the inclusion of the content-related offense of child pornography among its provisions (Article 9).[41] By criminalizing various aspects of electronic child pornography, the convention combats the sexual exploitation of children and aims to strengthen and modernize measures protecting children in cyberspace at the national level.[42]

Accordingly, given that child pornography is a global concern with no easy solution, this treaty calls on states parties to adopt appropriate legislation and regulations to eradicate child pornography. Pursuant to the Convention on Cybercrime, it is essential that states take effective holistic measures to combat child pornography and its root causes while contributing to strengthening international cooperation.[43] Cross-border cooperation is especially important given the "placeless" nature of cyberspace discussed previously.[44] The treaty defines child pornography as material that visually depicts: a. A minor engaged in sexually explicit conduct; b. A person appearing to be a minor engaged in sexually explicit conduct; c. Realistic images representing a minor engaged in sexually explicit conduct.[45]

The use of the term "visually depicts" denotes a reference to visual material or visual representation and may exclude the criminalization of sound or audio material at the national level. Furthermore, with the phrase "sexually explicit conduct," this legal instrument prohibits child pornographic materials in which children are explicitly sexually exploited—children who can also be with other children or with adults. Additionally, acts of abuse in a sexual context can involve those related to masturbation, sadisms or masochisms, and lascivious exhibitions.[46]

Additionally, subparagraph c of this definition makes illegal a practice known as "virtual child pornography" or "pseudo child pornography" by using the words "realistic images representing a minor engaged in sexually explicit conduct."[47] This clause means that pornographic materials may include artificially or digitally created sexualized imagery of children. Virtual child pornography encompasses wholly computer-generated child abuse material, which does not depict actual children, and morphed child pornography, which involves images of actual persons adjusted beyond recognition and potentially resembling no real individual. In addition, pursuant to subparagraph b of this provision, sexually explicit representations of people who appear to be minors are also illegal since this type of pornography and subparagraph c (virtual child pornography) can create the same effect on viewers as if they were watching actual children, thus facilitating a subculture of child abuse. However, pursuant to Article 9(4), states parties may reserve the right not to apply these definitions (Article 9[2], subparagraphs b and c).

In practice, modern technology and particularly the Internet has facilitated the creation of computer-generated child exploitative imagery in such a way that it can sometimes be difficult to distinguish it from real children involved in sexual activities. In general, this legal provision may present discrepancies in the definition of child pornography in national legislative approaches. CSAM, including the kind of material that is computer-produced, contributes to the tolerance of child sexual abuse and incites the victimization of more children in other forms of sexual exploitation online or offline.[48] Moreover, the CoE Lanzarote Convention includes provisions criminalizing acts related to child pornography and adopts a similar approach with respect to the criminalization of "simulated representations or realistic images of a nonexistent child," allowing states parties to make reservation in whole or in part.[49]

In defining child pornography, the Convention on Cybercrime describes the term "minor" as including all persons under the age of eighteen years and permits states parties to allow for a lower age limit not less than sixteen years.[50] This permissible criminal provision indicates that the age of the protected child can be sixteen years old in certain jurisdictions, reflecting a divergence in definitions of child pornography at the national level. The CRC has expressed particular concern to states parties on age limits lower than eighteen years. It thereby recommends that criminal laws apply to *all* children (i.e., persons below eighteen years of age) as they can never consent to any form of sexual exploitation or sexual abuse.[51]

This treaty mandates states parties to criminalize producing, offering or making available, distributing, transmitting, procuring ("whether for oneself or another"), or possessing child pornography through a computer system.[52] With the criminalization of these offenses, the drafters sought to strengthen protective measures for children online by penalizing various aspects of the electronic supply and distribution of child pornography. However the Convention on Cybercrime affirms that "each party may reserve the right not to apply, in whole or in part" the criminalization of procuring and possessing pornographic material involving children.[53] This permission points out the diversity in national criminal legislation of countries and the possibility that not all are addressing the possession of child pornography in their national jurisdiction.

In addition, the CoE Lanzarote Convention includes a wide range of acts related to producing, offering or making available, distributing or transmitting, procuring, possessing, or knowingly obtaining access to child pornography through ICTs.[54] Thus, significantly, the CoE Lanzarote Convention goes a little further by criminalizing the online viewing (not just downloading) of child pornography. This new element of the offense makes the requirement that "to be liable the person must both intend to enter a site where child pornography is available and know that such images can be found there."[55] This condition means that to demonstrate liability for accessing such content, the intent of the offender may be deduced by recurrent access to the site or making a payment for a service. However this legal provision remains optional as the Lanzarote Convention permits that "each party may reserve the right not to apply, in whole or in part" this definition.[56] On the whole, however, these CoE multilateral instruments (the Convention on Cybercrime and Lanzarote Convention) promote human rights concepts toward a common good—the protection of the well-being, best interests, and fundamental freedoms of children—and encourage holistic responses that address the prosecution of perpetrators, the protection of child victims, and the prevention of the crime.

Key to my argument in this book is that the drafters of the explanatory report of the CoE Convention on Cybercrime recognized the importance of the use of the Internet for child pornography and for new forms of sexual exploitation and endangerment of children. Specifically, they noted, "It is widely believed that such material [child pornography] and online practices, such as the exchange of ideas, fantasies and advice among pedophiles, play a role in supporting, encouraging or facilitating sexual offenses against children."[57] Thus the drafters further realized that the content-related offense of child pornography is not the only form of sexual exploitation because offenders may also develop online practices to promote or otherwise lead to other forms of child sexual abuse and exploitation. Nonetheless the convention does not go beyond the sphere of child pornography.[58] Thus it does not criminalize any other type of cyberoffense related to sexual exploitation via the Internet and other computer networks.

Altogether the CoE Convention on Cybercrime expresses an understanding of the challenges and dangers of living in an age of digitalization and new information technologies, and it is a symbol of international progress in the global fight against cybercrimes by providing common criminal policy responses. Furthermore, this convention, as a foundation for facilitating speedy and effective international cooperation, is a cornerstone in combating cybercrime, protecting legitimate interests of states and society, and aiding the modernization of domestic law. Specific to the issue at hand, because this convention is designed to protect society against cybercrime with due respect to human rights, states' compliance with its principles will promote harmonization of national cybercrime laws and strengthen international cooperation among them, thereby representing a solid first step toward eliminating cybercrimes against children.

CSAM: Act and Purpose of Exploitation

Online child pornography is an exploitative act that engages children in explicit activities for sexual stimulation. In this sense, a child is being used, procured, or offered for the production and dissemination of sexual abuse materials or for performing sexual activities in cyberspace. Indeed, CSAM involves exploitative representations of children (e.g., text and sound), evidencing a sexual objectification of them to satisfy the sexual fantasies and desires of viewers online.[59] Therefore, the use of the term "child sexual abuse material" rather than "child pornography" is more appropriate when referring to this form of crime, as minors are being sexually exploited and subjected to an ongoing trauma.

The Internet allows perpetrators to simplify the process of commodifying children for sexual exploitation purposes while quickly accumulating a significant amount of evidentiary offensive and graphic materials. For example, in a case from the UNODC 2018 *Global Report on Trafficking in Persons* from Thailand, digital forensics investigations found more than 500,000 pictures of children younger than ten.[60] This child exploitation case was initially prosecuted under cybercrime legislation and then extended to include counts of trafficking for sexual exploitation purposes.

In 2019, Europol reported that its repository contained 46 million unique images or videos related to child sexual exploitation material (CSEM).[61] There is some (albeit mixed) evidence that circulation of these images is increasing.[62] Importantly, the UK's Internet Watch Foundation (IWF) in its 2019 report found a total of 132,676 confirmed websites hosting or linking to CSAM.[63] This number reflects an increase in such sites of 25 percent from 2018.[64] Additionally, according to IWF figures, the number of Internet domains featuring child sexual abuse imagery increased by 130 percent from 2014 to 2018 (1,694 to 3,899 domains).[65] Following this, made-to-order CSAM has become an emerging cyberthreat that can be associated with organized criminal groups and is increasingly demanded by criminals.[66]

Furthermore, online environments provide dynamic storage and distribution of these materials, including pay-per-click advertisements on platforms hosting CSEM. The 2015 Environmental Scan of the European Cybercrime Centre (EC3) and the Virtual Global Taskforce (VGT) notes the misuse of "cyberlockers," or file-hosting sites, to remotely store offenders' collections of child pornographic materials on separate servers rather than on the offenders' personal computers.[67] The IWF suggest that these cyberlockers contain a high proportion of the most severe CSEM, including rape and sexual torture of babies and toddlers (up to two years old).[68]

Moreover, peer-to-peer (P2P) file-sharing networks are also a significant online distribution method for child pornographic materials. In fact, in 2019 Europol identified P2P networks as the most popular method for distribution of CSEM and as being commonly associated with Darknet platforms.[69] This popularity is apparently due to the greater level of anonymity that offenders have on the hidden Internet, giving them greater freedom to connect with others and discuss their sexual interests and desires either in one-on-one communication or larger groups. ECPAT International data from 2017 indicates that P2P platforms such as Gnutella, eDonkey, and eMule have presented a high volume of these type of offenses.[70] Thus file-sharing networks have become a tool for offenders to use in the distribution and storage of exploitative images and videos of children.

For example, when a sophisticated offender loses or has his collections seized, he may use these types of platforms to rebuild his materials faster. Typically when using private P2P platforms, midlevel offenders operate in small and closed groups that allow them to set up direct relationships with other users with the aim of accessing and sharing child abuse materials.[71] File-sharing platforms are used legitimately on the open Internet as well as anonymous networks via encrypted messages whereby cybercriminals conceal their activities by enhancing their security and privacy. For example, the use of Tor to create and share CSAM, especially that of an extreme nature, was identified as a key threat in the 2019 VGT Environmental Scan Report.[72] In addition, in 2020 Europol revealed increased use of P2P file-sharing networks to distribute and store exploitative images and videos of children, mainly due to the COVID-19 pandemic.[73] In 2019 Europol also revealed the increasing ability of perpetrators to store content online quickly through cloud storage use, which may lead to law enforcement difficulties when identifying perpetrators' physical location or obtaining digital evidence.[74]

Whereas the use of file-sharing to exploit children occurs online, the production of the shared pornographic material usually begins with physical force against, sexual abuse of, or coercion of children.[75] Given that a substantial portion of child pornographic materials is available and distributed via P2P networks and hidden services on the Darknet, it is difficult to establish the whereabouts of child victims as well as quantify the numbers of images that are circulating. Overall, the online distribution of materials includes new images and old or recycled ones.[76] It is also important to remember that offenders in possession of child sexual abuse images can also sexually abuse and exploit children if they have direct contact with them.[77]

Child Erotica

Another concern linked to child pornography is child erotica. This consists of erotic images of children that do not explicitly depict them in sexual activity but still sexualize them in some way. They are images of semi-nude or erotically posed children that, in some instances, can reach the level of CSAM. Although these images may not always be exploitative per se, the fact that they are displayed on sexually oriented sites is relevant in determining their exploitative intent.

Child erotica is a form of sexual abuse that may promote harmful attitudes toward children and that may involve the child being persuaded by known adults (such as relatives or acquaintances) to pose in certain ways, often for some form of compensation. These sexualized situations represent adults taking advantage of the innocence and vulnerability of children and the child's lack of power in the production of such imagery with the risk that these adults will use the images for exchange or commercial distribution purposes in cyberspace. Provocative imagery that may have an erotic value and serve a sexual purpose should be considered CSEM. One example is an Australian case where the court found the defendant guilty of possessing thousands of images of child pornography and more than 500,000 images of young children in nonsexual poses.[78]

The Interpol International Child Sexual Exploitation (ICSE) database has helped to identify victims of child sexual abuse worldwide, and it includes children in nude or in erotic poses.[79] Sexualized images may remain legal in some nations, usually on the grounds that the child is not engaged in an explicit sexual activity, and they can thus be freely distributed or exchanged with ease.[80] Pictures with children posing in a sexualized manner violate the sexual integrity of the child, have the purpose of exploiting the child, and can fuel the real fantasies of sexual predators online. Furthermore, these sexualized images of children have the potential to be used on sites to cover up the sexual exploitation of children and as a first step in the online grooming of a child for exploitation.[81]

Online Sexual Coercion and Extortion against Children or Sextortion

"Sextortion" is an exchange or quid pro quo. In this instance, after cyberoffenders obtain compromising material from the child victim, they use it to extract a sexual benefit or advantage. Moreover, offenders can use the obtained exploitative materials in sextortion for commercial and noncommercial distribution in cyberspace. Cyberoffenders entice children to provide graphic photos and videos of themselves[82] that can then be used in nonphysical forms of coercion such as blackmail to acquire more explicit sexual content of the child (78 percent of cases), obtain money or goods from the child (7 percent), or meet the child in person for sex (most often when the cyberoffender and the victim already know each other in real life; 5 percent).[83] In the context of cyberoffenders that exploit their victims online, only a small percentage of perpetrators request to meet the minor offline for sexual activities possibly due to the distance between the offenders and the victims. However this may be more reflective of a unique characteristic of sextortion as shown in a 2016 study from the Czech Republic: despite being in close physical proximity, none of the studied cyberoffenders sought an in-person meeting with their cybervictims.[84]

Reports found that most self-generated indecent images in sextortion cases portrayed domestic settings, such as bedrooms and bathrooms, and that access to the Internet was facilitated by mobile devices like smartphones.[85] Children's increased access to the Internet—which for many is becoming more private and less supervised[86]—may expose them to the risk of sextortion. Sextortion has been identified as the most rapidly increasing threat to children online.[87] According to the NCMEC, child victims of sextortion range from eight to seventeen years old, with an average age of fifteen years.[88] Additionally, the NCMEC found that according to CyberTipline reports, most child victims of sextortion are girls.[89]

In the beginning stages of cybersextortion of children, the predators do not initiate the interaction from a position of power or abuse. Instead they typically start by posing as someone trustworthy in order to gain possession of compromising photos or videos of the child. They then use these materials to compel their victim to produce and transmit sexually explicit content.[90] A 2016 online survey of 1,631 sextortion victims (eighteen to twenty-five years old) found that approximately 43 percent of the victims in online relationships (where the perpetrator and victim met and interacted only online) were seventeen years old or younger at the time of the abuse.[91] In addition the researchers found that most websites or apps used by perpetrators for the first contact with a victim were social media platforms such as Facebook, Tagged, and Instagram (31 percent) as well as messaging or photo messaging platforms such as Kik and Snapchat (24 percent).[92] The survey found that sextorters often promise their target an opportunity to work for a modeling or acting agency. For example, one victim reported her experience with such a sextorter. What appeared to be a routine online job interview for a modeling job quickly turned deceitful and exploitative when the offender asked to see the victim's breasts. Once she had shown them, the offender admitted he was not, in fact, a modeling agent and that he now had material that could ruin the victim's life.[93]

Respondents to this survey also described various barriers to police assistance, such as a "lack of criminal laws addressing sextortion, lack of jurisdiction when perpetrators lived in other states or countries, and difficulties proving the identity of perpetrators."[94] This demonstrates that online child sexual exploitation and abuse should be adequately covered by national legal provisions and met with a strong policed response that involves an enhanced role for the technology industry in preventing additional offenses, including effective reporting mechanisms, educational programs, and support for child victims.

In a significant case of sextortion as cybercrime in Sweden, a court found a man guilty of coercing children in Canada, the United States, and the UK, all under the age of fifteen, to perform sexual acts in front of a webcam while he watched. He coerced them by threatening to distribute the materials that he already had or to kill their relatives if they did not comply, leaving them with no other real or acceptable alternative but to submit to the abuse. Despite the fact that the offender never met any of the children in person, the court sentenced him to ten years imprisonment as a hands-on offender on the basis of the concept of virtual rape.[95] This was undoubtedly a progressive ruling that set a precedent in Sweden and was probably the first of its kind in the world where an online perpetrator was convicted as a hands-on abuser. A rape conviction in cyberspace may—and I argue should—encourage states to think about how to deal with this new phenomenon of different forms of exploitation connected to online environments in current judiciary systems or domestic legislation.

Livestreaming of Child Sexual Abuse and Exploitation

The livestreaming of child sexual abuse and exploitation is an offense that connects the physical and digital world. It involves filmed child abuse, typically in a home environment (e.g., a bedroom or bathroom), with real-time video made available online and usually at the request of Western customers. According to IWF data on trends from 2018, there is a tendency in these types of videos not to show the presence of an adult, who usually seems to be outside the room.[96] IWF indicates that the videos range from a few minutes to over an hour in duration and the majority of the imagery involves children eleven to thirteen years old, predominantly girls.[97]

Although this form of exploitation does not require direct physical contact between the cybercustomers and the child victims, the abuse that these children experience often escalates and can lead to offline sexual exploitation. For instance, in some cases live video streaming is a precursor to cyberviewers traveling to the destination country to sexually exploit the same child offline.[98] Nevertheless this is not necessary for the crime of sexually abusive cyberactivity. Rather it takes place when a cyberabuser watches children in live online sex shows anywhere in the world from his own computer or mobile device.

This predation trend usually has a commercial component as the customer frequently pays the individual who compels the minor to make the recording and who sells the child abuse online.[99] Although recent cases have involved children from developed countries,[100] this form of cybercrime is frequently presented as a transnational form of abuse because it predominantly involves customers from developed nations purchasing material from suppliers in developing nations.[101] Global economic inequalities contribute to a situation in which individuals in developing nations, in some cases parents and family members, use the Internet to sell live videos of their children while customers in developed nations exploit their relative commercial power to buy the right to watch those videos.[102] Payment is often via a money transfer agency and can be between $10 and $40 although in some cases offenders fail to fulfill their promise to transfer money and the payment is not received at all.[103]

The Philippines is the country where most child victims have been located. A 2019 case demonstrates the vulnerabilities of children and some root causes of the problem in that country. A British man sent money to the mother of two girls (seven and eleven years old) and a boy (five years old) in the Philippines. The mother used that money to buy food for the children and allowed him to request materials and have a direct conversation with the children in return.[104] This form of online sale and sexual exploitation of children often occurs hand in hand with extreme poverty and the absence of opportunities, including high levels of unemployment within a country. Western offenders take advantage of such socioeconomic conditions and lure the parents or close relatives of the child into allowing them to watch pornographic or sexual performances of the child in front of a camera and often through social media applications, online chat sites, or video chat applications with end-to-end encryption.[105] In this way these offenders misuse the encryption communications that some private platforms offer for legitimate purposes to access sexual material of the child, viewing the live act without downloading the file and thus minimizing forensic traces for identification and punishment of the offense.

In some cases the coercion to perform such an act can be reflected in getting "likes" and validation comments from viewers. This situation is shown in the following case:

> One child, who gave her age as 12 years old, referred to having 50 viewers to her current broadcast stream. After repeatedly exposing herself to the webcam, she stated that she would stop the broadcast if people didn't start commenting or "liking" the stream as there would be "no point" in her continuing.[106]

Examples like this demonstrate the limited understanding of parents or other family members of the severe psychological and developmental impact these activities may have on any child associated with live interactions through a webcam or cellphone. They may believe that the act does not harm their child because it is transmitted to perpetrators remotely, as demonstrated in the 2019 WPGA report.[107] As a result this limited understanding may lead them to be an accomplice in the exploitation of their own children.

Eliminating livestreaming of child sexual abuse requires cross-border law enforcement cooperation and presents new challenges for law enforcement authorities when detecting and investigating offenders. These challenges relate to low levels of reporting; difficulties obtaining the cooperation of parents, family members, and other close family friends who facilitate the exploitation of the child; and the use of encryption tools and Darknet platforms. Additionally, payment for the abuse is commonly transmitted to its providers in small amounts through money transfer services, which may help to reduce suspicious activity levels. These challenges demonstrate the need for countries to work in collaboration with key stakeholders, including the technology industry and civil society, to strengthen prevention strategies and education initiatives. For example, awareness-raising campaigns could help educate the public about the crime particularly in terms of the implications and harm of online production and distribution of streamed video images, the difficulty of their removal, and the loss of control in their further distribution via networks.

Although this crime is on the rise in countries of Latin America, Africa, and the Middle East, the Philippines as noted above is considered one of the main countries for the online sex trafficking industry because of its large supply of livestreams that depict the abuse of children.[108] Operation Endeavour, a significant 2014 VGT operation, captured twenty-nine individuals involved in the livestreaming of child sexual abuse of which eleven were part of a facilitation group in the Philippines and led to the identification of fifteen children six to fifteen years old.[109] This operation was the result of international cooperation between law enforcement authorities and private sector partners.

While the livestreaming of child sexual abuse is not explicitly defined in the international legal instruments I've analyzed, components of this crime and the obligations of states can be found in some of these texts. In particular, the UNCRC mandates states parties to take all appropriate measures to prevent "the exploitative use of children in pornographic performances and materials."[110] More specifically the OP-CRC-SC obliges states parties to prohibit at a minimum acts and activities related to "offering, delivering or accepting, by whatever means, a child for the purpose of sexual exploitation of the child,"[111] as well as the production, distribution, sale, or possession of CSAM.[112] The term "child pornography" includes "live performances, photographs, motion pictures, video recordings and the recording or broadcasting of digital images."[113] This understanding means that states parties have a legal obligation to criminalize the offending behavior of the facilitators and the customers who require the abuse of children involved in livestreaming child sexual abuse under national legislation.

Additionally, the ILO's Worst Forms of Child Labour Convention 1999 (No. 182) requires states to urgently prohibit and eliminate "the use, procuring or offering of a child for prostitution, for the production of pornography or for pornographic performances." Moreover, according to the CoE Lanzarote Convention under Article 21, if an individual intentionally recruits or coerces a child to perform pornographic performances or profits from or otherwise exploits a child for such purposes, this person should be criminalized.[114] This provision seeks to penalize both supply and demand as it is also extended to spectators or customers when they have the intention to attend such performances involving minors.[115] However paragraph 2 of the provision allows states parties to reserve the right to limit the application of paragraph 1(c), customers, to cases where the children involved in the pornographic performances have been recruited or coerced into such performances.[116]

Cyberperpetrators abuse livestreaming methods to arrange video conferences for members of closed networks who view the abuse and exploitation of children in another country in real time on webcam. Access to these sessions costs customers anywhere from $30 to $3,000 per occasion.[117] Furthermore, when the livestreaming video of a child has an extreme nature, such as depicting the torture of children, especially babies and toddlers, an online community of offenders can pay up to $10,000 for such material, often transmitted through a site on the Darknet.[118] This form of online child sexual exploitation and abuse can be commissioned to satisfy the specific desires of the virtual offender. For example, the offender may request the performance of specific sexual acts in front of a webcam, acts that may include live child rapes. Additionally, clients may require that the child says a specific name or wears specific attire. This includes dressing up boys as little girls.[119]

This form of online abuse of children is a CSEC offense that may co-occur with other forms of exploitation, such as CSEM, because live, distant child abuse can be the generating source of the former. In 2018, IWF found that 100 percent of these images were redistributed from the original upload location to third-party websites and 73 percent appeared in online forums dedicated to pay-per-view videos of webcam child sexual abuse.[120]

Livestreaming and recorded livestreams represent a relatively new offense that new technology facilitates. The captured imagery commonly ends up on image host URLs (85 percent), forum sites (9 percent), or cyberlockers (4 percent). There are online forums for the purpose of distributing the captures of livestreamed child sexual abuse, allowing uploaders to use them commercially—and be paid each time their video is downloaded. Some offenders offer a free trial download or make the video available only to premium members.[121] In such cases, offenders profit financially or boost the industry by making the video accessible to online community members. This is a crime trend that was identified as a key threat by Europol in 2019[122] and 2020.[123] The 2020 U.S. Department of State TIP Report found, as an effect of the COVID-19 pandemic, alongside an increase in the number of persons vulnerable to trafficking,[124] the use of the Internet to livestream child sexual abuse a trafficking trend.[125]

Sexting, an Area of Concern

"Sexting" entails the exchange of sexually suggestive text messages or emails with nude or nearly nude images. In any scenario, "sext" receivers may share these sexualized images with others. Alarmingly, "one in ten sext senders say they have sent these messages to people they don't even know,"[126] posing the risk of the forms of sextortion discussed above. Although child users can delete a post or message after a digital image is sent, it is impossible to prevent that image from being received, copied, or forwarded to others online. Intimate pictures can be shared voluntarily or involuntarily (for example, if the receiver's phone is lost or stolen). Either way, the images end up in cyberspace and possibly in the possession of online child sex offenders. Thus, after an indecent picture is shared, children may feel fear and a lack of control as they do not know who might potentially be the ultimate recipient.

A 2017 UKCCIS Evidence Group review noted that most children do not engage in sexting. However those who engage in sexting often do so in association with developing intimate or romantic relationships as teenagers. In addition as children get older, it is more likely they will have an interest in sharing sexual images (e.g., 26 percent of fourteen-year-olds compared to 48 percent of sixteen-year-olds).[127] The fact that children's Internet use and activities are changing rapidly and become more private as they age, especially as they navigate from the privacy of their own room, may facilitate more risk taking especially in sending self-generated compromising materials. Studies indicate that only 36 percent of teen girls and 39 percent of teen boys are aware that recipients of nude or semi-nude images often share these images with third persons.[128] Therefore, the sexual content obtained through sexting can be used for abuse and exploitation.

In some cases, sexting may precede a new form of online crime known as revenge pornography.[129] In such child sexual exploitation situations, a sext receiver intentionally distributes sexually explicit material of the child without his or her permission with the intent to embarrass or harass the child. Despite the term, revenge motives are not constitutive, and this can be considered a type of online harassment that may be linked to online sex trafficking as there is an intentional dissemination of these nonconsensual pornographic materials of children in cyberspace. For example, the relationship between sexting and revenge porn is exemplified in the 2015 federal indictment of Hunter Moore and Charles Evens, who posted sexually explicit images of individuals, some amounting to child pornography, on the website www.isanyoneup.com. The images were received by, among others, hackers and ex-girlfriends and ex-boyfriends.[130] These cases demonstrate the need to study the phenomenon of sexting and its potential links to abuse, harassment, intimate partner violence, and sex trafficking.

Sexting is also an area of concern because posting sexual or nude photographs of cybervictims on websites or sending them to others facilitates the distribution of sexual abuse materials, particularly of girls and women, that can be received by collectors. In addition, sexually explicit material of children may be used to exploit them, particularly for sexual coercion and extortion offenses.[131]

Although boys and girls are equally likely to receive sexts, evidence suggests that girls are more likely to be the senders of sexts. Reasons given for doing so include to feel sexy, to flirt, and to comply with a request or pressure from their partner. It is possible in some circumstances that such coercive sexting, particularly among those within a relationship, will be accompanied by the use of threats for the creation of the images and, hence, will potentially intersect with other forms of victimization. Girls more frequently report that their partners share their images without their consent.[132] Even if concerns exist for boys, it seems that girls are more at risk for sexting as indicated in findings from the United States and UK.[133] Moreover, 75 percent of teens are aware that such videos or photos could have a negative impact on their future—a potential sexting risk.[134] In general a lack of understanding of the possible results of consensual sexting serves as a key factor that may lead many children into forms of victimization. A 2019 IWF study highlights this potential risk by reporting that in Europe, 29 percent of self-generated indecent materials appeared on websites other than those where the creator originally posted them.[135] This finding shows how easily images and videos self-produced by minors can end up in the hands of offenders.

An array of behaviors can be associated with sexting and lead to sexual pleasure while also exposing children to the potential risk of circulating images of themselves online. Sexting behaviors may be influenced by gender, peer pressure, cultural environment, the normalization of online sexual interactions, or a child's wanting to be accepted, included, or loved. According to the UK National Society for the Prevention of Cruelty to Children (NSPCC) in 2016, concerns about sexting were discussed in 1,392 helpline counseling sessions of children and youth, representing an increase of 15 percent from the previous year.[136] Notably, concerns about sexting are increasing, and parents are increasingly more concerned by sexted images of their children.[137]

INTERNET-FACILITATED CONTACT EXPLOITATION

The problem of technology being abused for criminal purposes has led to increases in sex trafficking of children and child sexual exploitation in the real world. These cybercriminal activities include those designed to entice children with the intention of recruiting and engaging them in the sex industry. Depending on the vulnerabilities and needs of the potential victim, traffickers apply different online recruitment methods such as offers of love, friendship, protection, or opportunity, specifically "false job offers, false promises of a better life, misrepresentation, Internet ads, marriage offers, [and] trip offers."[138] These interactions occur via chat rooms, instant messaging, and online forums. Online exploitative situations also occur when minors initiate online contact or respond to traffickers' solicitations such as when using the contact information traffickers provide in online ads or when responding to or inquiring about false job announcements on an online site.

The traffickers use such online interaction to facilitate the physical recruitment of these minors, who later perform sexual activity in the sex industry.[139] Recruited children are then often trapped in the world of sex trafficking—a world that they had never expected or imagined to live in and from which they cannot escape with ease.

Furthermore, misuse of the Internet may be related to the aim of buying and selling sexual services from children (cybercommercial transactions and usually from a cybercriminal to a cybercriminal), leading to a contact or a face-to-face meeting between the minor and the offender. In this context, traffickers develop online tactics to expand their network of sex buyers, potential sex clients, other criminals, and criminal organizations. On the Internet they advertise and sell child sexual services to clients, receive payments for these services, coordinate the transportation of minors where applicable, and handle any other necessary arrangements to aid in the commission of child sex trafficking.[140]

Commoditization of children online for their sexual exploitation offline may target both girls and boys. For example, a twenty-six-year-old male took advantage of a fourteen-year-old male he met at an LGBTQ+ support group. The older male convinced the boy to post his picture on a popular sex-for-pay site, www.rentboy.com. The older man included his own contact information with the picture and would then drive his victim to different buyers. The older man and the young male would then split the profits from each encounter.[141]

In accordance with the international definition of trafficking from the Palermo Protocol as seen in chapter 2, the term "receipt" includes bringing a child into a situation of exploitation. This means that during the trafficking process, a child can be sold by a trafficker to another trafficker or exploiter such as a final buyer through cyberspace.[142] Sexual exploitation includes the sexual exploitation of children in prostitution. As seen above, the definition of child prostitution from the OP-CRC-SC in Article 2(b) involves the sexual activities of a child in exchange for remuneration or any other form of consideration.[143] To adequately address the offense of the advertisement of children for prostitution, states parties are required to ensure the prohibition of the use of the Internet in the acts of "offering, obtaining, procuring or providing a child"[144] for the provision of sexual services in exchange for remuneration or other considerations under national law. Such online acts demonstrate that the child is being treated as a sexual object rather than a human person for the purpose of exploitation.

Offenders may form virtual communities to connect in real time with others with whom they share preferences, behaviors, or values, exchange information and strategies on how to persuade children to engage in sexual activity, or collaborate in the child sex trade. Offenders' networks are usually formed based on the establishment of trust and camaraderie among them in their routine activities and interactions with the intent to commit or facilitate sexual exploitation of children in cyberspace.[145] Thus through the misuse of the Internet, offenders create conditions to facilitate the occurrence of crimes that lead to the victimization of children in sex trafficking activities.

INTERNET-FACILITATED NONCOMMERCIAL
SEXUAL EXPLOITATION OF CHILDREN

Supported by the legal analysis of the international definition of trafficking, I argue that through the Internet, offenders also facilitate noncommercial exploitative sexual practices against minors in physical places through the use of mail-order bride services, early marriages, and illegal adoptions.

Mail-Order Bride Services and Child
Marriages for Sexual Exploitation

Through the Internet, offenders can sell young women's and children's bodies via catalogs and mail-order bride agencies, fostering transactions that would be difficult to conduct in the real world. For instance, in one bride-trafficking case involving children, the alleged trafficker's catalog contained nineteen girls seventeen years old or younger including a thirteen year old and fourteen year old.[146] Via online mail-order bride sites "trafficking victims can be [bought] online [using] credit cards, while marriage agency sites may be offering sexual services."[147] Young women and girls induced or coerced by a family member may be offered as a bride online and thereby exploited in the real world.

Evidence indicates that the motives of family members who give a girl as a bride typically relate to maintaining family ties or are linked to economic or immigration reasons.[148] The child may nevertheless end up commodified as the object of an online transaction, leading her into an exploitation that could continue through adulthood. In general, the younger the child is, the more vulnerable a child marriage is to becoming slavery.[149] This recognition refers to the operation of factors or indicia of slavery that connect with the young age of the child. Younger children are at greater risk as they are in a position of vulnerability and have a limited ability to understand the implications of becoming an online bride. Once the online child bride is sold, her husband is in a position of power over her and may subject her to threats, force, coercion, and psychological control, thereby reducing her to slavery or at best to a servile marriage (a slavery-like practice). Therefore, young age may increase the likelihood of the child being seen and treated as an object online. In addition, brides with children can be offered so that these younger children potentially end up being sexually exploited with their mother—all as one "package."[150] Thus children advertised for marriage are likely to become victims of trafficking and modern slavery as they are portrayed as commodities rather than persons online. They are victims of adults who take advantage of their vulnerability and abuse their own position of power. Moreover, although not all

marriage agencies that operate online are involved in trafficking, they may
help to increase chances for online traffickers to meet and recruit vulnerable
women and children, including boys.

There has been a greater focus on girl brides due to the higher risk of their
being exploited within a marriage setting. Closer examination of the impact
on boys of child marriage is called for, however, and especially considering
the gender dimension of their victimization. For example, the practice of
child marriage for boys has negative effects as it may lead to adult responsibilities for which they are not ready, the economic pressure to provide for a
family, or the detriment of interrupted or eliminated access to education and
career development. UNICEF estimates that in 2019, globally, 115 million
men were married before eighteen years of age. Of these, one in five (or 23
million) got married before they were fifteen years old.[151]

In general, the traditional cultural arrangements of child marriages usually involve a transactional or trade component offering economic or in-kind
benefit "such as the traditional dowry system, which encourages families to
marry their daughters at a young age."[152] In other words, there is the exchange
of a child for cash or goods. If this is for the purposes of sexual exploitation, it
establishes links between child marriage and slavery under the precepts of the
1926 Slavery Convention.[153] In fact the 1924 Temporary Slavery Commission
was established to explore and appraise slavery worldwide, and it identified
the "acquisition of girls by purchase disguised as payment of dowry" as a
form of slavery (excepting "normal marriage customs" involving dowries).
This means that the potential link between the particular vulnerability of children with respect to nonconsensual marriage and forms of slavery has been
understood since at least the formulation of the 1926 Slavery Convention.[154]

In this form of child sexual abuse and exploitation, the husband is usually
an abuser who intends to obtain sexual gratification from a minor within the
context of marriage rather than economic gain from her commercial sexual
exploitation, which is why it can be considered a noncommercial form of
sexual exploitation against that child. Importantly there is often a relationship between child marriage and domestic violence. In some countries, there
may be no legal basis to prosecute these kinds of child abusers and exploiters as child marriages are a legal practice under some domestic laws.[155] The
CRC is of the view that the minimum age for marriage should be eighteen
because this age is when persons should have attained the maturity and the
capacity to make a conscious and informed decision to enter into marriage.
The CRC defines child marriage as "any marriage where at least one of the
parties is under 18 years of age."[156] The CRC has strongly recommended
that states parties set and enforce the age of eighteen as the minimum age
limit for marriage under national laws.[157] This recommendation is especially
important because the practice of child marriage can constitute the sale of a

child,[158] and although states are required to protect children from physical and psychological harm, entering into marriage at a young age often results in serious consequences for the child's welfare.[159] Children may be forced into a marriage, and the child may be powerless to refuse, leave, or dissolve such an agreement. Lower ages for consent to marriage mean there's a greater chance that these children will be sexually exploited.

In these cases, child marriage may be considered slavery on the basis of the exercise of one or more powers attached to the right of ownership over the child according to the definition of slavery in the 1926 Slavery Convention. These marriages have the element of exploitation although this can be disguised under the veil of marriage. Thus, there may be a gray zone in determining the existence or absence of the crime. Nonetheless there is no question that there is an individual—the husband—who exercises effective control over his child spouse for the purpose of sexual gratification as well as a father or other relative who exercised this control in giving the child into the marriage.[160] The 1956 Supplementary Slavery Convention explicitly obliges states parties to abolish forms of servile marriage and child servitude, which can include child and forced marriage as a slavery-like practice,[161] considered one of the worst forms of child labor.[162] Following this, under the terms of the Palermo Protocol, Internet-facilitated child marriages may involve an act and purpose that fit within the parameters of the definition of trafficking. In cases where the child is promised or given in marriage for a payment online, the act may be transfer or receipt of the child and the purpose may be slavery or sexual exploitation. Legally the act element can be evidenced in cyberspace, as there is a sale of a child—an online transaction in the form of financial payment or in-kind benefits—for the purpose of exploitation within the form of a marriage agreement. Therefore, the possession of the child is transferred to another person for value received so that the child is treated as an online commodity and exchanged for money or goods with the intent of exploitation.

Thus these exploitative practices against children occur under the legal institution of marriage, which is a noncommercial setting, and as such they can be seen as providing the abuser with a more-permanent method of personal sexual gratification involving the child as opposed to a situation in which the child is commercially and sexually exploited by being offered and sold to others in the sex industry. Nevertheless in some trafficking cases, personal gratification and economic gain may be present at the same time such as when the trafficker both sexually abuses a minor and also intends to sexually exploit him or her to generate profits. In addition, evidence suggests that in some cases, after a child has legally entered another country due to marriage, he or she can later be trafficked for commercial purposes, such as child prostitution.[163]

Illegal Child Adoption for the Purpose of Exploitation

The sale of children for purposes of illegal adoption online can satisfy the act and purpose elements of the international legal definition of trafficking. In terms of substance, the act element includes transfer or receipt so that the definition extends beyond those involved in bringing the child into the situation of exploitation to potentially include those involved in receiving or holding the child. Therefore, under this expanded definition, individuals who coercively recruit a child offline and offer and sell him or her online as well as those who accept the child and purchase the child online for purposes of illegal exploitative adoption would potentially be associated with an online sex trafficking crime.

In this respect, the guardian of the Palermo Protocol, the UNODC, links the commodification of children and the illegal adoption market, affirming that in some countries "children may be forcibly separated from their mothers who were coerced into signing blank documents that were later made into illegal contracts."[164] Significantly, practices like these in the illegal adoption market have the intent to harm—that is, to exploit—a child offline. This means that the child is made an object in an online transaction with the offender's intent that the child provides (sexual or labor) services to another, usually by the use of coercion and deception, and constituting trafficking under the definition provided in the Palermo Protocol.[165]

The link between child marriage and forced adoption with trafficking can be also identified in the broad definition of trafficking in UNGA's 1995 report on the trafficking of women and girls as

> the illicit and clandestine movement of persons across national and international borders, largely from developing countries and some countries with economies in transition, with the end goal of forcing women and girl children into sexually or economically oppressive and exploitative situations for the profit of recruiters, traffickers and crime syndicates, as well as other illegal activities related to trafficking, such as forced domestic labor, false marriages, clandestine employment and false adoption.[166]

Due to their age and the unequal powers and dependency between them and adults, children end up being exploited for sexual or labor purposes in a noncommercial setting (e.g., a servile marriage or in a role of servitude) through the practices of child marriage and illegal adoption. Via cyberspace, offenders facilitate the sale of children online with the intent of the slavery or sexual exploitation of the child, which falls within the third element of the definition of trafficking. In addition, exploitative situations evidence that the child is being offered, bought, or sold online for the purpose of exploitation, all of which demonstrate indicators of ownership associated with slavery and control over the child. Indeed, powers of ownership and control are likely to be evidenced especially in the sense of placing a value on the child or his or her services online. This commoditization of the child on digital platforms illustrates the exploitative use of the child who is owned and exchanged, usually in return for money. Thus, the Internet becomes a vehicle through which children are transferred and acquired, leading them to forms of exploitation (e.g., slavery or practices similar to slavery) in the digital or real world.

CONCLUSION

This chapter discusses the types of activities that are facilitated by the Internet involving individuals younger than eighteen that can be considered trafficking-related practices. It also identifies legal gaps in states' child protection systems, including preventive measures, explicit prohibition of the offenses in domestic criminal law, effective law enforcement measures (e.g., investigation of offenders and their prosecution), and support and assistance to child victims. International law obliges states to prevent and eradicate these forms of online violence against children in their domestic legal systems. Indeed, in line with the international legal instruments discussed in the previous chapters, states have an obligation to take all appropriate measures to adequately protect children in cyberspace and at the same time punish and deter perpetrators.[167]

Currently, efforts to mitigate cybersecurity issues such as cybercrime laws are being made in some countries particularly via laws concerning criminalization, procedural powers, jurisdiction, and international cooperation. However these efforts do not necessarily translate into the effective implementation of policies and strategies at the national level as demonstrated by the 2018 ITU Global Cybersecurity Index (GCI). While considering ICTs one of the most crucial challenges to global security, the GCI survey highlights the urgent need for cooperation among countries to reduce differences in national responses in order to deploy appropriate responses to threats and crime in the borderless realm of cyberspace and provide a safer space for Internet users.[168] In general, diverse national approaches to these activities lead to a variety of responses between states that also introduce challenges to, inter alia, the elimination of criminal safe havens and global evidence collection.[169] While taking advantage of the Internet's speed, worldwide reach, and relative anonymity, cybercriminals continue to find fertile grounds to hide in the shadows of cyberspace and perpetrate their criminal offenses—characteristics that also complicate law enforcement activity.

This problem presents new challenges to the investigative powers that law enforcement and judicial sectors have under national law and especially those associated with the following areas: (1) uncertainty over the extent and evolution of forms of online child sexual exploitation and abuse, (2) differences between national legal frameworks, (3) difficulties in identifying child victims and the IP addresses of perpetrators, (4) difficulty tracking the criminal abuse of cryptocurrencies and digital payment systems (e.g., Bitcoin, Monero, Zcash, and Dash), (5) obstacles in monitoring the activities of offenders and organized groups and collecting electronic evidence, which may have a volatile nature and is often not easily detected when transmitted using encryption technologies, and (6) difficulties in processing takedown requests due to hosting providers' geographic locations, which may facilitate the hosting of illegal content or criminal activity—so-called bulletproof hosting.[170] Not only do these situations provide a world of opportunity for offenders, but they also demonstrate the clear shortcomings of and investigative need for effective enforcement. In particular, an international criminal investigation may meet with significant delays because it requires engaging in formal or informal cooperation mechanisms between governments for investigative and prosecutorial actions. At the same time, this emphasizes the need to strengthen a multistakeholder collaboration approach with the involvement of all relevant stakeholders, including the Internet industry, by establishing with clarity their roles and responsibilities with a view to ensuring effectively and timely responses to this type of cybercrime.

States have an obligation to establish a well-defined legal framework that protects children from harm through adequate (enacted or adjusted) national legislation, to increase sufficiency in detection, investigation, and prosecution of offenders and reporting mechanisms, to improve prevention programs, including raising awareness through public–private partnerships that include the Internet industry and that require the implementation of corporate social responsibility principles,[171] and to ensure protection, recovery, and access to redress for child victims in full compliance with relevant standards of international human rights law.[172] Indeed, the global nature of this problem underlines a challenge to the international community and its member states, as the primary duty bearers of human rights, that requires a global response to the growing sexual exploitation of children in cyberspace.

NOTES

1. Roy Balleste, "In Harm's Way: Harmonizing Security and Human Rights in the Internet Age," in *Cybersecurity and Human Rights in the Age of Cyberveillance*, ed. Joanna Kulesza and Roy Balleste (Lanham, MD: Rowman & Littlefield, 2015), 42.

2. CoE, "Convention on Cybercrime," signed November 23, 2001, E.T.S. 185; UNODC, *Comprehensive Study on Cybercrime* (New York: United Nations, 2013).

3. Jonathan Clough, *Principles of Cybercrime*, 2nd ed. (Cambridge: Cambridge University Press, 2015), 5–11.

4. Fiona Brookman et al., *Handbook on Crime*, 1st ed. (London: Willan, 2010), 194.

5. Ibid.

6. UNODC, "Global Programme on Cybercrime," www.unodc.org/unodc/en/cybercrime/global-programme-cybercrime.html.

7. UNODC, *Comprehensive Study on Cybercrime*, 16–18.

8. Majid Yar and Kevin F. Steinmetz, *Cybercrime and Society*, 3rd ed. (London: Sage Publications, 2019), 13.

9. Adam M. Bossler, Kathryn Seigfried-Spellar, and Thomas J. Holt, *Cybercrime and Digital Forensics: An Introduction*, 2nd ed. (Abingdon, UK: Routledge, 2017), 15.

10. Ibid., 16.

11. EC3, *Internet Organised Crime Threat Assessment* (Europol: 2019), 30 (hereafter IOCTA 2019).

12. U.S. Department of State, *TIP Report* (2017), 32.

13. President's Interagency Task Force, *Report on U.S. Government Efforts to Combat Trafficking in Persons* (U.S. Department of State, 2019), 8.

14. Department for Digital, Culture, Media & Sport and Home Office, *Online Harms White Paper* (CP57) (London: Crown Copyright, 2019), 31.

15. WPGA, *Global Threat Assessment 2018*: *Working Together to End the Sexual Exploitation of Children Online* (London: Crown Copyright, 2018), 12.

16. Jean Allain, "Bellagio-Harvard Guidelines on the Legal Parameters of Slavery," in *The Law and Slavery* (Leiden: Brill/Nijhoff, 2015), guideline 2, at 556.

17. OP-CRC-SC Guidelines, para. 48, at 11; para. 63, at 13.

18. Ibid., para. 58, at 12.

19. OP-CRC-SC, art. 2(b).

20. CoE, "Convention on the Protection of Children against Sexual Exploitation and Sexual Abuse," entered into force October 25, 2007, C.E.T.S. 201, art. 22 (hereafter Lanzarote Convention).

21. CoE, "Explanatory Report to the Council of Europe Convention on the Protection of Children against Sexual Exploitation and Sexual Abuse," October 25, 2007, C.E.T.S. 201, para. 151–154, at 22.

22. OP-CRC-SC, art. 2(c).

23. HRC, "Report of the Special Rapporteur on the Sale of Children, Child Prostitution and Child Pornography, Maud de Boer-Buquicchio," A/HRC/28/56, December 22, 2014, para. 26, at 8.

24. OP-CRC-SC, guidelines, para. 61, at 12.

25. Ibid., para. 60, at 12.

26. Ibid., para. 53, at 11.

27. "The Lanzarote Committee: Invites Parties to review their legislation to address all serious harm to the sexual integrity of children by not limiting their criminal offences to sexual intercourse or equivalent acts (R9)" (Lanzarote Committee, *1st Implementation Report: Protection of Children against Sexual Abuse in the Circle of Trust: The Framework* [Strasbourg: CoE, 2015], para. 47, at 17).

28. OP-CRC-SC, art. 3(1), (C).

29. OP-CRC-SC Guidelines, para. 65, at 13.

30. HRC, "Report of the Special Rapporteur on the Sale of Children, Child Prostitution and Child Pornography, Maud de Boer-Buquicchio," para. 27, at 8.

31. Canadian Centre for Child Protection, *Survivors' Survey: Full Report* (Winnipeg: Canadian Centre for Child Protection, 2017), 24.

32. INHOPE, *Annual Report 2019* (Amsterdam: INHOPE, 2020), 31.

33. Interpol, "ICSE database," www.interpol.int/Crimes/Crimes-against-children/ International-Child-Sexual-Exploitation-database; ECPAT International, *Trends in Online Child Sexual Abuse Material* (Bangkok: ECPAT International, 2018).

34. ECPAT International, *Trends in Online Child Sexual Abuse Material*, 13.

35. CoE, "Convention on Cybercrime."

36. CoE, "Chart of Signatures and Ratifications of Treaty 185," www.coe.int/en/ web/conventions/full-list/-/conventions/treaty/185/signatures.

37. CoE, "Explanatory Report to the Convention on Cybercrime," November 23, 2001, E.T.S. 185, 4.

38. CoE, "Convention on Cybercrime," art. 15; Ibid., para. 145–148, at 23.

39. CoE, "Explanatory Report to the Convention on Cybercrime," para. 5, at 1–2.

40. CoE, "Convention on Cybercrime," preamble.

41. Ibid., art. 9.

42. CoE, "Explanatory Report to the Convention on Cybercrime," para. 91–106, at 15–17.

43. HRC, "Report of the Special Rapporteur on the Promotion and Protection of the Right to Freedom of Opinion and Expression, Frank La Rue," A/HRC/17/27, May 27, 2011, 10.

44. See Joanna Kulesza, "Preface," in *Internet Governance: Origins, Current Issues, and Future Possibilities*, ed. Roy Balleste (New York: Rowman & Littlefield, 2015).

45. CoE, "Convention on Cybercrime," art. 9(2).

46. CoE, "Explanatory Report to the Convention on Cybercrime," para. 100, at 16.

47. Ibid., para. 101, at 16.

48. ECPAT International, *Terminology Guidelines for the Protection of Children from Sexual Exploitation and Sexual Abuse* (Bangkok: ECPAT International, 2016), 41.

49. Lanzarote Convention, art. 20(3); CoE, "Explanatory Report to the Council of Europe Convention on the Protection of Children against Sexual Exploitation and Sexual Abuse," para. 144, at 21.

50. CoE, "Convention on Cybercrime," art. 9(3).

51. OP-CRC-SC Guidelines, para. 72 at 14.

52. CoE, "Convention on Cybercrime," art. 9(1).

53. Ibid., art. 9(4); CoE, "Explanatory Report to the Convention on Cybercrime," para. 106, at 17.

54. Lanzarote Convention, art. 20(1).

55. CoE, "Explanatory Report to the Council of Europe Convention on the Protection of Children against Sexual Exploitation and Sexual Abuse," para. 140, at 21.

56. Lanzarote Convention, art. 20(4).

57. CoE, "Explanatory Report to the Convention on Cybercrime," para. 93, at 15–16.

58. Erin I. Kunze, "Sex Trafficking via the Internet: How International Agreements Address the Problem and Fail to Go Far Enough," *Journal of High Technology Law* 10, no. 2 (2010): 241–289.

59. Suzanne Ost, *Child Pornography and Sexual Grooming, Legal and Societal Responses* (Cambridge: Cambridge University Press, 2009), 105.

60. Reference is made to Thailand, Court Region 5. UNODC, *Global Report on Trafficking in Persons 2018* (New York: United Nations, 2018), 39.

61. IOCTA 2019, 30.

62. Ibid.

63. IWF, *Annual Report 2019* (Cambridge: IWF, 2020), 46.

64. Ibid.

65. IWF, *Annual Report 2018* (Cambridge: IWF, 2019), 30.

66. UNODC, *Study on the Effects of New Information Technologies on the Abuse and Exploitation of Children* (New York: United Nations, 2015), 21.

67. EC3, and VGT, *Virtual Global Taskforce Child Sexual Exploitation Environmental Scan 2015* (Europol, 2015), 8.

68. IWF, *Annual Report 2019*, at 58.

69. IOCTA 2019, 30.

70. ECPAT International, *Online Child Sexual Exploitation: An Analysis of Emerging and Selected Issues* (2017), 34; European Financial Coalition (EFC), *Commercial Sexual Exploitation of Children Online: A Strategic Assessment* (2013), 9.

71. EFC, *Commercial Sexual Exploitation of Children Online*, 9.

72. VGT, *Virtual Global Taskforce Online Child Sexual Exploitation: Environmental Scan Unclassified Version 2019* (VGT, 2019), 5.

73. EC3, *Internet Organised Crime Threat Assessment* (Europol, 2020), 36 (hereafter IOCTA 2020).

74. IOCTA 2019, 57.

75. Subgroup against the Sexual Exploitation of Children and NGO Group for the UNCRC, *Semantics or Substance? Towards a Shared Understanding of Terminology Referring to the Sexual Abuse and Exploitation of Children* (2005), 27.

76. Justė Neverauskaitė, *Child Sexual Abuse Material and the Internet (Part 2): Challenges for the Law Enforcement Agencies* (Brussels: ECPAT Belgium, 2015), 3.

77. The number of CSAM offenders who also commit contact sexual offenses against children was estimated to range from 60 to 85 percent (Michael L. Bourke, "The Myth of the Harmless Hands-Off Offender," in *The NetClean Report 2016* [NetClean, 2016], 35).

78. R v. Hill, [2011] 110 SASR 588, at 590.

79. Interpol, "ICSE database."

80. ECPAT International, *Trends in Online Child Sexual Abuse Material*.

81. ECPAT International, *Terminology Guidelines*, 42.

82. U.S. Department of State, "Online Sexual Exploitation of Children: An Alarming Trend," in *TIP Report* (2017), 1.

83. NCMEC, *Trends Identified in Cybertipline Sextortion Report* (2016), at 4.

84. Kemal Veli Açar, "Sexual Extortion of Children in Cyberspace," *International Journal of Cyber Criminology* 10, no. 2 (2016): 114, https://doi.org/10.5281/zenodo.163398.

85. U.S. Department of Justice, *The National Strategy for Child Exploitation Prevention and Interdiction* (no. 249863) (2016), 74.

86. UNICEF, *The State of the World's Children 2017: Children in a Digital World* (New York: UNICEF, 2017), 64.

87. U.S. Department of Justice, *The National Strategy*, 75.

88. NCMEC, *Trends Identified*, 1.

89. Ibid., 1.

90. Ibid., 2.

91. Janis Wolak and David Finkelhor, *Sextortion: Keys Findings from an Online Survey of 1,631 Victims* (Crimes against Children Research Center and Thorn, 2016), 12.

92. Wolak and Finkelhor, *Sextortion*, 12.

93. Author's summary of one respondent's description; Wolak and Finkelhor, *Sextortion*, 12.

94. Wolak and Finkelhor, *Sextortion*, 6.

95. IOCTA 2019, 31.

96. IWF, *Trends in Online Child Sexual Exploitation: Examining the Distribution of Captures of Live-Streamed Child Sexual Abuse* (Cambridge: IWF, 2018), 11.

97. Ibid., 10–11.

98. EC3, *Internet Organised Crime Threat Assessment* (Europol: 2015), 30.

99. WPGA, *Global Threat Assessment 2019: Working Together to End the Sexual Exploitation of Children Online* (London: Crown Copyright, 2019), 20.

100. EC3, *Internet Organised Crime Threat Assessment* (Europol: 2018), 35.

101. VGT, *Virtual Global Taskforce Online Child Sexual Exploitation: Environmental Scan Unclassified Version 2019*, 19; EFC, *Commercial Sexual Exploitation of Children Online* (EFC, 2015), 23.

102. EFC, *Commercial Sexual Exploitation*, 23.

103. Ibid.

104. Author's summary of case reference in IOCTA 2019, 33.

105. IOCTA 2019, 33.

106. IWF, *Trends in Online Child Sexual Exploitation*, 12–13.

107. WPGA, *Global Threat Assessment 2019*, 33.

108. ECPAT International, *Online Child Sexual Exploitation*, 54.

109. VGT, "Operations," http://virtualglobaltaskforce.com/operations/; HRC, "Report of the Special Rapporteur on the Sale of Children, Child Prostitution and Child Pornography, Maud de Boer-Buquicchio," para. 71. at 18.

110. UNCRC, art. 34(c).

111. OP-CRC-SC, art. 3(1)(a), (i), (a).

112. Ibid., art. 3(1), (c).

113. UNICEF Innocenti Research Center, *Handbook on the Optional Protocol on the Sale of Children, Child Prostitution and Child Pornography* (Florence, Italy: UNICEF, 2009), 12.

114. Lanzarote Convention, art. 21(1)(a), (b).

115. Lanzarote Convention, art. 21(1)(c); CoE, "Explanatory Report to the Council of Europe Convention on the Protection of Children against Sexual Exploitation and Sexual Abuse," para. 147–149, at 22.

116. Lanzarote Convention, art. 21(2). See CoE, "Explanatory Report to the Council of Europe Convention on the Protection of Children against Sexual Exploitation and Sexual Abuse," para. 150, at 22.

117. EC3, *The Internet Organised Crime Threat Assessment* (Europol: 2014), 32.

118. WPGA, *Global Threat Assessment 2018*, 17.

119. UNODC, *Study on the Effects of New Information Technologies on the Abuse and Exploitation of Children*, 21; ECPAT International and Religions for Peace, *Protecting Children from Online Sexual Exploitation: A Guide to Action for Religious Leaders and Communities* (Bangkok: ECPAT International and Religions for Peace, 2016), 8–9.

120. IWF, *Trends in Online Child Sexual Exploitation*, 3.

121. Ibid., 12, 15.

122. IOCTA 2019, 33.

123. IOCTA 2020, 39.

124. U.S. Department of State, *Trafficking in Persons Report* (2020), 1.

125. U.S. Department of State, *TIP Report* (2020), 28.

126. GuardChild, "Teenage Sexting Statistics," www.guardchild.com/teenage-sexting-statistics/.

127. Sonia Livingstone et al., *Children's Online Activities, Risks and Safety: A Literature Review by the UKCCIS Evidence Group* (London: LSE Consulting, 2017), 35.

128. GuardChild, "Teenage Sexting Statistics."

129. Bossler, Seigfried-Spellar, and Holt, *Cybercrime and Digital Forensics*, 267–268.

130. U.S. Department of Justice, "Operator of 'Revenge Porn' Website Sentenced to 2 1/2 Years in Federal Prison in Email Hacking Scheme to Obtain Nude Photos," www.justice.gov/usao-cdca/pr/operator-revenge-porn-website-sentenced-2-years-federal-prison-email-hacking-scheme.

131. EC3, *Online Sexual Coercion and Extortion as a Form of Crime Affecting Children: Law Enforcement Perspective* (The Hague: Europol, 2017), 10.

132. Sonia Livingstone et al., *Children's Online Activities*, 35.

133. See GuardChild, "Teenage Sexting Statistics"; Sonia Livingstone et al., *Children's Online Activities*, 35.

134. GuardChild, "Teenage Sexting Statistics."

135. IWF, *Annual Report 2019*, 57.

136. NSPCC, *"What Should I Do?" NSPCC Helplines: Responding to Children's and Parents' Concerns about Sexual Content Online* (London, UK: NSPCC, 2016), 26.

137. In the UK, "the biggest group of adults contacting both the NSPCC helpline and the O2 & NSPCC Online Safety Helpline was parents" (NSPCC, *"What Should I Do?"* 8).

138. Neda Ilic et al., *Human (Child) Trafficking: A Look through the Internet Window* (Belgrade: ASTRA–Anti-Trafficking Action, 2006), 53.

139. Athanassia P. Sykiotou, *Trafficking in Human Beings: Internet Recruitment, Misuse of the Internet for the Recruitment of Victims of Trafficking in Human Beings* (Strasbourg: Council of Europe, 2007).

140. Mark Latonero, *Human Trafficking Online: The Role of Social Networking Sites and Online Classifieds* (Los Angeles: USC Annenberg Center of Communication & Policy, 2011), 12.

141. Author's summary of *United States v. Stoterau*, 524 F.3d 988 (9th Cir. 2008), at 995.

142. UNICEF Innocenti Research Center, *Handbook on the Optional Protocol*, 10.

143. OP-CRC-SC, art. 2(b).

144. Ibid., art. 3(1)(b).

145. Ella Cockbain, *Offender and Victim Networks in Human Trafficking* (Abingdon, UK: Routledge, 2018), 56.

146. Donna M. Hughes, "Use of the Internet for Global Sexual Exploitation of Women and Children," www.academia.edu/3415661/Use_of_the_Internet_for_Global_Sexual_Exploitation_of_Women_and_Children.

147. UN Global Initiative to Fight Human Trafficking, *017 Workshop: Technology and Human Trafficking, in the Vienna Forum to Fight Human Trafficking* (Vienna, Austria: United Nations Office on Drugs and Crime, 2008), 9; Sykiotou, *Trafficking in Human Beings*, 40.

148. Farhat Bokhari, *Stolen Futures: Trafficking for Forced Child Marriage in the UK* (London: ECPAT UK, 2009), 28.

149. Catherine Turner, *Out of the Shadows: Child Marriage and Slavery* (Anti-Slavery International, 2013), 8.

150. UN CHR, "Report of the Special Rapporteur on the Sale of Children, Child Prostitution and Child Pornography, Ofelia Calcetas-Santos," E/CN.4/1996/100, January 17, 1996, para. 66, at 12.

151. UNICEF, "115 Million Boys and Men around the World Married as Children," www.unicef.org/press-releases/115-million-boys-and-men-around-world-married-children-unicef.

152. ECPAT International, *Preventing and Eliminating Child, Early and Forced Marriage: Challenges, Achievements, Best Practices & Implementation Gaps* (2013), 3.

153. UNGA, "Preventing and Eliminating Child, Early and Forced Marriage," A/HRC/26/22, April 2, 2014, para. 11, at 5.

154. OHCHR, *Abolishing Slavery and Its Contemporary Forms* (HR/PUB/02/4) (New York: United Nations, 2002), para. 11, at 4.

155. UNICEF, "Legal Minimum Ages and the Realization of Adolescents' Rights," www.unicef.org/lac/media/2806/file.

156. UN Committee on the Elimination of Discrimination against Women and CRC, "Joint General Recommendation no. 31 of the Committee on the Elimination of Discrimination against Women/General Comment no. 18 of the Committee on the Rights of the Child Committee on Harmful Practices," CEDAW/C/GC/31-CRC/C/GC/18, November 14, 2014, sec. 6.2., para. 19, at 7.

157. For example, CRC, "Concluding Observations on the Combined Fifth and Sixth Periodic Reports of Costa Rica," CRC/C/CRI/CO/5–6, March 4, 2020, para 31, at 8; CRC, "Concluding Observations on the Report Submitted by the Niger under Article 12(1) of the Optional Protocol to the Convention on the Rights of the Child on the Sale of Children, Child Prostitution and Child Pornography," CRC/C/OPSC/NER/CO/1, December 12, 2018, para. 18 at 3.

158. OP-CRC-SC, art. 2(a), 3(1)(a)(i)(a).

159. The CRC also notes that "in exceptional circumstances a marriage of a mature, capable child below the age of 18 may be allowed provided that the child is at least 16 years old and that such decisions are made by a judge based on legitimate exceptional grounds defined by law and on the evidence of maturity without deference to cultures and traditions" (UN Committee on the Elimination of Discrimination against Women and CRC, "Joint General Recommendation no. 31 of the Committee on the Elimination of Discrimination against Women/General Comment no. 18 of the CRC Committee on Harmful Practices," sec. 6.2., at 7).

160. For reading on trafficking in persons for marriage, see UNODC, *Global Report on Trafficking in Persons* (New York: United Nations, 2016), 15.

161. Supplementary Slavery Convention, art. 1(c), (d); Catherine Turner, *Out of the Shadows*, 22.

162. The 1999 ILO's Worst Forms of Child Labour Convention (No. 182) calls for the prohibition and immediate action toward the elimination of practices in which children can be at risk of slavery or practices similar to slavery (ILO, "Worst Forms of Child Labour Convention, 1999 [No. 182]," entered into force November 19, 2000, C182, art. 1, 3[a]).

163. CRC, "Concluding Observations on the Combined Fourth and Fifth Periodic Report of Lebanon," CRC/C/LBN/CO/4–5, June 22, 2017, para. 42(b), at 13.

164. UNODC, *Anti-Human Trafficking Manual for Criminal Justice Practitioners: Definition of Trafficking in Persons and Smuggling of Migrants (Module 1)* (New York: United Nations, 2009), 7.

165. Palermo Protocol, art. 3(c); UNGA, "Addendum: Interpretative Notes for the Official Records (*Travaux Préparatoires*) of the Negotiation of the United Nations Convention against Transnational Organized Crime and the Protocols Thereto," A/55/383/Add.1, November 3, 2000, art. 3, para. 66, at 12.

166. UNGA, Resolution 49/166, Traffic in Women and Girls: Resolution/Adopted by the General Assembly, A/RES/49/166 (Feb. 24, 1995), 2.

167. A due diligence obligation of states toward children involves "the obligation to prevent violence or violations of human rights, the obligation to protect child victims and witnesses from human rights violations, the obligation to investigate and to punish those responsible, and the obligation to provide access to redress human rights

violations." See CRC, "General Comment no. 13 (2011): The Right of the Child to Freedom From All Forms of Violence," CRC/C/GC/13, April 18, 2011, para. 5, at 4.

168. ITU, *Global Cybersecurity Index 2018*, 16–17.

169. UNODC, *Comprehensive Study on Cybercrime*, 56.

170. IOCTA 2020, 22; For a helpful analysis, see IOCTA 2019, 57.

171. HRC, "Report of the Special Representative of the Secretary-General on the Issue of Human Rights and Transnational Corporations and Other Business Enterprises, John Ruggie," A/HRC/17/31, March 21, 2011.

172. CRC, "General Comment no. 13 (2011)," para. 40, at 14; CRC, "General Comment no. 25 (2021) on Children's Rights in Relation to the Digital Environment," CRC/C/GC/25, March 2, 2021, para. 23, at 4.

Chapter 5

Internet-Facilitated Grooming of Children

We now turn to an analysis of the crime of "grooming" as a form of cyber-crime against children and one that many children are vulnerable to as online users. Among Internet-related crimes affecting children, online child grooming continues to grow as a significant concern for many countries. UN member states most frequently requested support for investigative measures in countering child trafficking activities conducted via computer, including the production and dissemination of child pornography and child grooming.[1] The COVID-19 pandemic may have increased cybercrime opportunities, including those related to online child exploitation. Particularly during the peak months of the pandemic, online connectivity became part of children's everyday lives especially in countries with physical lockdowns and school closures.[2] This chapter discusses the role of the Internet in grooming children to facilitate their involvement in exploitative practices online or in the real world and considers how this offense may lead to online trafficking. Especially in view of the latest trends in this area, I argue that there is a need to enhance global efforts to address the online grooming of children.

ONLINE GROOMING OF CHILDREN

The term "grooming," when applied to children, refers to a complex phenomenon that involves multiple forms of activities and situations with the ultimate purpose of the solicitation of children for sexual purposes.[3] In the context of child sexual exploitation, it refers to the process through which an individual prepares a child with the intention to facilitate a sexual contact online or offline.[4] This definition implies that there is an individual who interacts with the minor over a period of time, establishing a relationship and gaining trust, with the intention to solicit them for sexual purposes. In Internet grooming, online interactions between the offender and the child develop to the point at which the offender gains the minor's confidence. To accomplish such an emotional connection and other exploitative goals, cyberoffenders exercise subtle psychological manipulation of children that is "calculated, controlling, and premeditated."[5] As a result of this approach, most minors end up being under the offenders' effective control while keeping their online interactions and sexual relationship secret.

Findings from a four-year study by Middlesex University, London, suggest that online grooming can develop more quickly than predigital forms. This research indicates that it may take just three minutes for an online groomer to start sexual talk with a child and eight minutes to create a bond with them.[6] This demonstrates that cyberperpetrators who solicit sexual contact with minors after brief interactions may be more focused on quickly establishing influence or control over them rather than spending substantial time to build trust in the relationship. A profile of victims generated from responses to questionnaires created by the Virtual Global Taskforce notes that both genders are targeted by cybergroomers for sexual purposes in similar proportions.[7] The taskforce observed that victims were predominantly between the age of ten and seventeen.[8] Moreover, in the opinion of the countries responding to this international survey, chatting usually took place late at night in children's bedrooms when they might have less parental supervision, and it was often facilitated by the use of mobile devices.[9]

In general the time it takes from the first interaction between an abuser and a victim to the time of the abuse or an agreement to meet in person depends on the vulnerabilities of the minor concerned. Offenders, including traffickers, analyze a minor's needs and particular circumstances and adjust their strategies accordingly.[10] Hence, in common with offline types of grooming, trust is an essential component in the process of establishing a relationship with a child. To gain this trust, the groomer explores and targets the minor's vulnerabilities so as to use them to his favor in perpetuating and concealing the predation. A groomer is likely to establish a confiding and supportive tone in initial approaches such as "Hey angel, sounds like things are hard for you right now you wanna chat?"[11] An interesting point is that some cybergroomers may choose to tell children their real age instead of posing as teenagers.

Child: What age r u?

Adult: Whats too old?

Child: I don't know

Adult: 20s to 30s

Child::)

Adult: I'm 35, is that too old?[12]

Although perpetrators frequently pretend to be another child in cases of online soliciting of children for sexual purposes, this is not always the case as offenders base their strategies on their motivations and on minors' vulnerabilities.[13]

Aiming at accomplishing the goal of building a cyberrelationship with a child for the purpose of the sexual exploitation of the child, a perpetrator may closely monitor the child during the course of their online interactions in order to identify and appraise potential external risks with a view to reducing the chances of being detected. Moreover, the perpetrator may tell the child to change their time or hours of interaction or ask the child to ensure more privacy for their conversation, for example, by moving communications from a computer to a mobile phone and bedroom.[14] The offender may display patience and spend time with the child online—for example, chatting, listening to music, or playing video games. The child begins to trust the cyberoffender and starts openly talking about his or her personal life and other topics.

As a consequence, a romantic or amicable relationship is formed between the offender and the child. This cyberrelationship is commonly characterized by the authority the offender holds over the child and the child's position of vulnerability. In some cases, children may perceive the offender as a mentor as the offender guides them in exploring and understanding their sexuality.[15] This process is intended to enhance the offender's sexual fantasies and prepare the child for his or her abuse or exploitation. It is common for cyberoffenders to target children who are vulnerable to manipulation and victimization due to low self-esteem, a need for attention, or family problems as such conditions may facilitate initiating sexual talk with a child.

As noted previously, the question of consent is irrelevant in sexual activity involving children insofar as they are legally unable to consent to their own sexual abuse or sexual exploitation.[16] The UNCRC in Article 34 affirms that "States Parties undertake to protect the child from all forms of sexual exploitation and sexual abuse."[17] Today, discrepancies in the age of sexual consent in national legislation may prevent the prosecution of some offenders as not all children younger than eighteen are protected from these exploitative acts. States have a positive obligation to protect the fundamental rights and dignity of children and to ensure that an adequate legal child-protective framework is in place to prevent and combat all forms of sexual exploitation of children. Moreover, states must ensure that any consent of a child victim—at or above the nationally prescribed legal age to consent to sexual activities—to exploitative practices, including online grooming, should be null and void and should not alter the criminal liability of the offender, who is the one responsible for such acts.[18] Because grooming can be an integral or preparatory act to subsequent sexual offenses and can in itself also be harmful, it is essential to consider the challenges in its criminalization to ensure adequate protection of children against this form of abuse.

CRIMINAL LAW DIMENSIONS OF GROOMING

There have been legal developments related to the grooming of children through the use of computer systems.[19] Many states now recognize online sexual solicitation of children or child grooming as a culpable cybercrime. There is a baseline consensus among many legal systems globally with regard to the criminalization of online solicitation or grooming of children for sexual purposes. Nevertheless it seems that national approaches to dealing with such crimes are often general (noncyberspecific) rather than via cyberspecific legal frameworks. This criminalization may indicate that most countries are, to some extent, applying traditional laws while fewer may be grappling with new intangible objects such as computer data or computer information and cyberspecific concepts in the context of solicitation or the grooming of children.[20] It is important to consider the dynamics of online grooming behaviors both when the intention of the groomer is to move into a "virtual" meeting and when the intention of the groomer is to initiate a real-life meeting with a view to committing a sexual offense against the child.

A Preparatory Act with the Intent to Lead to Another Cyberoffense

The current international legal landscape is at issue here because grooming leading to exploitation committed online is not currently illegal in most countries. The intentional proposal of an adult to a child online often results in unlawful behavior that may occur in the digital environment and may not be followed by a material act leading to an offline meeting. The Lanzarote Convention has significant importance here as it is the only international legal instrument that explicitly criminalizes grooming or solicitation of children for sexual purposes committed intentionally through the use of ICTs. However it only addressed this offense when the offense involves material acts leading to a meeting in person, which is an essential element of Article 23.[21]

Aware of the challenges of criminalizing grooming children online, the Council of Europe Committee of the Parties to the Lanzarote Convention (Lanzarote Committee), established to monitor implementation of the convention, is concerned that cyberoffenses can go beyond the scope of Article 23 particularly when cyberperpetrators groom or solicit children to commit sexual offenses online without intending to meet the child offline. Such cybercrimes may not always be adequately recognized by states and therefore may not always be investigated and criminalized in national laws.[22] Thus, the Lanzarote Committee provides guidance to those states parties that wish to effectively criminalize online grooming beyond the scope of Article 23. This involves guidance to those states parties that are fully aware that these new situations can be presented—when cybergrooming behaviors are committed or were intentionally perpetrated online—and want to criminalize them under national laws. Additionally, states parties must criminalize grooming behaviors when they lead to a meeting in person between an offender and a child to engage in illegal sexual activity, as mandated by Article 23 of the Lanzarote Convention.

In international law, the term "sexual exploitation" when applied to children refers to the exploitative use of children in prostitution and related practices such as the production of pornographic performances and materials.[23] Although the offense of grooming is not directly mentioned in the OP-CRC-SC, the CRC recognizes child grooming as a form of sexual exploitation of children that may constitute an offense covered by the OP-CRC-SC.[24] For example, the offender may lure a minor in order to obtain sexual materials (images and videos) of themselves or to promote other exploitative situations that may involve the criminal acts of production and dissemination of CSAM (child pornography offenses).[25] Once the materials are in the hands of the offender, they can be used for sexual gratification or be distributed online to make a profit or for noncommercial purposes. At the same time, the offender may persuade the child victim over the course of time to keep producing and sending more material. It is clear that online grooming belongs in the same category as other forms of online child sexual abuse and exploitation practices.

A study of children ten to eighteen from Portugal (986), Spain (756), and the UK (823) found that cyberoffenders were commonly someone that the minors had just met online and that the offender started sexualizing their relationship with the minor by behavior such as talking about sexual matters, sending emails or links with sexual content, or asking the minor to do something sexual online such as provide explicit photos and videos of themselves.[26] This method served to break down the child's resistance and demonstrates that as a result of grooming conversations, cyberoffenders manipulate or control children, leading to an exploitative situation such as engaging in sexual activities or voluntarily providing self-generated, explicit sexual images to the offender.[27] In addition, online grooming can involve causing a child to view sexual abuse or sexual activities even without their participation, and it therefore connects with the offense of the corruption of children.[28]

A 2019 case from the District Court of Western Australia in Perth provides an example of how this criminal activity may begin and gain traction with children online. The Australian Federal Police were able to identify the perpetrator, who was charged and sentenced for various offenses, including a new offense at section 474.25C of the criminal code.[29] In cases of cybergrooming, a predatory adult commits an offense via the Internet when establishing a relationship with a child as a preparatory step to procuring or engaging in sexual activity with the child online. This does not necessarily require physical contact to be considered an offense; the offense can be the preparatory act of misrepresenting one's age online, as in the example above.[30] Because this new Australian legal provision aims at preventing online sexual exploitation crimes against children by allowing law enforcement agencies to intervene, detect, investigate, and prosecute such online groomer offenders during the initial stage of luring children for sexual exploitation and abuse—thus before sexual activity takes place—it provides greater protection for children under the age of sixteen. Therefore, it may reveal a possible gap in the law in relation to older children regarding such exploitative practices.[31] Furthermore, some cases of child sextortion will be preceded by enticement, especially those situations where parties first meet online.[32]

In these cases, the child's knowledge that images and videos depicting themselves can circulate online with few ways to completely remove them from cyberspace can create long-lasting trauma that can be very difficult for the child to overcome. This harm from the exploitative use of children for pornographic material may continue into adulthood. Under international human rights law, the offense of child pornography still exists regardless of whether or not the underage victim has already become an adult.[33]

In a 2016 report to Congress by the U.S. Department of Justice, the term "online enticement of children" was also used to refer to online grooming, revealing that children are often enticed or groomed online when the offender has the intention to commit sextortion.[34] In this sense, the report demonstrates that when online grooming turns into the criminal behavior of sextortion, a single sextortion offender may accomplish his exploitative goals by communicating with hundreds of potential minor victims all over the world to solicit their performance of sexual acts online. In the general context of online trafficking, perpetrators use a combination of praise and abuse strategies to the point that they exercise such effective control over the child that the child becomes completely dependent and incapable of leaving the exploitative situation. Threats are sometimes extended to parents or family members, introducing a means element such as deception, abuse of authority, and a position of vulnerability. In some instances, the severity of these coercive methods, along with demands for materials more degrading or violent, may lead the child to self-harm or suicide as they may find no other way to escape from it.

To help fight the grooming of children that may involve the offense of child pornography, the EU Directive on Child Exploitation (Directive 2011/93/EU) promotes the common goal of covering the prosecution of perpetrators, the protection of child victims, and prevention of crimes, including via ICTs, in a comprehensive approach among EU member states. Moreover, this directive recognizes child pornography and the solicitation of children for sexual purposes as serious violations of children's fundamental rights and well-being.[35] Article 6(2) of the directive mandates the criminalization of the practice of online luring of a child to provide CSAM depicting them and thus obliges states as part of the EU law to work to prevent and combat these activities.[36] In such cases, online grooming of children is an attempt to commit criminal offenses such as "acquisition or possession of child pornography" and "knowingly obtaining access" to child pornography. However the fact that this provision provides protection only to children under the age of sexual consent, which may vary among EU states, results in difficulties for law enforcement in the prosecution of some online grooming behaviors by leaving a legal gap in the protection of all child victims below the age of eighteen.[37]

Online grooming may cause serious, long-lasting harm to children. In fact, the impact of this criminal offense can be classified as one of the most severe in a child's life according to the above-mentioned study undertaken at the University of Minho in Portugal.[38] In addition, the impact of online grooming on the child victim can be as severe as that on those who have suffered offline sexual abuse.[39] Although it is not necessary to prove the means requirement in situations that relate to child trafficking, evidence indicates that these methods are frequently used to induce or coerce a child to engage in any unlawful sexual activity, or at the very least, such activity may be a reflection of an abuse of power or a position of vulnerability. In any case, these groomed children cannot legally consent to such practices relating to their own sexual exploitation or sexual abuse. They have no choice in this business nor do they have the capacity to make a real choice even if they have what appears to be a choice. It is therefore important to consider that any presumed consent of any child up to the age of eighteen to exploitative or abusive practices committed against themselves is legally irrelevant.[40] Children exploited on the Internet are under the effective control of the offender, who usually makes them comply by using coercion, threats, extreme psychological manipulation, and deception.

To prevent and combat sexual exploitation of children on the Internet more effectively, states should enact or strengthen national legislation and other measures that ensure the protection of children from the criminal offense of online grooming even when it is intended to lead to noncontact sexual offenses by remaining exclusively in cyberspace.[41] The criminalization of the phenomenon of online grooming would make illegal the mere act of sexually chatting with a child for the purpose of sexually exploiting that child in the digital space. Under the parameters of the current international legal understanding of trafficking, factors such as loss of free will, use of threats of violence, forms of coercion, or psychological manipulation influence the inducement of the child to exploitative practices. In addition, the element of exploitation is intrinsically connected to the nature of trafficking and is undertaken in cyberspace.

A Preparatory Act to Facilitate Subsequent Sexual Offenses Offline

In the framework of current international legal instruments, grooming that occurs online is intended to prepare for an offline meeting. Cybergroomers try to target and lure the most vulnerable in society, often with a view to committing a sexual offense against them in the real world. In such cases, during the online grooming process, once the minor is seen as ready to meet in person, the abuser arranges a face-to-face encounter. It is important to highlight that sexual predators may persuade a child to meet in as short a time as eighteen minutes, which demonstrates how quickly online grooming can function to convince a child of the need for a physical meeting.[42]

The Lanzarote Convention recognizes cybercriminals' use of grooming strategies and addresses such abuse and exploitation of children in Article 23, which states in part,

> Each party shall take the necessary legislative or other measures to criminalize the intentional proposal, through information and communication technologies, of an adult to meet a child . . . where this proposal has been followed by material acts leading to such a meeting.[43]

As noted in this European multilateral instrument, for an individual to bear criminal responsibility with respect to cybergrooming, an intentional proposal is required—organized and expressed via ICTs—followed by material acts undertaken to meet the child in person for unlawful sexual activities. Therefore, while sexual chatting with a child could, for example, be considered a preparatory act for sexual abuse offline, it would not be sufficient to meet the requirements of Article 23 for criminalization itself. By contrast, the arrival of the adult involved at the meeting place would be considered a material act in terms of the convention.[44] Overall, this international binding instrument results in a certain degree of harmonization among the national laws of the countries that are party to it.[45]

Moreover, as part of the EU's efforts, Directive 2011/93/EU—like Article 23 of the Lanzarote Convention—establishes a legal rule in Article 6(1) relating to the criminalization of online solicitation or grooming of children for sexual purposes. This provision specifies the following core elements as constituting the offense: the intention of committing an offense in an adult's arrangement of meeting a child, and the use of ICTs in setting up said meeting.[46] Both the convention and the directive promote human rights concepts toward a common good—the protection of the well-being, best interests, and fundamental freedoms of children—and encourage holistic responses to this crime. However they provide protection only to children who are under the legal age of consent to engage in sexual activities in accordance with national law. Therefore, they may leave children who are above the applicable age of consent without legal protection against this form of abuse under national legislation.

Notably, the Lanzarote Convention establishes the obligation of states to take the necessary legislative measures or otherwise to allow, where appropriate, for the possibility of covert operations (Article 30[5]). Although this is a general obligation, it may enable specialized units and investigative services to use any investigation methods that may be required for a specific task and under the particular circumstances necessary for effective investigation and prosecution of an offense under the convention. In addition, the convention's protective approach toward child victims requires that governments ensure that law enforcement units or investigative services combating online child sexual exploitation be specialized in this field or trained for this purpose (Article 34[1]).

Grooming to Facilitate Recruitment of Children into Sex Trafficking

The Internet and new technologies can facilitate the recruitment of children for the purpose of their sexual exploitation in the real world, for example, the use of children in prostitution and other forms of CSEC, including stripping or service in residential brothels, working for an escort agency, and soliciting at truck stops.[47] In this context, once a child is recruited, they are subjected to sexual exploitation practices, allowing the trafficker to exercise effective control over them, giving the child no option to leave or to refuse their orders. They are denied their most basic human rights, and their personal freedom and autonomy are taken away, thus diminishing their dignity. The 2018 *Global Report on Trafficking in Persons* indicates that cases of trafficking involving online grooming take place in various regions around the world, including those in Eastern Europe, Southeastern Europe, North America, Central America, and South America.[48] Unfortunately, traffickers apply online grooming behaviors to children to facilitate an important part of the trafficking chain: recruitment for their use in the sex business.

Cyberspace is thus being misused to lure children into the sex trade as demonstrated in the following case that involved a large number of young victims who were enticed and entrapped in a sexually exploitative ploy. Two traffickers from Eastern Europe were in charge of recruitment in their trafficking network. The recruiters enticed and recruited one hundred girls who were convinced to share intimate pictures of themselves, which the recruiters then used to coerce them to travel to a destination country. The recruiters used social media to contact these potential victims, creating fake profiles, participating in groups, and promoting lucrative modeling jobs abroad. Upon arrival, the young victims were bought for $500 each, with payment made via a mobile payment application, and the girls ended up sexually exploited in prostitution. They never met in person either of the two initial traffickers who had lured them online and who were able to facilitate the entire trafficking operation online.[49]

It is worth mentioning that the CRC has confirmed the link between trafficking in children and a search for better economic opportunities.[50] The root causes of trafficking can make people more vulnerable to exploitation and reflect the combination of "push" and "pull" factors in the economic principles of supply and demand.[51] Push factors include poverty, unemployment, violence, and conflicts that could make the person feel the need to migrate or accept a proposal, thus being at greater risk to be lured and coerced for the purposes of labor or sexual exploitation. Pull factors relate to consumerism and the demand for cheap unskilled labor in an informal economy or activities related to commercial sexual exploitation from which traffickers can profit.[52]

With respect to children in the online context, this recognition of the CRC implies that when children are being enticed for the purposes of exploitation, their choice is made on the basis of a combination of factors such as poverty, lack of economic opportunities, or the need for affection. In such cases, one may argue that the means element of coercion may not be very clear as the child voluntarily undertakes the journey and leaves for a certain destination. Nonetheless, under the sway of manipulation tactics and deception—including the promise of a better financial situation or better living conditions, modeling or dancing employment, participation in beauty contests, or study-abroad opportunities—the child or teenager may leave home and, upon arrival, find themselves trapped in exploitative activities such as performing commercial sex acts in the sex industry.

The Internet has brought a new dimension to human trafficking activities as it involves low risk and may facilitate the acquisition of high profits. Even though there is no single strategy that these groomers use to lure children for sexual purposes, in these cases online solicitation of children links to the process of trafficking—recruitment or receipt of a child victim—and to its end result of exploitation.[53] The question that arises is, How visible is the recruitment process of children previously facilitated via an abuser's grooming behaviors? Even though there is a need for further exploration and this examination may represent just the tip of the iceberg, based on a 2015 survivor survey conducted by Thorn, 77 percent of trafficking survivors recruited who met their offenders online were eighteen years old or younger at the time of their meetings.[54] Therefore, it is likely that children and young people face a higher risk of meeting traffickers or controllers online and of being groomed for engagement in commercial exploitative activities in the real world.

After the child is physically recruited and is under the trafficker's effective control, the trafficker frequently abuses the child physically, sexually, and verbally to prepare them for further exploitation. A common method of grooming is what we might call the boyfriend model of exploitation. The offender establishes a relationship in which the victim thinks of them as their boyfriend. The offender then uses this perception of a relationship for exploitative purposes. For example, at some point during the grooming process, which starts online, the victim will usually be required to prove his or her love by engaging in sexual activity in cyberspace or with others offline. These are circumstances that may link to the involvement of a child in commodified relationships as the child may engage in sexual activities in exchange for any form of consideration—for example, money, goods, or affection.[55] While perpetrators use this love interest as a method to control and manipulate the child or young victim, some children may not see this as a means of exploitation; rather, they may think that by doing this they are earning their boyfriend's love while keeping him happy and maintaining their sexual relationship.

Another possible consequence of the online grooming of children relates to the phenomenon of child sex tourism. Evidence indicates that some online child predators entice or groom children via Internet platforms with the purpose of traveling to their location for physical sexual contact.[56] Although child sex tourism is not explicitly referred to as a separate offense in Article 3 of the OP-CRC-SC, this practice is explicitly mentioned in its preamble and in Article 10 as an area of concern that requires stronger cooperation and coordination between state authorities.[57] Moreover, the CRC recognizes the direct connection of this form of child sexual exploitation in travel and tourism with offenses related to child prostitution, child pornography, and, to some extent, the sale of children as covered by the OP-CRC-SC.[58] In fact, the sexual exploitation of children in travel and tourism can be seen within the context of child prostitution as it often involves "the use of a child in sexual activities for remuneration or any other form of consideration."[59] In relation to this provision, the perpetrator—the traveler—has the opportunity to sexually exploit a minor in exchange for monetary compensation or by providing "any other consideration," meaning that this act still falls under the definition of child prostitution in the OP-CRC-SC. This practice can involve the use of the child to engage in sexual activities or in the production of pornographic material either for the direct gratification of the offender or for commercial distribution.

Consequently, the crime of child sex trafficking can have a clear digital component, the initial stages being developed in an online environment with enticement or grooming of the child, targeting his or her vulnerabilities, to facilitate forms of CSEC, a criminal process that may also be connected to the criminal activity of money laundering.[60] At the international level, the UNTOC mandates states parties to establish offenses relating to money laundering, including for human trafficking.[61] States should criminalize the laundering of proceeds of any offenses related to trafficking in persons. Such money laundering is often associated with organized crime groups at the domestic level and is often an essential part of the trafficking process.[62]

CONCLUSION

Within a broad definition of the term "cybercrime," child grooming acts are a global phenomenon that facilitates the involvement of a child in exploitative practices in cyberspace or in the real world. Online grooming of children for the purpose of sexual exploitation is an offense against the person of the child and can cause them severe psychological harm—sometimes even physical harm—and long-lasting effects. On the Internet, child grooming may involve the use of children in sexual relationships with the aim of exploitation, which can connect to the intended purpose of human trafficking.[63]

Due to the evolution of this online offense, soliciting children may include exploitation situations that occur only online. Consequently the criminalization of online child grooming requires that national law responses extend to situations in which the offense leads only to virtual sexual activity with the child for exploitative purposes. Taking into account the UNCRC general principle of the best interests of the child as a primary consideration through-out all states' relevant legislation and measures, in order to address the legal challenge of the online offense of child grooming as a form of sexual exploitation affecting children in today's realities, states should take the necessary measures, legal and otherwise, to ensure that all children—persons under the age of eighteen—are protected against this form of abuse in the digital space. Without this, legal frameworks risk undermining the gravity of the sexual exploitation of children online and deny justice to child victims.

It is important to enhance global efforts to deal with online grooming of children, and countries should penalize the commission of this criminal offense. Whether the intention of the perpetrator is sexual chatting with a child or arranging an offline meeting for sexual activity, all should be punishable in terms of national legislation. In this respect, it is essential to ensure the necessary legislation and its effectiveness in practice to safeguard children—regardless of the legal age of sexual consent at the national level—from all forms of sexual exploitation online, including the offense of online grooming. This chapter notes that the frequently secretive nature of online sexual chatting between an adult and a child and the difficulty and delays relating to children disclosing it pose additional challenges in the prosecution of these groomers and in the identification of actual numbers of groomed child victims exploited online. The difficulty of detecting Internet-facilitated child grooming reflects the invisible nature of this crime in general.

Even though public awareness of the problem of child grooming in society is growing, it is essential that states strengthen educational programs for users, including children, to promote online safety. In particular, educational programs should focus on better recognizing signs of inappropriate online communications that might lead to grooming behaviors and reporting mechanisms. The private sector could also be involved in such programs aimed at preventing the abuse and exploitation of children over the Internet.

In a human rights–based approach to online grooming, states should further strengthen appropriate measures and actions to prevent child sex trafficking both online and offline. It is essential to enhance the understanding of the connections between the Internet phenomenon of grooming of children and sexual exploitation of children. This must be done in order to work toward improved intervention and child protection policies particularly with respect to prevention and the criminalization of perpetrators of sexual exploitation of children online, including perpetrators of online grooming, who may be part of the trafficking chain. At the same time, states must work toward effective support and protection of child grooming victims, who may become victims of sex trafficking.

NOTES

1. UNODC, *Comprehensive Study on Cybercrime* (New York: United Nations, 2013), 213.

2. IOCTA 2020, 36.

3. Anne-Marie McAlinden, *"Grooming" and the Sexual Abuse of Children: Institutional, Internet, and Familial Dimensions* (Oxford: Oxford University Press, 2012), 11.

4. OP-CRC-SC Guidelines, para. 68, at 13.

5. International Centre for Missing and Exploited Children (ICMEC), *Online Grooming of Children for Sexual Purposes: Model Legislation & Global Review*, 1st ed. (Alexandria, VA: ICMEC, 2017), 9.

6. Ibid., 4.

7. EC3 and VGT, *VGT Child Sexual Exploitation Environmental Scan 2015* (Europol, 2015), 14.

8. Ibid.

9. Ibid., 14–15.

10. UNODC, *Guidance Note on "Abuse of a Position of Vulnerability" as a Means of Trafficking in Persons in Article 3 of the Protocol to Prevent, Suppress and Punish Trafficking in Persons, Especially Women and Children, Supplementing the United Nations Convention against Transnational Organized Crime* (2012), para. 2.3, at 2.

11. Rachel O'Connell, *A Typology of Child Cybersexploitation and Online Grooming Practices* (Preston, UK: University of Central Lancashire, 2003), 7.

12. Ibid., 7.

13. IOCTA 2019, 31.

14. Stephen Webster et al., *European Online Grooming Project: Final Report* (European Commission Safer Internet Plus Programme, 2012), 17.

15. O'Connell, *A Typology of Child Cybersexploitation*, 10.

16. For example, CRC, "Concluding Observations on the Combined Fifth and Sixth Periodic Reports of Australia," CRC/C/AUS/CO/5–6, November 1, 2019, para. 50(e), at 15.

17. UNCRC, art. 34.

18. See European Committee of Social Rights, "Decision on the Merits of the Complaint: *Federation of Catholic Family Associations in Europe (FAFCE) v. Ireland*," no. 89/2013, September 12, 2014, para. 58, stating, "Article 7§10 requires that all acts of sexual exploitation of children be criminalised. In this respect, it is not necessary for a Party to adopt a specific mode of criminalisation of the activities involved, but it must rather ensure that criminal proceedings can be instituted in respect of these acts. Furthermore, States must criminalise the defined activities with all children under 18 years of age irrespective of lower national ages of sexual consent."

19. "Almost 70 percent of countries report that grooming is an offence" (UNODC, *Comprehensive Study on Cybercrime*, 104).

20. Ibid., xx, 78.

21. Lanzarote Convention, art. 23.

22. Lanzarote Committee, *Opinion on Article 23 of the Lanzarote Convention and Its Explanatory Note* (Strasbourg: Council of Europe, 2015), para. 7–11, at 5–6.

23. UNCRC, art. 34(b), (c), 35. See generally OP-CRC-SC, art. 1–3.

24. OP-CRC-SC Guidelines, para. 68, at 13.

25. OP-CRC-SC, art. 2(c).

26. Fátima Ferreira, Paula Martins, and Rui Gonçalves, "Online Sexual Grooming: A Cross-Cultural Perspective on Online Child Grooming Victimization," paper presented at the 20th World Congress for Sexual Health, Glasgow, United Kingdom, June 12–16, 2011.

27. Elena Martellozzo, *Online Child Sexual Abuse: Grooming, Policing and Child Protection in a Multi-Media World* (Oxfordshire, UK: Routledge, 2012), 57.

28. For example, Lanzarote Convention, art. 22.

29. Author's summary of Australia Federal Prosecution Service, "Paedophile Groomed Girls on Twitter," www.cdpp.gov.au/case-reports/paedophile-groomed-girls-twitter.

30. *Criminal Code Act 1995* (Cth), sec. 474.25C; Explanatory Memorandum, Criminal Code Amendment (Protecting Minors Online) Bill 2017, para. 14.

31. Explanatory Memorandum, Criminal Code Amendment.

32. U.S. Department of Justice, *The National Strategy for Child Exploitation Prevention and Interdiction: A Report to Congress* (2016), 75.

33. ECPAT International, *Terminology Guidelines for the Protection of Children from Sexual Exploitation and Sexual Abuse* (Bangkok: ECPAT International, 2016), 11.

34. U.S. Department of Justice, *The National Strategy*, 75.

35. Directive 2011/93/EU, para.1, 6, 12, 19, art. 5, 6.

36. Ibid., art. 6(2).

37. Ibid.

38. Ferreira, Martins, and Gonçalves, "Online Sexual Grooming."

39. For example, "there is no evidence in this study to suggest that young people who are abused via the Internet suffer less harm than those who are abused offline" (Helen C. Whittle, Catherine Hamilton-Giachritsis, and Anthony R. Beech, "Victims' Voices: The Impact of Online Grooming and Sexual Abuse," *Universal Journal of Psychology* 1, no. 2 (2013): 59.

40. OP-CRC-SC Guidelines, para. 54, at 11.

41. See Lanzarote Committee, *Opinion on Article 23 of the Lanzarote Convention and Its Explanatory Note,* para. 20, at 4.

42. Rowenna Baldwin, "Children at Risk of Grooming in as Little as 18 Minutes," British Science Association, www.britishscienceassociation.org/news/children-at-risk-of-grooming-in-as-little-as-18-minutes; Nicola Davis, "Online Grooming of Children Often 'Alarmingly Fast,' Researchers Find," *Guardian*, www.theguardian.com/society/2016/sep/08/online-grooming-of-children-often-alarmingly-fast-researchers-find.

43. Lanzarote Convention, art. 23.

44. CoE, "Explanatory Report to the Council of Europe Convention on the Protection of Children against Sexual Exploitation and Sexual Abuse," October 25, 2007, C.E.T.S. 201, para. 157, 160, at 23.

45. See CoE, "Chart of Signatures and Ratifications of Treaty 201: Council of Europe Convention on the Protection of Children against Sexual Exploitation and Sexual Abuse," www.coe.int/en/web/conventions/full-list/-/conventions/treaty/201/signatures?p_auth=03F2P5uy.

46. Directive 2011/93/EU, art. 6(1).

47. Polaris Project, *Child Sex Trafficking At-a-Glance: Child Sex Trafficking in the United States* (2011).

48. UNODC, *Global Report on Trafficking in Persons 2018* (New York: United Nations, 2018), 38–39.

49. Author's summary of case material provided by Belarus, Pervomaisky District Court, Minsk in UNODC, *Global Report on Trafficking in Persons 2018*, 38.

50. CRC, "General Comment no. 6: Treatment of Unaccompanied and Separated Children outside Their Country of Origin," CRC/GC/2005/6, September 1, 2005, para. 2, at 4.

51. Sofija Voronova and Anja Radjenovic, *The Gender Dimension of Human Trafficking* (2016), www.europarl.europa.eu/RegData/etudes/BRIE/2016/577950/EPRS_BRI(2016)577950_EN.pdf.

52. Roza Pati, "Human Trafficking: An Issue of Human and National Security," *The University of Miami National Security & Armed Conflict Law Review* 4 (2014): 41.

53. Palermo Protocol, art. 3(c).

54. Thorn, "Digital Defenders of Children and Vanessa Bouché: A Report on the Use of Technology to Recruit, Groom and Sell Domestic Minor Sex Trafficking Victims" (2015), 10.

55. OP-CRC-SC Guidelines, para. 58, at 12.

56. U.S. Department of Justice, Office of Public Affairs, "Nearly 1,700 Suspected Child Sex Predators Arrested during Operation 'Broken Heart,'" www.justice.gov/opa/pr/nearly-1700-suspected-child-sex-predators-arrested-during-operation-broken-heart.

57. OP-CRC-SC, preamble, art. 10.

58. For example, CRC, "UN Committee on the Rights of the Child: Concluding Observations on the Combined 3rd and 4th Periodic Reports of Morocco," CRC/C/MAR/CO/3–4, October 14, 2014, para. 22–23, at 5; CRC, "UN Committee on the Rights of the Child: Concluding Observations: Morocco," CRC/C/OPSC/MAR/CO/1, March 17, 2006, para. 15, at 3; OP-CRC-SC Guidelines, para. 59, at 12.

59. OP-CRC-SC, art. 2(b).

60. UNODC, *Anti-Human Trafficking Manual for Criminal Justice Practitioners: Definition of Trafficking in Persons and Smuggling of Migrants (Module 1)* (New York: United Nations, 2009), 20.

61. UNTOC, art. 6, para. 1–2. According to Article 6, paragraph 2(a), states parties shall seek to apply the money-laundering provisions to the "widest range of predicate offences," including therefore to offenses of the convention itself and the protocols, if the state has become a party, and also, to all "serious crime" (art. 6, para. 2[b]) as defined by the convention.

62. Offenses underlying trafficking include torture, rape, bodily injury, murder, kidnaping, withholding of identity papers, violations of immigration law, money laundering, and cruel, inhumane, or degrading treatment (UNODC, *Anti-Human Trafficking Manual*, 20).

63. Palermo Protocol, art. 3(a).

Chapter 6

Child Victims and Offenders

Technological advances are available for exploitation by criminal actors just as much as by legal ones, meaning that cybercrime activities have developed along with ICTs. By misusing global connectivity tools, cyberoffenders achieve a global reach to accomplish their criminal goals, including human trafficking. In particular, traffickers misuse various online platforms and tools to facilitate forms of sexual exploitation of children. Through these exploitative practices, children are seen and treated as online sex commodities, causing them severe harm.

This chapter starts by examining the children victimized in cyberspace for sexual exploitation purposes. Specifically, it explores children's vulnerabilities and the effects of the psychological harm and trauma they suffer from online victimization. By considering children's special status under international human rights law, states can strengthen legislative frameworks to protect and support child victims in a victim-centered approach. States should identify child victims of trafficking and exploitation online and ensure their rights, safety, and well-being. In addition, this chapter examines some of the primary types of cyberoffenders responsible for these crimes, including individuals and groups that misuse online platforms and tools to facilitate or otherwise contribute to child sexual exploitation. This discussion aims to provide a general picture of cyberoffenders' characteristics and motivations to enhance our understanding of the challenges faced by the criminal justice system.

CHILD VICTIMS IN CYBERSPACE

A cursory look at human history reveals that children have often suffered from various forms of violence including abuse, negligence, and exploitation. Such treatment of children is often found in writings from ancient Egyptian, Greek, and Roman civilizations.[1] Millennia later, many children continue to be subject to forms of violence. In 2020, UNICEF and the WHO estimated that, globally, approximately one out of every two children suffers violence every year.[2] Furthermore, the WHO's *World Report in Violence and Health* affirms that in most nations, girls face an increased risk of sexual abuse, infanticide, forced prostitution, and educational and nutritional neglect. This assertion is evidenced by multiple international reports showing that girls experience rates of sexual abuse one and a half to three times higher than those boys face.[3] Although violence against children must end, it is often viewed as a family matter or justified by the culture of a particular society or by the normalization of behavior that marginalizes women and girls.

Ease of access to the Internet for both offenders and children has facilitated the victimization of boys and girls. Investigators of a 2018 Interpol and ECPAT International research study analyzed photos and videos from all over the world in the Interpol's ICSE database. They found that although girls are more susceptible to online victimization, boys and very young children are usually the victims who experience the most extreme forms of online sexual exploitation or are involved in paraphilic themes (e.g., bestiality or humiliation). Specifically, more than 60 percent of unidentified victims were prepubescent, including babies and toddlers.[4] Experts agree that the report demonstrated a connection between gender and the severity of abuse since boys were more likely to be featured in the more severe online abuse materials.[5] Overall, the child's age is a vulnerability factor that can increase their susceptibility to being trafficked for purposes of sexual exploitation.[6] Furthermore, the child's age can indicate the cyberoffender's abuse of power or of a position of vulnerability, that of the child, which constitutes a means of trafficking.[7]

Like trafficking in the real world, cybertrafficking is a form of violence against children. For the involvement of children in this form of online violence, various root causes and vulnerabilities are directly relevant to their online sexual exploitation. Offenders find fertile ground for exploiting online children when the children are unable to meet tangible and intangible basic needs or can do so to a limited extent. These circumstances render children more vulnerable and make them more likely to take risks with strangers and with exploitative offers online. For example, in the trafficking paradigm minors are lured and recruited through advertisements and websites with information they are likely to find interesting such as work and study opportunities.[8] Due to these lofty and manipulative promises, young victims are lured by Internet scams and other recruitment methods. Sometimes traffickers target and recruit minors from a particular ethnicity or age group to satisfy the preferences of a specific community of clients.[9] Thus, online traffickers target the particular vulnerabilities of minors and take advantage of child victims' struggles and desires. Nevertheless the element of exploitation still exists and, therefore, the gravity of the offense remains.

Notably poverty and migration have been identified as common risk factors for child victims of trafficking for sexual exploitation purposes. UNICEF explicitly affirms that "children who live in extreme poverty are often those who experience violence, exploitation, abuse and discrimination."[10] Consequently, to address trafficking-related vulnerabilities especially in women and children, the Palermo Protocol mandates that states parties take positive steps to alleviate vulnerability factors such as "poverty, underdevelopment and lack of equal opportunity."[11] Therefore this treaty obligation of states intends to prevent trafficking by addressing its causes, which may create or increase susceptibility to exploitation. There is limited research on the links between poverty and migration with Internet-facilitated child abuse and exploitation. However, the UNODC provides, as an example of this, a child recruited in his or her own country to do domestic work in a destination country. Upon arrival in the destination country, the child is forced to engage in commercial sex (advertised online) or to appear in CSAM (which may be later distributed online).[12] Cases such as these signal the existence of a broad relationship between poverty and migration patterns along with child sexual exploitation in cyberspace.

Based on an ITU 2020 report on global information and communication technology, over half of the world's population is online.[13] Although limited data is available on how many children younger than fifteen use the Internet, the report offers a tentative figure that 69 percent of the world's youth (fifteen to twenty-four years of age) are Internet users. This estimate is significantly higher than the proportion of Internet users in the total global population (51 percent).[14] In addition, one in three children (younger than eighteen) is estimated to be online, and approximately 800 million children have a social media account.[15] These statistics suggest that for children, social media and video games serve as essential venues for meeting, interacting, and communicating with friends, making these venues a key component in online interactions. At the same time, UNICEF asserts that approximately 80 percent of children from twenty-five countries feel in danger of online sexual exploitation and abuse.[16] Furthermore, mobile devices are an evolving means by which online child predators target, recruit, and coerce their child victims with ease to sexually exploit them.[17]

Research by the UN suggests that adolescents face the highest risk of becoming victims of Internet-facilitated child abuse and exploitation.[18] These statistics align with the fact that teenage users of the Internet receive less supervision than younger children and possess more skills to pursue their interests online, including forming relationships with strangers, exploring their concerns about sexuality, and starting a relationship. In this way,

LGBTQ+ adolescents, particularly boys looking for answers regarding sexual orientation or romance, may be a group at greater risk of online victimization.[19] Overall, these activities place teenage users at a higher risk than younger Internet users.

Offenders may interact with minors using a broad spectrum of Internet-based communications such as social media sites and applications, webpages, chat rooms, and emails. For example, minors incur risks when meeting strangers online within the gaming community. Although there is limited research on online interactive game sites as a venue to promote virtual interactions for child sex trafficking, it is an emerging concern.[20] Online gaming sites are a growing concern for those combating online sex trafficking because significant portions of children use them.[21] Indeed, online gaming may be one of the favorite activities in the digital world of children, particularly young boys.[22] While playing, gamers interact with one another and contact other players.[23] As more children use online gaming platforms, they face a greater risk of interacting with online offenders. Chats with unknown users facilitate the initial contact with traffickers, who pose as fellow gaming enthusiasts and, through online gaming interactions, groom minors and encourage them to transfer their interactions to other platforms.[24] Approximately three in four teen online gamers (thirteen to seventeen years old) interact with other players online.[25] Through the use of web chat (50 percent), voice chat (44 percent), and webcam (20 percent), these interactions potentially increase minors' chances of being groomed by perpetrators requesting that they perform sexual acts in real time or arrange a meeting offline.[26] Thus, children seek activities in cyberspace that increase their chances of being sexually abused or exploited.

Overall, due to children's naive nature, potential offenders more easily target, create bonds, and engage in online talks with them. In addition, children are not always able to recognize and disengage from potentially and actually dangerous situations in cyberspace. Thus, the misuse of ICTs facilitates online exploitation, advertisement, and recruitment into the commercial sex industry as emphasized by the 2020 UN *Global Report on Trafficking in Persons*.[27]

VULNERABILITIES AND EFFECTS OF ONLINE SEXUAL EXPLOITATION OF CHILDREN

Regarding the risk factors of children, research has shown a correlation between online and offline victimization. Specifically, children who have experienced traumatic incidents offline such as violence, domestic violence, abuse (including psychological abuse), a dysfunctional family, low self-esteem, and depression may be more vulnerable to the seduction of cyberpredators.[28] A study found that girls who have more conflicts with their parents and boys who have less communication with their parents are more likely to form "close online relationships."[29] Separately, a report found that adolescents exhibiting aggressive online behavior were significantly more likely to become victims of online abuse.[30] Although any child can be a victim of violence in cyberspace, those who have previously been sexually abused or exploited, who have experienced financial or social insecurity or marginalization, or who feel lonely face elevated risks of online victimization, including sexual exploitation.[31] In this way vulnerability in the real world may negatively impact children's lives in online environments.

According to the NCMEC, runaways and homeless children are at a higher risk of becoming trafficked victims: one in six endangered runaways reported to the center in 2020 was likely a sex trafficking victim.[32] Abused children also often struggle to disclose their past experiences, increasing the challenge of identifying this vulnerable population and protecting them from exposure to solicitations for "survival sex"—that is, to exchange sex in order to meet basic needs.[33] Similarly, among all child Internet users in the digital environment, those with a history of abuse—including domestic violence, neglect, or physical, psychological, or sexual abuse—are especially vulnerable to sexual victimization.[34] As a result, these minors are at high risk of engaging in risky Internet behavior and may be in greater need than other children of affection, protection, and care.

Additionally, children who face ostracism from or clash with their parents also face a higher risk, along with socially repressed children, who are more likely to act out or live with depression. Furthermore, children who frequently engage in sexual risks and boys who are questioning their sexuality (or who are gay) may find themselves at higher risk.[35] Given that children's behavior demonstrates continuities offline and in the digital world, strategies that offenders use in the real world may also be applicable to some forms of online child abuse and exploitation. Experts from Europol's EC3 identified the potential characteristics and vulnerabilities of child victims of online sexual coercion and extortion:

- naive, either on a relational level or on a technical level
- experiencing little or no parental control
- willing to share self-generated sexual content
- online a significant amount of time each day
- a frequent user of social networks and other ways of online communication, especially through mobile devices
- willing to befriend strangers (unknowns)
- willing to have sexualized conversations with strangers[36]

Child sexual exploitation experts similarly identify as prevalent causes of child victimization lack of awareness of Internet dangers and the absence of parental or caregiver influence. This means full parental engagement with the child at the level that the child is able to discuss his or her Internet behavior, concerns, and friends.[37] Children's personal situations, such as those related to school, family, or friends, and psychological state (which can be connected to self-esteem issues) are another such risk factor.[38] Nevertheless, reasons for why children are coerced or extorted for possible abuse should be analyzed on a case-by-case basis. Thus, by no means are the criteria above intended to determine a typical child victim profile or to interpret victims' motivations as more research should be conducted and more data should be gathered on potential risk factors, causes, and the victimization process. Nevertheless, these characteristics help facilitate a comprehensive picture of the mentioned offenses for sexual exploitation of children in online environments.

Indeed, the Internet has become a tool for offenders to sexually exploit children in various ways, jeopardizing children's safety online and offline. In this web of exploitation, victimized children can be *recipients* of illegal content (pornographic or sexual), *participants* in erotic or sexual activity when induced to perform sex acts or meet strangers offline, and *actors* when manipulated and coerced into creating and sharing self-generated sexual images depicting themselves.[39] Child victims of exploitative acts facilitated in cyberspace may suffer severe psychological harm due to these traumatic situations that may affect them in the short and long term and even cause irreversible lifetime consequences. For example, in cases where a child engages in sexual activity in front of a webcam with an offender, the child could be coerced or blackmailed for producing images of him- or herself that may be later offered, distributed, or sold as CSAM.[40] These situations mean that children suffer humiliation, violence, and traumatic episodes from producing such content, which exposes them in the immediate aftermath of the abuse to fear, anxiety, and shame. In addition, in the long run, children may suffer ongoing abuse, including issues related to self-esteem due to the additional humiliation of knowing that many users could receive or trade their images online and for an indefinite amount of time. Thus, a child victim could still be victimized online into adulthood as his or her pictures continue to be shared for sexual purposes in cyberspace, secretly and globally.

Child victims face a long and difficult road to recovery due to the psychological damage and harmful effects of these criminal acts. Such outcomes are not surprising as they result from offenders' making children the subject of images circulating in cyberspace (e.g., creating, distributing, and displaying CSAM). In other words, since the Internet has no borders, the psychological and emotional effects on child victims of Internet pornography may remain with them for years, especially when they know with certainty that their images are being disseminated online. For example, Europol data highlights reports of some countries where offenders continue to deceptively run fake modeling agencies or photo studies to lure minors into producing self-generated sexually explicit materials online.[41] In addition, child victims may be advertised and treated as products for prostitution, becoming the supply side of trafficking schemes.[42]

In summary, these children represent the object of exploitation in these illegal activities for sexual purposes and thus these offenses deny them their fundamental human rights and dignity. Consequently, states are obliged to ensure adequate national legislation to effectively detect, investigate, prosecute, and punish those responsible for children's harm and to protect and assist child victims.

A VICTIM-CENTERED APPROACH FOR CHILD VICTIMS

In the trafficking context, the Palermo Protocol enforces a victim-centered, multidisciplinary, human rights approach to comprehensive protection of victims for healing and prevention of revictimization.[43] The protocol mandates that states parties establish appropriate cooperation and collaboration with community organizations and civil society to strengthen antitrafficking efforts, including providing adequate physical and psychological care and support services to victims and taking into account the unique needs of children (Article 6[4]). This central obligation of states to protect trafficking victims guarantees that they receive assistance and care regardless of whether they cooperate in legal proceedings with the competent authorities.[44] In addition, under a human rights–based approach, states are required to eliminate the demand that leads to trafficking (Article 9[5]).

In addition to being affected by violence and harm, trafficked victims are exposed to dangers such as being involved in criminal activity due to their trafficking victimization. Although the Palermo Protocol does not include any clause related to the principle of nonprosecution or nonpunishment of victims, "Recommended Principles and Guidelines on Human Rights and Human Trafficking" expressly recognizes, according to principle 7, that

> trafficked persons shall not be detained, charged or prosecuted for the illegality of their entry into or residence in countries of transit and destination, or for their involvement in unlawful activities to the extent that such involvement is a direct consequence of their situation as trafficked persons.[45]

Chapter 6

In a comprehensive and human rights–based approach to trafficking, trafficked persons should be treated as victims of crime rather than criminals.[46] According to international law, states must protect trafficked victims from prosecution or punishment for offenses committed while under the control of traffickers as they are directly connected to their trafficking situation or the offenses were under compulsion.[47] The 2020 UNGA "Trafficking in Women and Girls Report of the Secretary-General" also confirmed this position.[48] The report calls on states to ensure the proper identification of victims and to continue enhancing measures to strengthen support systems and the protection of victims in line with human rights standards and the principle of nonpunishment. However, this protective noncriminalization principle to trafficking victims remains weakly implemented in states' criminal justice systems.[49]

This protective principle of noncriminalization of trafficking victims may pose practical challenges to courts, law enforcement, and criminal justice practitioners at the national level. This difficulty is particularly relevant in cases where it must be decided whether possible trafficking victims should be prosecuted for being suspected of having committed an offense while the alleged trafficking case is still pending.[50] In addition, the 2020 UNGA report outlines states' challenges regarding the effective implementation of the nonpunishment principle: (1) lack of awareness of the realities that victims may face while being trafficked, (2) failure to take diligent steps to investigate the circumstances of the criminal conduct, including examining whether the victim could have been forced to commit an illegal act, (3) insufficient training for relevant officials, including police officers, and (4) deficient processes for dealing with the identification of trafficking victims.[51] Therefore states should enact clear national laws and practices to ensure trafficking victims receive immediate care and support and should avoid holding them accountable for offenses resulting from being subject to trafficking. Otherwise such criminalization could adversely affect victims by undermining their rights (i.e., these victims are entitled to access to justice, protection and support, and access to appropriate remedies).

The nonpunishment principle has been applied through legislative and policy measures. For example, in the United States, New York passed legislation in 2010 vacating the convictions of prostitution offenses for survivors of trafficking, becoming the first state to do so. A 2013 Florida law went further by expunging any sentence altogether.[52] In addition, an EU directive on preventing and combating trafficking in human beings and protecting its victims (2011/36/EU) explicitly recognizes the application of this principle to trafficked persons.[53] The directive refers to any unlawful activities concerning human trafficking, including "the exploitation of criminal activities,"[54] which refers to "the exploitation of a person to commit, inter alia, pick-pocketing, shop-lifting, drug trafficking and other similar activities which are subject to penalties and imply financial gain."[55] Therefore the directive makes it mandatory that member states implement this nonpunishment provision in their national legal system.

This area of cybercrime requires a victim-centered approach.[56] A victim-centered approach means that states should take all appropriate measures to properly identify online child victims while having as a primary focus their safety and well-being.[57] The CRC explicitly provides recommendations to states parties of the OP-CRC-SC regarding the protection of children from OP-CRC-SC offenses including those facilitated by ICTs.[58] More specifically, the CRC encourages states parties to "ensure that national legislation does not criminalize children exploited in acts that would constitute an offence under the Optional Protocol, but treats them as victims."[59] States' obligations to protect and assist exploited children are specified in Article 8 of the OP-CRC-SC. Because sexually exploited children in cyberspace are victims of crime and human rights violations, states should give these children protection and support and not hold them criminally responsible for exploitative sexual acts committed against themselves. As is argued consistently in this book, these children cannot be accountable for their sexual exploitation by an offender.

Online offenders take advantage of children's vulnerabilities, including their innocence and young age, to gain power and to engage them in forms of exploitation. States should take all measures necessary to respond to online child exploitation appropriately, meaning that they provide support and remedy to exploited children and ensure the investigation and punishment of those responsible for these offenses.[60] Specifically, regarding child trafficking for purposes of sexual exploitation, including when it may take place in cyberspace, the child's consent is irrelevant and therefore meaningless.[61] As discussed in chapter 1, children enjoy special protection under international human rights law. In precise terms, the UNCRC provides a binding provision to states parties regarding their legal obligation to provide protection and support to children who are sexually exploited:

> Take all appropriate measures to promote physical and psychological recovery and social reintegration of a child victim of: any form of . . . exploitation . . . in an environment which fosters the health, self-respect and dignity of the child.[62]

Because of the principle of the child's best interest,[63] states should ensure adequate legislation and policies to assist and protect child victims of these online criminal acts in a victim-centered manner. Under a human rights–based approach, states are required to identify child victims and ensure adequate measures for their rehabilitation, psychological recovery, and care, including confidential and safe counseling, reintegration, and access to redress for the harm they suffer from such acts.[64] For example, those legally responsible for downloading child pornography depicting a victim may be responsible for reparation to the child as contributing to the harm caused by exploitation (18 USC §2259—Mandatory Restitution).[65]

Thus, as is the case in the real world, a victim-centric approach in cyberspace that considers children seeks to support their rights and dignity. Using a human rights–based approach to uphold children's right to dignity and protection in the digital space, states should protect potential and actual child victims of exploitation. This obligation of states includes working in collaboration with the private sector, primarily with technology companies, service providers, and civil society, for improving children's digital literacy, safety techniques, psychological support and recovery, and coping strategies. Thus, states should ensure legislation at the national level to prevent and respond to unlawful acts through which a child may become an object by being exploited or bought and sold for sexual purposes.

PERPETRATORS AND BENEFICIARIES

The 2020 UNODC *Global Report on Trafficking in Persons* found that traffickers operate as individuals or as part of organized criminal groups. Furthermore, during various stages of the trafficking process, traffickers can take on the role of recruiter or transporter or assume roles that appear sympathetic at first, such as that of a marriage broker.[66] According to the UNODC, "anyone knowingly involved in any stage of the trafficking process is a trafficker and is guilty of a crime."[67] Therefore the term "trafficker" can be understood broadly to refer to various perpetrators who perform criminal acts in the sequence of actions that represents the trafficking process. These individuals, under whatever chosen guise, benefit from their involvement in child sex trafficking.

Some offenders knowingly aid and abet by providing practical assistance or encouragement—acting, for instance, as recruiters, including cyberrecruiters and transporters—that substantially facilitates the commission of the crime, which makes them criminally responsible for the victimization of children.[68] Third parties such as facilitators or intermediaries may be compensated in a variety of ways. Given the personal benefit of criminal involvement, there is a potential link between corrupt practices and human trafficking. For example, in cases where corruption is involved, authorities and individuals—from both the public and private sectors—engage in corrupt practices, ranging from active involvement to passive negligence, to facilitate different crime stages.[69] Given the myriad ways in which traffickers approach child victims, it is essential to refrain from stereotyping criminals' traits or to use a particular image to profile them.

Sex trafficking has become a very profitable illegal business.[70] Forced sexual exploitation provides a global average profit of \$21,800 per year per victim.[71] In addition, this sector has the highest profitability of all forms of forced labor. This profitability can be attributed to the demand for these services, the frequent willingness of clients to pay high prices, and the low capital investment and operating costs traffickers incur.[72]

On a global level, responding officers are becoming aware of increased cybercrime committed by organized crime groups and individuals pursuing profit-driven and personally satisfying criminal opportunities. At present no advanced skill or technique is required to commit cybercrime.[73] Cyberoffenders are frequently driven by their desire to gain significant revenue or satisfy their sexual fantasies, leading them to violate children's fundamental human rights in cyberspace.

For example, some exploitation websites allow traffickers to auction children to the highest bidder.[74] Online auctioning is a form of Internet-facilitated child sex trafficking for exploitation. Research from 2017 determined that criminals connect with other like-minded individuals to purchase minors for sexual services through this form of exploitation using cryptocurrencies (e.g., Bitcoin).[75] The process of online auctioning of child sex trafficking victims was identified by Corporación Centro de Consultoría y Conflicto Urbano (C3) investigations in the city of Medellín, Colombia. C3 studies found that perpetrators auctioned off the virginity of young girls to the highest bidder online and offered the girls for commercial sex.[76] According to this study, the trading of girls (who were usually twelve to fourteen) occurs via brochures at approximately \$2,600, with bidders using secret PINs to access the auction. Once the auction was over, the site disappeared, leaving almost no traces of its occurrence.[77] C3 findings demonstrated that online auction participants included local residents, international sex tourists, and members of organized crime groups.[78] Furthermore, the online auctions often involved child victims who lived in poverty and whose parents or family members were being tricked or coerced into selling or giving away their children for commercial exploitation (e.g., child prostitution).

Generally speaking, criminals victimize children online in various ways. These violators hiding in the shadows of the digital space come from all walks of life and present no consistent profile.[79] Additionally, these offenders misuse the publicly accessible Internet—the Clearnet—or use anonymity tools on the Darknet.

The Darknet

In 2001, Michael K. Bergman, founder of BrightPlanet, compared searching on the Internet to fishing in the ocean. Specifically, he noted that

> searching on the Internet today can be compared to dragging a net across the surface of the ocean. While a great deal may be caught in the net, there is still a wealth of information that is deep, and therefore, missed.[80]

This statement is still relevant because within the vast Internet, digital information can be found in the visible part of the Web, which is publicly and easily accessible via conventional search engines such as Google, Bing, Yahoo, Baidu, Yandex, and DuckDuckGo. These sites reside on the Web's surface, which most Internet users know and utilize daily. However, it is estimated that this surface Web information represents only 10 to 16 percent of the total Internet information available.[81] Notably, a great deal of Internet content remains hidden beneath the surface of the Web. These other components of the Web are known as the Deep Web or the Darknet. While access to information in the Deep Web is limited, it represents approximately 84 to 96 percent of the entire Internet.[82]

Regarding the Darknet, major traditional search engines do not allow conventional Internet users direct access to hidden websites. A 2015 ECPAT Belgium study revealed that sexual exploitation of children, including the transmission of CSAM, frequently took place on the Darknet.[83] Darknet users obtain access to a portion of cyberspace that operates apart from everyday Internet traffic. Currently, various well-known online tools exist on the Darknet such as Freenet, Tor, and the Invisible Internet Project (I2P). Without exception, any Darknet platform can be utilized for the sexual exploitation of children. For example, based on the findings of the 2015 ECPAT Belgium study, in the Freenet, users use a file-sharing system via Frost and communicate with others via private encrypted messages.[84] Thus, these chat capabilities are allegedly being abused to store and exchange CSAM.

Another Darknet tool for these cybercrimes is the anonymity tool Tor. In a 2015 research study by the University of Portsmouth, Gareth Owen and Nick Savage analyzed the types of content and their popularity on Tor for six months.[85] The study found that although child abuse–related sites represented only 2 percent of the estimated 45,000 active hidden services sites present at any one point in time, these sites attracted more than 80 percent of the traffic and were therefore the most popular. Although the authors did not know the exact reasons in every case why this category of content was frequently requested, the volume likely included law enforcement visits.[86] Furthermore, active websites were, in general, found to exist for only a short period of time, with only 15 percent appearing to have long-lived services.[87]

Tor is a free software that runs on most common operating systems and enhances the anonymity of online communications.[88] This anonymity tool uses "onion routing" to protect the anonymity and privacy of users and online activities for an array of users—military personnel, government officials, journalists, human rights advocates, and activists—in their activities.[89] Tor users (organizations and individuals) enhance their safety and security on the Internet as they do not make a direct connection to sites and other services. Instead they create a circuit of encrypted connections through relays on the network (a Tor private network pathway). Thus, with the use of a Tor circuit, users have the ability to remain anonymous themselves and also to host websites or Internet services anonymously. Without a doubt, Tor has legitimate uses and provides significant benefits to online users, particularly those who live in places where they may suffer from governmental persecution or where their political views or freedoms may be restricted. However, the same capabilities that provide these benefits also enable criminals to trade CSAM and deal in drugs while remaining hidden in virtual space.

The name "Tor" is an acronym for "the Onion Router," which was the original name of the software project.[90] This anonymity tool is essentially an Internet communication system with layers of encryption akin to the layers of an onion.[91] Data is moved via anonymous connections through several other onion routers—network nodes—in the form of encrypted messages that are transmitted to the next destination in random order via other Tor computers. As a result, the mechanism creates private and secure Internet communications over a public network while avoiding online analysis tools. Data is altered at each onion router by layering cryptographic operations making that data difficult to trace en route. This technique is a particularly effective anonymizing mechanism because "preserving privacy means not only hiding the content of messages, but also hiding who is talking to whom (traffic analysis)."[92]

The IOCTA 2020 from Europol's EC3 analyzed the threats and trends of online child sexual exploitation and found evidence demonstrating potential links between child sexual exploitation and the Tor network. This finding points to the commercial trade and distribution of CSAM behind layers of encrypted protection.[93] Thus, at present, a huge concern is the use of Darknet tools to exploit minors, including the livestreaming of abuse and the exchange of sexual abuse materials. For instance, in 2020 a child online sex offender operating from the Philippines was sentence to life imprisonment for sexually exploiting local children, recording the abuse, and distributing it to child predators in the United States, Canada, Europe, and Australia in exchange for payment. These like-minded individuals were interested in watching the sexual abuse and exploitation of children, including babies, via online livestreaming services.[94] The suspect apparently used the Tor network and BitTorrent as a data tool for moving and sorting child abuse content.[95] The conviction was on the ground of trafficking offenses, and the offender was ordered to pay the child victims monetary compensation for the harm suffered.[96]

To understand the purpose and function of the Tor network within the online sex trafficking context, it is helpful first to discuss its history and intended use. Tor was developed in 1995 by military researchers at the U.S. Naval Research Laboratory and further refined by the Defense Advanced Research Projects Agency in 1997 to protect government communications.[97] In 2001, the U.S. Navy received a patent for an "onion routing network for securely moving data through communication networks," which credits as its inventors Michael Reedy, Paul Syversony, and David Goldschlag.[98] In this onion routing system, after the connection is established between the initiator and the responder, each router removes one layer of encryption to obtain instructions to define the route to the next onion router. In this manner, each node or onion router knows its predecessor and successor nodes but no other node on the route. When the final data is decrypted, it arrives at the receiver as plain text and the receiver can only point to the location immediately preceding it so that the origin of the data and the sender remain anonymous. Data can also be moved backward, in the opposite direction, to be transmitted to the initiator.

Currently, users worldwide download the Tor Browser and run Tor on Microsoft Windows, Mac OSX, Linux, or Android without installing any software.[99] Tor is also portable as it can operate on a USB flash drive.[100] Tor has demonstrated a global appeal: from July 1 to September 29, 2021, the countries that used Tor the most were the United States (22.76 percent), Russia (15.03 percent), and Germany (7.65 percent).[101] In addition, the Tor Project indicates that the number of Tor users fluctuated between approximately 2 million and 2.5 million during this same period.[102] On the Tor network, more users imply more security and privacy for all of them. This is because each new user helps increase the number of possible sources and destinations of communications and the number of new relays to cover users' tracks, providing the network with more diversity while enhancing its sustainability.

In their constant efforts to find sophisticated ways to evade detection by law enforcement by achieving greater anonymity and hiding their tracks as much as possible, cybertraffickers use Tor to accomplish their trafficking goals.[103] In 2019, the Tor site Welcome To Video was dismantled, having been monitored by law enforcement since 2017. This site had used Bitcoin as the means of payment for child sexual exploitation images and videos.[104] It was a massive child pornography file-sharing marketplace that handled approximately 250,000 videos of the sexual exploitation of children. Customers apparently paid 0.02 Bitcoin (at the time approximately $160) for "points" that allowed them to download up to 230 videos. In addition, they could also pay 0.03 Bitcoin ($352) for a six-month VIP membership allowing unlimited downloads. In addition, users could earn points through referrals and by uploading videos. A South Korean operator, twenty-three-year-old Jong Woo Son, ran the site with the server's IP address registered in his name and the server located in his bedroom. Some of the Welcome To Video's top keyword search terms were "PTHC" (pre-teen hardcore porn); "PEDO" (pedophile); "2yo percent" (two-year-old); and "4yo percent" (four-year-old)."[105] Investigators' analysis of the site's Bitcoin transactions led to the arrest of 337 users in nearly forty countries.[106]

Online sex trafficking acts constitute a particularly thorny and evolving problem given the rapid global expansion of Internet usage as well as the growing sophistication of cybercriminals' technical skills in encryption and anonymity tools. Additionally, cyberoffenders at a distance need not download any materials, leaving no trace on their personal electronic device, which makes the live viewing of the abuse and exploitation of children more convenient and more cost-effective for the consumer. In short, child predators develop online marketplaces with extra layers of anonymity using the Darknet's sophisticated tools. This makes the Darknet a prime location for activities related to child sexual exploitation and one of the most critical challenges facing law enforcement. Thus, it may be fruitful to shed light on some of the cybercriminal actors who act in an individual capacity or as members of organized crime groups. The following sections present broad categories of offenders to illustrate a general picture of their distinctiveness and motives for committing online child sexual exploitation and abuse.

Organized Criminal Groups

Working across national borders, these groups expand their activities and networks with ease and increase the collaboration and coordination of criminal activities among their members and allied organized criminal groups around the globe. The UNTOC, adopted in November 2000, serves as the leading international instrument in the fight against transnational organized crime. According to the UNTOC, a serious crime has a global nature if it is committed in more than one state or if it is committed within one state with substantial preparation, planning, and control in another state.[107] Additionally, transnational crimes are also those committed in one state by criminal groups that operate in multiple states or those committed in one state that significantly affect another state.[108] The UNTOC defines an organized criminal group as a structured group of three or more persons existing for a period of time while acting in concert with the aim of committing at least one offense punishable by at least four years of deprivation of liberty and doing so in order to obtain, directly or indirectly, a financial or other material benefit.[109]

Therefore an organized crime group, under the convention, need not have a formal or sophisticated organization; it merely needs to consist of three individuals working to commit a serious crime for a material benefit. Although the definition was intended to exclude groups with political or social purposes, the term "material benefit" should be interpreted broadly to extend beyond monetary or equivalent benefits, allowing for the pursuit of personal benefits such as sexual gratification.[110] Nonetheless, personal benefits may coincide with economic benefits when traffickers have the intent to commercially exploit children.[111]

According to the Palermo Protocol, states parties must ensure the prevention, investigation, and prosecution of trafficking offenses under their national legislation including when it is "transnational in nature and involve[s] an organized criminal group" and to protect trafficking victims.[112] In addition, organized crime groups may also be involved in sexual exploitation in cyberspace. For instance, criminal groups may act as Internet-based social networks of actors for trading CSAM, from which they collect credit card payment information to use in other crimes.[113] Furthermore, many of these groups have been found to be involved in the sex trafficking business both online and offline.[114] Research on human trafficking in Texas found the involvement of Mexican cartels, transnational gangs, and individual criminals engaging in child trafficking activities in the cyberspace sex market of children.[115] International bands such as Mara Salvatrucha (MS-13) establish a presence on the Internet, developing criminal cyberactivities that include recruiting trafficking victims.[116] Evidence has revealed that members of this transnational gang, who are predominantly Central American nationals, engage in the business of gang-controlled child sex trafficking. The gang's involvement in child sex trafficking can be seen, for instance, in *United States v. Juarez-Santamaria*, 513 F. App'x 306, 307 (4th Cir. 2013).[117]

Dominique Roe-Sepowitz et al. found that "nearly one out of five arrests for sex trafficking of a minor involved a person who was gang involved."[118] Additionally, the study found that gang-involved sex traffickers post online advertisements to sell both adult and minor victims. Group sex traffickers are 79.9 percent more likely than solo sex traffickers (non-gang-involved sex traffickers) to abuse the Internet to promote and sell victims.[119] Criminal gangs also employ digital means to maintain close surveillance of victims to ensure their continuing obedience.[120] These perpetrators operate with near impunity due to the physical distance between themselves and the victims. This use of technology poses another risk to the victims: if they do not continue to comply with the criminals, the criminals may coerce them by threatening to disseminate their compromising pictures to others and their families.[121]

Additionally, organized crime groups may be involved in possible Internet-facilitated commercial sexual exploitation of children schemes. These actions may relate to the abuse of online services such as eros.com, cityvive.com, adultsearch.com, localescortpages.com, findhotescorts.com, eroticmugshots.com, and myproviderguide.com.[122] Members of criminal enterprises use their reputation for violence to intimidate and coerce victims, exercising effective control over them while subjecting them to sexual slavery or sexual exploitation. Using strict discipline and coercion, organized crime groups accomplish their goals of involving their members effectively in achieving crimes.

Traffickers Working Either Individually or in Opportunistic Associations

Traffickers may work as an individual or cooperate with other traffickers to obtain authority and control over children using power and control tactics that may involve manipulation, violence, drugs, feigned affection, and psychological abuse. Sometimes to mask the fact that they are prostituting minors, the perpetrators coerce children into claiming themselves to be adults who engage in consensual commercial sex.[123] In this way the traffickers have a comprehensive arsenal with which to keep minors under their effective control. Beyond being kept literally locked up, the children sometimes continue to attend school and participate in other activities as usual while being trafficked.[124] Therefore, besides organized crime groups that systematically engage in committing crimes, individuals working alone or through associations of traffickers can be involved in stages of the trafficking process such as recruiting, harboring, transporting, providing, or obtaining a child for the purpose of sexual exploitation.

For traffickers, the Internet is a safe haven for numerous reasons. For example, the Internet provides lower risk of exposure than putting minors on the street for commercial sex. In addition, through the Internet, traffickers develop and camouflage actions such as (1) finding and expanding client networks, (2) communicating with allied individuals and groups, (3) exchanging information, (4) advertising child sexual services, (5) coordinating encounters, and (6) receiving payment for minors' commercial sex acts.[125] In short, the Internet has allowed traffickers to shift away from the traditional process of child sex trafficking.

Consequently, traffickers use the Internet to entrap minors and also to connect with the "johns"—the demand side of the crime—to rent out the bodies of minors and receive a significant amount of money for the children's commercial sex acts.[126] Indeed, traffickers have developed numerous new ways of continuing the child sex trafficking business by strengthening their networks of potential buyers, current sex buyers, and other criminals. These efforts often result in attractive financial benefits for the traffickers. In addition, traffickers use Internet platforms to sell children for sexual activity by creating a friendly online shopping venue in which the traffickers can interact, network, and coordinate operations with potential and actual sex buyers. Through these strategies, traffickers ensure the demand flow in the children's market in the sex trade.

Research has shown that 67.3 percent of minor sex traffickers use technology such as email accounts, posted advertisements online, and cell phones.[127] Aiming at sexually exploiting children, offenders facilitate their crimes by sharing information, arranging operations, and managing online criminal networks. To achieve their goals, criminals are careful to avoid leaving digital footprints of their actions, yet despite this, clues still exist that allow law enforcement officers to track their movements. Online traces include "patterns in credit card transactions, mobile phone calls, GPS patterns, plane tickets, apartment rentals, and other activities that create opportunities of detection."[128]

One trafficker technique is crafting carefully worded advertisements and posting them on online classified sites. Traffickers often use coded writing and writing styles, using euphemisms such as "barely legal" and "young" as creative methods to camouflage their online advertisements of minor and adult victims for commercial sex.[129] Thus, without leaving their homes, traffickers advertise minors for offline commercial sex activities in different cities and states—and do so quickly, effectively, and cheaply. Coded language in online advertisements makes recruitment and advertisement much more effective in numerous ways. Coded language in online advertisements serves to hide or minimize the risk of exposure of a human trafficking activity related to commercial sexual activities of children from law enforcement.

Online advertising is not the only method utilized with coded language. Traffickers also use coded language in online conversations with current and potential sex clients[130] and to refer to their own industry and activities.[131] Although traffickers make it appear as though their transactions involve consenting adults, investigation of their online advertisements reveals potential trafficking crimes. In fact, an analysis of such online advertisements brings to light ways of identifying a structured organization or a sophisticated business model behind the advertisement. For example, some advertisements may show the availability of services in different places or invite the user to visit an external link, all of which point to a more effective mechanism at work.[132] Moreover, similar writing styles emerge from some advertisements as well as a pattern of visual clues. For example, pictures may appear to be taken in the same place, the physical or behavioral characteristics of posters may seem similar, or the advertisements may show multiple people with the same management—as can be inferred from the contact information listed on different advertisements.[133] Therefore images and posting styles in online classified advertisements may contain characteristics and cues that serve as clues in identifying potential trafficked victims.

To avoid law enforcement, traffickers avoid using any one specific website or online advertisement section to advertise and sell minors and adult victims for sex. This increases the difficulty of detecting cybertrafficking as the activities are dispersed and easily overlooked. In addition to advertising trafficked persons for commercial sex, traffickers also use online classified ads to solicit and recruit independent posters, some of whom may be minors, with different enticing strategies including managerial offers and promises of lucrative income.[134]

CSAM Offenders (Producers and Possessors)

Child pornography on the Internet is a crime that can connect the real and virtual worlds in one single offense. For example, CSAM can be created offline and then distributed and circulated online. In addition, statistically speaking, most producers are individuals already known by the child, such as family members and acquaintances, or who have been in contact with the child for more than a year before the first sexual contact occurs.[135] In fact, based on data from CoE member states, "the majority of sexual abuse against children is committed within the family framework, by persons close to the child or by those in the child's social environment."[136] The worst cases are when parents play a role in the trafficking chain or are the ones who make the CSAM of their own children and distribute it online, as found in some states' data reports of the 2018[137] and 2020[138] UNODC global reports on trafficking in persons.

Some of the cybercriminals who participate in these crimes can be preferential abusers who have sexual interests in children or are inclined to obtain sexual gratification from them.[139] In addition, situational abusers, who are not technically preferential abusers, end up obtaining anonymous access to watch, download, and distribute such materials.[140] Research has found that most CSAM possessors are preferential abusers.[141]

Possessors of pornographic images of children online may have particular psychological and behavioral characteristics. For instance, childhood issues often related to early sexual experiences and abusive sexual experiences during adulthood may be factors.[142] In addition, online offenders are likely to have no or a negligible criminal record and higher levels of education and self-esteem than offline offenders.[143] They may have a dependency on the

Internet and feel emotionally isolated. Furthermore, they may tend to identify with fictional characters and experience motor impulsivity and increasing levels of sexual fantasies.[144]

Offenders may produce child sexual exploitative materials for their own sexual gratification or with the intention of sharing them with other like-minded individuals, especially in forums and P2P networks.[145] This sharing among online peers helps offenders strengthen their status and build trust among group members in online communities where they interact. Offender communities work as groups in which sexual predators collaborate online to promote the sexual exploitation of children and young people.[146] In addition, offenders may produce and distribute CSAM for economic gain.[147] As a result, the constant online distribution of images facilitates the sexual revictimization of children as there is abuse every time their pictures circulate. To date, the cooperative work among law enforcement and the private sector—particularly ISPs, mobile phone operators, and search engines—has become key to obtaining rapid information on child victims and perpetrators, such as their IP address.[148]

Consumer Demand

Sex buyers may be locals or foreigners or those in positions of trust and power in society.[149] Sex buyers abuse the Internet to facilitate a subculture of exploitation by sharing information, tactics, and support to entice children and connect with other criminals such as child sex tourism operators to locate child sexual services.[150] Consequently, Internet tools afford sex buyers a forum in which to seek and purchase minors for commercial sex and express to traffickers their preferences, fantasies, and desires. These actions can be accomplished through blogs, social media sites, online advertisements, forums, and website announcements.

Another aspect of sex buyers' activities is found in the global child sex tourism industry, which is also facilitated by communication technologies such as the Internet. Child sex tourism can be understood as a form of trafficking in which "a person undertakes tours and travel plans consisting of tourism packages or activities utilizing a child for prostitution or sexual exploitation."[151] Therefore these offenders are sex travelers who travel domestically or abroad for the primary purpose of engaging in sex acts with trafficked children. It is estimated, alarmingly, that the average age of sex tourism victims is fourteen years old, and it is becoming common to find victimized children as young as five years old.[152] Research has found that perpetrators also use the Internet to groom overseas children for global sex tourism and coordinate cross-border criminal acts such as locating information for travel agents and hotels who might assist them.[153] International sex tourism continues to thrive today perhaps because the offenders seek a safe haven in countries with more relaxed legislation related to child sex trafficking and online child sexual exploitation or countries with a culture of tolerance toward trafficking practices.[154] Sex buyers in global sex tourism are regular tourists in countries such as Brazil, Costa Rica, and the Dominican Republic. Additionally, Thailand, Cambodia, and the Philippines are popular destinations for child sex tourism and are the bases of large-scale child prostitution rings.[155]

While some sex buyers may be aware that the person involved is underage, others may not. Therefore not all sex buyers consciously elect to commit an offense against a child. In these cases, a situational offender may take advantage of the opportunity to commit a crime.[156] As a result of their crimes, the sex buyers face severe risks and consequences from legal punishment such as arrest and imprisonment to health issues such as the elevated risk of contracting sexually transmitted diseases.

CONCLUSION

Aiming to meet the challenges of online sex trafficking, states should strengthen their national legal systems for preventing and protecting children in the digital space (post-factum exploitation). Using a human rights–based approach, states should avoid prosecuting children who have been sexually exploited in cyberspace. In this context, states should implement protection measures and provide comprehensive services to child victims to ensure rehabilitation, psychological recovery from these traumatic situations, and reparations.[157]

The Internet allows traffickers to use sophisticated techniques to conceal their criminal acts. Traffickers are masters in abusing Internet-based features to perpetuate trafficking offenses or to facilitate the commercial and noncommercial sexual exploitation of children. Although the breadth and depth of these forms of crime are currently unmeasured and unknown, this chapter illustrates characteristics of cybercriminals that facilitate child sex trafficking activities and related acts and the strong need for states to combat them.

By utilizing the digital space, including the Darknet's sophisticated tools, online traffickers disseminate their wares and reach minors, customers, and like-minded criminals and networks to sexually exploit children. These criminal actions allow them to expand their connections, exchange information, arrange encounters, coordinate operations and services, and pay for access to livestreaming of the abuse of children. Moreover, as Internet technology continues to develop and expand, cyberpredators are given more tools to make their crimes more sophisticated and more elusive for law enforcement to detect and prosecute.

To defend children against offenders' cybercrime strategies, states must enhance national legislation, rally for effective collaboration among civil society sectors (such as the Internet industry, the social workforce, grassroots organizations, and families), and improve the capacity of the law enforcement community. In this way, the international community of states can effectively gather systematic intelligence and dismantle the networks of organized groups and individuals who navigate cyberspace to commit sexual crimes against the person and dignity of children.

States have a positive obligation to enact or strengthen appropriate criminal law provisions to cover all forms of trafficking and exploitation of children online and ensure adequate law enforcement and judicial system responses to identify child victims and combat these offenses. By taking these actions, states will contribute to the fight against online trafficking and enhance respect for the dignity and rights of children in cyberspace.

NOTES

1. Ellen W. Clayton, Richard D. Krugman, and Patti Simon, eds., *Confronting Commercial Sexual Exploitation and Sex Trafficking of Minors in the United States* (Washington, DC: National Academies Press, 2013), xi.

2. WHO, *Global Status Report on Preventing Violence against Children* (Geneva: World Health Organization, 2020), 11.

3. Etienne G. Krug et al., *World Report on Violence and Health* (Geneva: World Health Organization), 66.

4. Interpol, "Study Finds Boys and Very Young Children at Greater Risk of Severe Online Sexual Abuse," www.interpol.int/en/News-and-Events/News/2018/Study-finds-boys-and-very-young-children-at-greater-risk-of-severe-online-sexual-abuse.

5. Ibid. For further reading, see Interpol and ECPAT, *Towards a Global Indicator on Unidentified Victims in Child Sexual Exploitation Material: Summary Report* (Bangkok: Interpol, ECPAT International, 2018), 3.

6. OHCHR, *Human Rights and Human Trafficking: Fact Sheet no. 36* (New York: United Nations, 2014), 7.

7. Palermo Protocol, art. 3(a).

8. UNGIFT, *017 Workshop: Technology and Human Trafficking, in the Vienna Forum to Fight Human Trafficking* (Austria: United Nations Office on Drugs and Crime, 2008), 7.

9. Polaris Project, *Comparison Chart of Primary Sex Trafficking Networks in the U.S.* (2011).

10. UNICEF, *Child Protection Strategy Reference Document* (2008), 3.

11. Palermo Protocol, art. 9(4).

12. UNODC, *Study on the Effects of New Information Technologies on the Abuse and Exploitation of Children* (New York: United Nations, 2015), 26.

13. ITU, *Measuring Digital Development: Facts and Figures* (Geneva: International Telecommunication Union, 2020), 7.

14. Ibid., 7.

15. ITU, *Guidelines for Industry on Child Online Protection* (Geneva: International Telecommunication Union, 2020), 8.

16. UNICEF, "Protecting Children Online: Every Child Must Be Protected from Violence, Exploitation and Abuse on the Internet," www.unicef.org/protection/violence-against-children-online.

17. U.S. Department of State, Office to Monitor and Combat Trafficking in Persons, *Online Sexual Exploitation of Children: An Alarming Trend* (Washington, DC: U.S. Department of State, 2017), 1.

18. UNODC, *Study on the Effects of New Information Technologies*, ix, 26.

19. Ibid., 24. See generally Janis Wolak et al., "Online 'Predators' and Their Victims: Myths, Realities, and Implications for Prevention and Treatment," *American Psychologist* 63, no. 2 (2008): 123.

20. ICMEC, *Online Grooming of Children for Sexual Purposes: Model Legislation & Global Review*, 1st ed. (Alexandria, VA: International Centre for Missing and Exploited Children, 2017), 3.

21. NPD Group, "Notable Increases in Both Engagement and Spending Coming from Kids," www.npd.com/wps/portal/npd/us/news/press-releases/2019/according-to-the-npd-group--73-percent-of-u-s--consumers-play-video-games/.

22. See Jasmina Byrne et al., *Global Kids Online Research Synthesis, 2015–2016* (London: UNICEF Office of Research Innocenti, 2016), 43.

23. ICMEC, *Online Grooming of Children*, 3.

24. Ibid., 4.

25. The Futures Company, "2014 Teen Internet Safety Survey," www.cox.com/content/dam/cox/aboutus/documents/tween-internet-safety-survey.pdf.

26. ICMEC, *Online Grooming of Children*, 4.

27. UNODC, "Traffickers' Use of the Internet," in *Global Report on Trafficking in Persons* (New York: United Nations, 2020).

28. UNODC, *Study on the Effects of New Information Technologies*, 25. See generally Wolak et al., "Online 'Predators,'" 117.

29. Janis Wolak, Kimberly J. Mitchell, and David Finkelhor, "Escaping or Connecting? Characteristics of Youth Who Form Close Online Relationships," *Journal of Adolescence* 26, no. 1 (2003): 105–119.

30. Michele L. Ybarra et al., "Internet Prevention Messages: Targeting the Right Online Behaviors," *Archives of Pediatrics and Adolescent Medicine* 161, no. 2 (2007): 142.

31. UNODC, *Study on the Effects of New Information Technologies*, 25.

32. NCMEC, "The Issues: Child Sex Trafficking," www.missingkids.org/theissues/trafficking.

33. UNODC, *Study on the Effects of New Information Technologies*, 25.

34. Ibid.

35. Wolak et al., "Online 'Predators,'" 123.

36. EC3, *Online Sexual Coercion and Extortion as a Form of Crime Affecting Children: Law Enforcement Perspective* (The Hague: Europol, 2017), 18.

37. Ibid., 18.

38. Ibid.

39. Iqbal Mohammed, *Saving Children from a Life of Crime: A Sociological Perspective* (New Delhi: D.P.S. Publishing House, 2011), 122.

40. HRC, "Report of the Special Rapporteur on the Sale of Children, Child Prostitution and Child Pornography, Maud de Boer-Buquicchio," A/HRC/28/56, December 22, 2014, para. 38, at 10–11.

41. EC3, *Internet Organised Crime Threat Assessment 2017* (The Hague: Europol, 2017), 38 (hereafter IOCTA 2017).

42. Ibid., para. 31, at 9.

43. Palermo Protocol, art. 2(b), 6, 9, para. 1(b).

44. OHCHR, "Recommended Principles and Guidelines on Human Rights and Human Trafficking," E/2002/68/Add.1, May 20, 2002, principle 8, at 1.

45. Ibid., principle 7, at 1.

46. Palermo Protocol, art. 2(b) explicitly establishes as one of the purposes of the protocol "to protect and assist the victims of such trafficking, with full respect for their human rights."

47. Inter-Agency Coordination Group against Trafficking of Persons (ICAT), *Issue Brief 8: Non-Punishment of Victims of Trafficking* (2020), 1–6.

48. UNGA, "Trafficking in Women and Girls: Report of the Secretary-General," A/75/289, August 7, 2020, para. 17, at 6.

49. Ibid.

50. ICAT, "The International Legal Frameworks Concerning Trafficking in Persons," *ICAT Paper Series* 1 (2012): 10.

51. UNGA, "Trafficking in Women and Girls," para. 17, at 6.

52. U.S. Department of State, *Trafficking in Persons Report* (2016), 27.

53. Directive 2011/36/EU of the European Parliament and of the Council of 5 April 2011 on Preventing and Combating Trafficking in Human Beings and Protecting Its Victims, and Replacing Council Framework Decision 2002/629/JHA, art. 8.

54. Directive 2011/36/EU, art. 2(3).

55. Ibid., para. (11).

56. See OP-CRC-SC Guidelines, para. 18, at 5.

57. The CRC underscores that states parties should "encourage training on effective responses that are both victim-centered and survivor-led for child victims of offences covered by the Optional Protocol." (OP-CRC-SC Guidelines, para. 29[b], at 7).

58. Ibid. See generally, UNCRC, "General Comment no. 25 (2021) on Children's Rights in Relation to the Digital Environment," CRC/C/GC/25, March 2, 2021.

59. OP-CRC-SC Guidelines, para. 18, at 5.

60. UNCRC, "General Comment no. 25," para. 112, at 19. The CRC affirms, "Children should be protected from all forms of exploitation prejudicial to any aspects of their welfare in relation to the digital environment."

61. Palermo Protocol, art. 3(C).

62. UNCRC, art. 39.

63. CRC, "General Comment no. 14 (2013) on the Right of the Child to Have His or Her Best Interests Taken as a Primary Consideration (Art. 3, Para. 1)," CRC/C/GC/14, May 29, 2013.

64. OHCHR, "Recommended Principles and Guidelines on Human Rights and Human Trafficking," guideline 8, at 10.

65. 18 U.S. Code § 2259.

66. UNODC, *Global Report on Trafficking in Persons*, 40.

67. UNGIFT, *First Aid Kit for Use by Law Enforcement First Responders in Addressing Human Trafficking* (2010), 3.

68. Palermo Protocol, art. 3(c).

69. UNODC, *Issue Paper: The Role of Corruption in Trafficking in Persons* (Vienna: United Nations, 2011), 4, 15.

70. U.S. Department of State, *Trafficking in Persons Report*, 17.

71. ILO, *Profits and Poverty: The Economics of Forced Labour* (Geneva: International Labour Organization, 2014), 15.

72. Ibid., 15.

73. UNODC, *Comprehensive Study on Cybercrime* (New York: United Nations, 2013), xvii.

74. Eric Olson and Jonathan Tomek, *Cryptocurrency and the BlockChain: Technical Overview and Potential Impact on Commercial Child Sexual Exploitation*, https://www.icmec.org/cryptocurrency-and-the-blockchain-technical-overview-and-potential-impact-on-commercial-child-sexual-exploitation/.

75. Ibid., 27.

76. Rodrigo M. Arango, "Delincuentes le ponen precio a cuerpos de niñas," *El Colombiano*, www.elcolombiano.com/BancoConocimiento/D/delincuentes_les_ponen_precio_a_cuerpos_de_ninas/delincuentes_les_ponen_precio_a_cuerpos_de_ninas.asp.

77. James Bargent, "Children, Sex and Gangs in Medellin," InSight Crime, www.insightcrime.org/news-analysis/children-sex-and-gangs-in-medellin.

78. Ibid.

79. UNODC, *Study on the Effects of New Information Technologies*, 28.

80. Michael K. Bergman, "White Paper: The Deep Web: Surfacing Hidden Value," *Journal of Electronic Publishing* 7, no. 1 (2001).

81. Penny Hoelscher, "What Is the Difference between the Surface Web, the Deep Web, and the Dark Web?" INFOSEC, https://resources.infosecinstitute.com/topic/what-is-the-difference-between-the-surface-web-the-deep-web-and-the-dark-web/.

82. Ibid.

83. Justė Neverauskaitė, *In the Shadows of the Internet: Child Sexual Abuse Material in the Darknets* (Brussels: ECPAT Belgium, 2015), 1.

84. Ibid., 2–3.

85. Gareth Owen and Nick Savage, *The Tor Dark Net* (Centre for International Governance Innovation, Royal Institute of International Affairs, 2015), 1.

86. Ibid., 3, 6.

87. Ibid., 3–4.

88. Tor Project, "About Tor: Overview," www.torproject.org/about/overview.html.en.

89. Tor Project, "Inception," www.torproject.org/about/torusers.html.en.

90. See generally Tor Project, "History," www.torproject.org/about/history/.

91. Tor Project, "Tor: Onion Service Protocol," www.torproject.org/docs/onion-services.

92. David Goldschlag, Michael Reedy, and Paul Syversony, "Onion Routing for Anonymous and Private Internet Connections," www.onion-router.net/Publications/CACM-1999.pdf.

93. IOCTA 2020, 38.

94. International Justice Mission, "Online Sex Offender Sentenced to Life in Prison in Landmark e-Conviction," https://ijm.org.au/news/online-sex-offender-sentenced-to-life-in-prison-in-landmark-e-conviction/.

95. *New York Post*, "Inside Suspected Pedophile's Lair, a Glimpse at a Global Child Rape Epidemic," http://nypost.com/2017/05/09/suspected-pedophile-busted-in-sickening-philippines-sex-den/.

96. International Justice Mission, "Online Sex Offender."

97. Onion Router, "Our Sponsors," www.onion-router.net/Sponsors.html.

98. European Patent Office, "Bibliographic Data: US6266704 (B1)—200107–24; Onion Routing Network for Securely Moving Data Through Communication Networks," https://worldwide.espacenet.com/publicationDetails/biblio?CC=US&NR=6266704&KC=&FT=E&locale=en_EP#.

99. Tor Project, "Download," www.torproject.org/projects/torbrowser.html.en.

100. Tor Project, "Make Tor Browser Portable," https://tb-manual.torproject.org/make-tor-portable/.

101. Tor Project, "Users: Top-10 Countries by Relay Users," https://metrics.torproject.org/userstats-relay-table.html.

102. Tor Project, "Users: Relay Users," https://metrics.torproject.org/userstats:-relay-country.html?start=2021-07-01&end=2021-09-29&country=all&events=off.

103. IOCTA 2020, 38.

104. U.S. Department of Justice, Office of Public Affairs, "South Korean National and Hundreds of Others Charged Worldwide in the Takedown of the Largest Darknet Child Pornography Website, Which Was Funded by Bitcoin," www.justice.gov/opa/pr/south-korean-national-and-hundreds-others-charged-worldwide-takedown-larges-darknet-child.

105. *United States of America v. Jong Woo Son*, 2018, Court of the District of Columbia, at 5, (August 9, 2018).

106. U.S. Department of Justice, Office of Public Affairs, "South Korean National and Hundreds of Others Charged."

107. UNTOC, art. 3(2).

108. Ibid.

109. Ibid., art. 2(a).

110. UNGA, "Addendum: Interpretative Notes for the Official Records (*Travaux Préparatoires*) of the Negotiation of the United Nations Convention against Transnational Organized Crime and the Protocols Thereto," A/55/383/Add.1, November 3, 2000, para. 3, at 2.

111. UNODC, *Study on the Effects of New Information Technologies*, ix.

112. Palermo Protocol, art. 4.

113. UNODC, *Study on the Effects of New Information Technologies*, 35.

114. Michael J. Frank and G. Zachary Terwilliger, "Gang-Controlled Sex Trafficking," *Virginia Journal of Criminal Law* 3, no. 2 (2015): 374.

115. Texas Department of Public Safety, *Assessing the Threat of Human Trafficking in Texas: A State Intelligence Estimate* (2014), 12.

116. Frank and Terwilliger, "Gang-Controlled Sex Trafficking," 374.

117. Jim Donovan and Carmel Matin, eds., *United States Attorneys' Bulletin: Gang Prosecutions* (Washington, DC: Executive Office for United States Attorneys, 2014), 19.

118. Dominique Roe-Sepowitz et al., *A Six-Year Analysis of Sex Traffickers of Minors: Exploring Characteristics and Sex Trafficking Patterns* (Arizona State University Office of Sex Trafficking Intervention Research, 2017), iii.

119. Ibid., 16.

120. UNODC, "Traffickers' Use of the Internet," 127.

121. UNODC, *Global Report on Trafficking in Persons 2020*, 44.

122. Judge Herbert B. Dixon Jr., "Human Trafficking and the Internet (and Other Technologies, Too)," *Judges' Journal* 52, no. 1 (2013): 37.

123. U.S. Department of State, Office to Monitor and Combat Trafficking in Persons, *The Benefits of Smart Raids vs. Blind Sweeps* (Washington, DC: U.S. Department of State, 2012), 1.

124. Katherine K. Walts, *Building Child Welfare Response to Child Trafficking* (Chicago: Loyola Center for the Human Rights of Children, 2011), 29.

125. Danah Boyd et al., "Human Trafficking and Technology: A Framework for Understanding the Role of Technology in the Commercial Sexual Exploitation of Children in the U.S.," Microsoft Research Connections, 2011, https://ec.europa.eu/anti-trafficking/human-trafficking-and-technology-framework-understanding-role-technology-commercial-sexual_en.

126. UNODC, "Traffickers' Use of the Internet," 120.

127. Roe-Sepowitz et al., *A Six-Year Analysis*, iii.

128. Boyd et al., "Human Trafficking and Technology," 4–5.

129. Polaris Project, *Child Sex Trafficking At-a-Glance: Child Sex Trafficking in the United States* (2011), 2.

130. Boyd et al., "Human Trafficking and Technology," 5.

131. Polaris Project, *Tools for Educators: National Human Trafficking Resource Center* (2011). See generally Breaking Free and Ramsey County Attorney's Office, "Sex Trafficking and Safe Harbors," https://www.presentica.com/doc/11372364/sex-trafficking-and-safe-harbors-pdf-document.

132. Emily Kennedy, "Predictive Patterns of Sex Trafficking Online," thesis, Carnegie Mellon University, 2012, 27.

133. Ibid., 22.

134. Joan M. Sherwood, "Study Finds Extensive Prostitution Ads on Backpage.com," ASU News, https://news.asu.edu/content/study-finds-extensive-prostitution-ads-backpagecom.

135. HRC, "Report of the Special Rapporteur on the Sale of Children, Child Prostitution and Child Pornography, Najat M'jid Maalla," A/HRC/12/23, July 13, 2009, 10.

136. CoE, "Explanatory Report to the Council of Europe Convention on the Protection of Children against Sexual Exploitation and Sexual Abuse," October 25, 2007, C.E.T.S. 201, para. 3, at 1.

137. UNODC, *Global Report on Trafficking in Persons 2018* (New York: United Nations, 2018), 39.

138. UNODC, *Global Report on Trafficking in Persons 2020*, 44.

139. UNODC, *Study on the Effects of New Information Technologies*, ix.

140. Ibid., 12.

141. Ibid., 30.

142. Mary Aiken, Mike Moran, and Mike Berry, "Child Abuse Material and the Internet: Cyberpsychology of Online Child Related Sex Offending," paper presented at the 29th Meeting of the Interpol Specialist Group on Crimes against Children, Lyons, France, September 5–7, 2011, 5.

143. Ibid., 4–5.

144. Ibid., 4–6.

145. IOCTA 2020, 37.

146. VGT, *Virtual Global Taskforce Environmental Scan 2012* (2012), 17.

147. IOCTA 2017, 38.

148. IOCTA 2019, 30.

149. UNODC, *Combating Trafficking in Persons: A Handbook for Parliamentarians* (Austria: Inter-Parliamentary Union and the United Nations Office on Drugs and Crime, 2009), 70; Kimberly J. Mitchell et al., "Internet-Facilitated Commercial Sexual Exploitation of Children: Findings from a Nationally Representative Sample of Law Enforcement Agencies in the United States," *Sexual Abuse: A Journal of Research and Treatment* 23, no. 1 (2011): 56.

150. UNODC, "Traffickers' Use of the Internet," 119.

151. Protection Project, "Model Law on Combating Child Sex Tourism," in *International Child Sex Tourism: Scope of the Problem and Comparative Case Studies* (Washington, DC: John Hopkins University and the Paul H. Nitze School of Advanced International Studies, 2007), art. II, para. 2, 188.

152. UNODC, *Study on the Effects of New Information Technologies*, 26.

153. UNODC, *Global Report on Trafficking in Persons 2020*, 57, 119.

154. Protection Project, "Model Law on Combating Child Sex Tourism," 187.

155. UNODC, *Global Report on Trafficking in Persons 2020*, 57; OHCHR, "Combating Child Sex Tourism," www.ohchr.org/en/newsevents/pages/childsextourism.aspx.

156. Virginia M. Kendall and T. Markus Funk, *Child Exploitation and Trafficking: Examining the Global Challenges and U.S. Responses* (New York: Rowman & Littlefield, 2011), 26.

157. OP-CRC-SC, art. 9(3), (4).

Chapter 7

An Appraisal of Human Dignity in Cyberspace

The core assumption of this book is that sexual exploitation of children in cyberspace threatens human dignity in a free society. Inspired by the jurisprudential technique of the New Haven School, in this chapter I appraise the empirical values of human dignity and propose new pathways—better for the community and for a public order of human dignity—toward a more effective global response to this form of cybercrime, helping to ensure the protection of children. This chapter and the following recommend alternative solutions to child sexual exploitation in cyberspace by considering it a social and legal problem in the international sphere. The New Haven School provides a definitional basis for identifying and examining relevant factors and elements in decision-making processes with the goal of maximizing access to shaping and sharing the values of human dignity.[1] Drawn from the literature and using a multistakeholder approach, this chapter's appraisal considers the values of human dignity within the context of fighting trafficking. It intends to promote a public order of human dignity in future decisions.[2]

ONLINE EXPLOITATION IN THE POLICY-ORIENTED JURISPRUDENCE PERSPECTIVE

Human beings have always interacted with each other to develop social connections between individuals and across groups. Reisman, Wiessner, and Arsanjani characterize these interpersonal relations as the basis for the emergence and solidification of cultures and civilizations worldwide because these interactions foster individuals' sense of belonging to a community as they cannot develop in isolation or as "monads."[3] In such communal contexts, the protection of social values and human relations inspire the participation of individuals and communities in governance. In *The Social Contract*,

Jean-Jacques Rousseau draws a close association between government and the beginning of social life: a government exists as a "legitimate rule of administration" to ensure the common good for all individuals.[4] Rousseau famously declared that "man is born free, and he is everywhere in chains,"[5] arguing that humans are born free, equal, and naturally good but are eventually corrupted and held back by structures and creations of human society. However, individual citizens unite by entering into a contract of association and voluntarily submitting to a legitimate political authority to coexist harmoniously and for mutual benefits.[6] For Rousseau, a good government exists to protect individuals' freedom, equality, and justice and to express the general will of the public good, which in communal life is placed ahead of personal interests. For Rousseau, people in an ideal society are themselves parties in a legitimate social contract and are sovereign so that they are only subject to their own collective will, surrendering their natural rights to the "general will."[7] This reasoning prefigures and indeed influenced the sentiment captured in the first words of the U.S. Constitution, "We the people."[8] By submitting to the common good, citizens lead more meaningful lives. They realize their full potential and human aspirations because they conduct their lives in a society that ensures their life, freedom, equality, and security. For this society to be equitable, all citizens share the same civic rights, responsibilities, and duties.

As set forth by legal scholars Myers McDougal, Harold Lasswell, and Lung-Chu Chen, public order provides the most significant access to all things cherished by humanity. Although what individuals consider valuable may differ, the most common demands of people worldwide can be grouped into eight general categories of values: power, enlightenment, wealth, well-being, skill, affection, respect, and rectitude.[9] These eight values inform our understanding of the law and help shape it.[10] Cybertrafficking of children can be analyzed according to these eight values in the context of law to help develop a greater understanding of the problem. By appraising the legal system according to the maximization of values, we can advance children's best interests and rights in cyberspace. States can establish greater public order in cyberspace by encouraging children's happiness and holistic development and achieving more-thorough protection of their human dignity.[11]

The methodology of policy-oriented jurisprudence aspires to ensure the common interest of all individuals rather than the primacy of particular groups. From this standpoint, its framework of inquiry seeks to achieve a wider sharing of human dignity protections. This stance is in line with values enshrined in various international instruments such as the UN Charter and the UDHR (codified in two international covenants, the 1966 ICCPR and the 1966 ICESCR). Together these instruments form an authoritative postulation of values held by the whole of humanity.[12] The realization of public order through fundamental policies that underlie all law requires a legal system dedicated to protecting, restoring, and improving public order. According to W. Michael Reisman, states achieve public order goals using seven specific strategies:

1. Preventing imminent discrete public order violations.
2. Suspending current public order violations.
3. Deterring, in general, potential future public order violations.
4. Restoring public order after it has been violated.
5. Correcting behavior that generates public order violations.
6. Rehabilitating victims who have suffered the brunt of public order violations.
7. Reconstructing in a larger social sense to remove conditions that appear likely to generate public order violations.[13]

Preventing seeks *ex ante* responses to intervene before violations occur, *suspending* seeks immediate *ex post* responses to stop the occurred violation, *deterring* more generally helps to identify credible threats and discourages violators from committing violations in the future, *correcting* focuses on adjusting patterns of behavior that may generate violations of public order, *rehabilitating* focuses on assisting victims and may encompass the right to remedy, and *social reconstruction*, in a broad sense, seeks to identify situations that may contribute to the rupture of public order and spearheads organizational efforts to prevent their occurrence.[14]

These seven strategies detail a means to protect, reestablish, or create public order, helping to inform the design and adjustment of policies as well as the shaping of institutions to ensure the protection of human dignity in cyberspace. Online sexual exploitation is a public order violation that has become a real global threat against human beings, particularly children. Therefore, policies geared toward a better global public order must enhance the protection of the dignity and rights of children in the digital space by promoting normative goals or values for ensuring the well-being of children in cyberspace. In the process of authoritative decision making, it is only when the law adopts or strengthens measures ensuring children's online safety that their human dignity can be fully protected both online and offline.[15]

When states improve protection of human dignity, policies influence the shaping and sharing of values that reduce deviations that threaten public order. The ICCPR connects freedom with human rights:

> The ideal of free human beings enjoying civil and political freedom and freedom from fear and want can only be achieved if conditions are created whereby

everyone may enjoy his civil and political rights, as well as his economic, social and cultural rights.[16]

This covenant recognizes the obligation of states to create conditions that allow human beings to realize all rights and freedoms, an idea affirmed in Article 28 of the UDHR.[17] In light of the preceding, human rights from a policy-oriented perspective offer a comprehensive map for the shaping and sharing of values integral to achieving a public order of human dignity and thus serve as an essential guide for those seeking to overcome the enormous contemporary challenge of protecting children online.[18] One important avenue for achieving a more successful and broader fulfillment of rights for everyone in the world community is discouraging the abuse of Internet platforms.

APPRAISAL: THE EIGHT FUNDAMENTAL VALUES OF HUMAN DIGNITY

To appraise activities related to the online sexual exploitation of children, the eight values of human dignity can be applied to achieve a comprehensive picture of cybertrafficking while laying a foundation for recommendations that harmonize policies and strategies with international human rights standards. Consequently, this appraisal outlines a frame of reference to balance all factors and variables to improve processes of authoritative decisions that concern the inviolability of the human dignity of Internet users, including children. Once followed, this jurisprudential framework will help states protect public order and avoid arbitrary or excessive decisions.[19]

Power

From a policy-oriented perspective, authoritative decisions (i.e., decisions made by states) facilitate the production and sharing of values intending to promote an order where everyone can thrive and reach their full potential to realize human dignity.[20] In a cybertrafficking context, institutional procedures, strategies, and decisions should lead to purposive social changes that are compatible with the adequate protection of the human dignity of children in cyberspace. States have the power to establish these protections and best practices. Otherwise, changes will be "retrogressions."[21] To develop sound policies, states should frequently evaluate conditions, demands, and factors that influence social problems because new elements can emerge.

Within a human trafficking context, states have taken significant steps to raise awareness and otherwise combat this crime. For example, national governments, the UN (including the UNODC), and NGOs have labored to implement a zero-tolerance policy while rejecting defenses on the grounds of traditions as violations related to child exploitation.[22] At present, 178 states have ratified the Palermo Protocol that sets forth clear guidelines to help countries worldwide adopt and revise legislation concerning trafficking.[23] This significant number of states parties demonstrates a robust legislative response and indicates individual and collective efforts toward combating trafficking in human beings. This response suggests that states have protected and assisted a substantial number of victims.

States can develop or adjust national policies to enhance the protection of children in cyberspace with effective strategies. Thus, states are the predominant participants in the power process, which is the most decisive value process in the world community.[24] As noted, the Internet has transformed trafficking. In response to this, the 2016 Europol *Situation Report: Trafficking in Human Beings* encourages law enforcement authorities to increase efforts to combat these illicit activities on online platforms.[25] These efforts should include detecting and investigating potentially exploitative practices that occur on social media sites, job boards, escort forums, and sex chats. There is an urgent need for governments to strengthen their antitrafficking efforts and effective safeguards for children online.[26] Many states have utilized their power to create and implement legislation to prevent, reduce, and eliminate this serious crime. Therefore, with their national sovereign power, states can also exercise their authority in cyberspace, making all criminal activities in the cyberworld subject to the law. Nonetheless, states have agreed not to claim ownership over the Internet.[27]

The broadly accepted premise that states should act under international law in cyberspace suggests that human rights law obligations are applicable in cyberspace as well. States should promote and protect human rights online while remembering "the same rights that people have offline must also be protected online."[28] This assertion is affirmed in the HRC's landmark resolution 20/8, "The Promotion, Protection, and Enjoyment of Human Rights on the Internet." In 2012, Sweden presented this resolution and the HRC unanimously adopted it. As the first of its kind, the resolution acknowledges "the global and open nature of the Internet as a driving force in accelerating progress towards development in its various forms."[29] Furthermore, the resolution calls upon all states "to promote and facilitate access to the Internet and international cooperation" toward developing technological infrastructures worldwide.[30] Thus, it underlines an evolution of international principles for cyberspace and their importance for exercising human rights and enabling development. In addition, the resolution urges states to promote and protect human rights and fundamental freedoms in cyberspace to the same extent and with the same commitment as in the physical world, a position the HRC reaffirmed in its resolutions 26/13 in 2014[31] and 32/13 in 2016.[32]

States should promote the quest for a safer cyberspace for children where the respect for and protection of their rights are enhanced. A public order's objectives that involve balancing the interests, rights, and values at stake and in practice can relate to crime prevention and criminal justice. Thus, it is essential to achieve an acceptable balance between legal safeguards to secure public order goals and individual freedom in online environments. In compliance with international standards, states should ensure respect for human rights. Concomitantly, measures must not unduly intrude upon the rights of the accused or online users, restrict individual rights, or unnecessarily involve the use of arbitrary state powers.

The International Covenant on Civil and Political Rights: General Parameters for Restrictive Measures on the Rights to Freedom of Expression and Privacy in Online Environments

The ICCPR is central in safeguarding fundamental human rights and provides legal standards to ensure effective protection of covenant rights, including when states parties address online communications.[33] According to Article 2, paragraph 1, of the ICCPR, states parties must respect and ensure the rights recognized in the covenant.[34] This responsibility implies that besides the obligation to respect, states parties have the positive obligation to take appropriate measures to protect the rights laid down in the covenant to ensure the enjoyment of these rights by all individuals within their territory and subject to their jurisdiction.[35] Furthermore, based on Article 2, paragraph 3, of the ICCPR, states parties must ensure effective remedies if human rights violations occur.[36]

In a democratic legal system, states are the duty bearers in international law and should ensure the common good of all individuals, whose benefits should be front and center in state activities. One such duty is to ensure that all individuals have opportunities to acquire other rights and to be protected from human rights abuses. When states enter into international relations and become parties to international treaties, they exercise their sovereign power. Therefore, they assume legal obligations for respecting, protecting, and fulfilling human rights. The obligation to respect means that states must refrain from interfering with the enjoyment of human rights, the obligation to protect requires states to prevent infringement of the human rights of individuals and groups, and the obligation to fulfill implies that states take positive action to facilitate the exercise of human rights.[37] Thus, at the international level, human rights protections exist to protect every person's dignity and rights. At the same time, this postulate approximates the realization of human dignity's goals as states move toward establishing a public order in which all human beings can fully develop in the complexity of their entire social context and lead dignified lives.[38] This legal provision of Article 2 of the ICCPR exclusively identifies states parties as bound by the covenant provisions.

Furthermore, the preamble underscores that "the individual [has] duties to other individuals and to the community to which he belongs." This postulate acknowledges the possibility that states parties may subject rights guaranteed by the covenant to certain restrictions for protecting the rights of other individuals or a specific public interest.[39] Accordingly the HRCttee, in General Comment no. 31(80), affirms that when making restrictions, "states must demonstrate their necessity and only take such measures as are proportionate to the pursuance of legitimate aims in order to ensure continuous and effective protection of covenant rights."[40] This explanation means that states should not place the right itself in jeopardy with restrictions connected to Article 19, paragraph 3, regarding the right to freedom of expression, which "carries with it special duties and responsibilities."[41] Therefore, it mandates that this right may be subject to restrictive measures that are "provided by law and are necessary: (a) For respect of the rights or reputations of others; (b) For the protection of national security or of public order (ordre public), or of public health or morals."[42] Accordingly, the ICCPR expressly imposes three requirements for any restriction: legality as "provided by law," legitimacy in meeting one of the two limitation conditions above (subparagraphs a and b), and necessity as subject to the principle of proportionality.[43] In this way, with the guidance of international human rights law, states' powers to restrict the exercise of freedom of expression on the Internet must demonstrate that the measures meet the requirements of legality, legitimacy, and necessity and proportionality.[44]

International law permits certain restrictions of freedom of expression provided by law (limitations specifically apply to Article 19[2]). When states limit this fundamental right to freedom of expression, which is valued highly on the Internet and off, they must meet established international standards including the requirements of legality, legitimacy, and necessity and proportionality. International law mandates that states prohibit certain exceptional types of expression such as child pornography by meeting these conditions, provided that the measure taken is limited to specific situations and does not interfere with the essence of the rights to privacy and freedom of expression in online environments. States should protect children against sexual abuse (legitimate interest) under international human rights law guidance. States' legal obligations under the ICCPR require them to enact and implement legislation where necessary and to proportionally address the threats likely associated with online sex trafficking, meeting the three-part test of legality, legitimacy, and necessity and proportionality.[45] In compliance with international law, states must protect children from harm while maintaining respect for individuals' liberties such as the right to freedom of expression on the Internet. Put another way, this legal framework of the grounds for legitimate restrictions to protect children from harm requires state laws to detect, investigate, prosecute, and punish perpetrators of Internet-facilitated child sex trafficking.

As previous chapters demonstrate, perpetrators including traffickers use sophisticated technologies such as encryption and anonymity to secure online communications to carry out their criminal activities more effectively. These online practices constitute a critical, contemporary challenge for states primarily to prevent and investigate. They must strike a balance between individuals' right to use the Internet and each state's obligation to protect children. In conformity with international human rights law, effective state restrictions to establish online security must be prescribed by law, necessary, or proportionate and with appropriate safeguards to ensure the promotion and protection of the rights to privacy and freedom of opinion and expression. The ICCPR provides standards of conduct for all 173 of its states parties to ensure that individuals enjoy their rights under the covenant and enshrines the rights to privacy and freedom of opinion and expression as fundamental rights derived from the inherent dignity of the human being and the foundations of a democratic society.[46] This position aligns with Article 26 of the VCLT, which sees a treaty as an international agreement legally binding for states parties.[47] States parties of the ICCPR have a legal obligation to harmonize national laws and policies with the provisions of this international human rights treaty to which they are party and to implement the treaty's obligations in good faith.[48] In addition, for those states that have signed but not ratified the ICCPR and are not bound by its legal provisions, they should respect its object and purpose as established under Article 18 of the VCLT.[49]

UN Special Rapporteur La Rue notes that the rights to privacy and freedom of expression are interlinked.[50] States must ensure adequate legislation and legal frameworks regarding measures of communications surveillance. The three requirements are essential to ensure that the privacy, security, and anonymity of communications remain intact.[51] The civil and political right to privacy is a fundamental right and supports realizing the right to freedom of expression and holding opinions.[52] Moreover the right to freedom of expression "is essential for the enjoyment of other human rights and freedoms and constitutes a fundamental pillar for building a democratic society and strengthening democracy."[53] The ICCPR defines the right to privacy as including the following:

1. No one shall be subject to arbitrary or unlawful interference with his privacy, family, home or correspondence or to unlawful attacks on his honour and reputation.

2. Everyone has the right to the protection of the law against such interference or attacks.[54]

This legal provision echoes Article 12 of the UDHR.[55] In addition, Article 17, paragraph 2, provides that legal rules are necessary to protect this right against governmental or private intrusion. In fact, the HRCttee, in General Comment no. 16, considers regarding this positive obligation from states to ensure protection of the right to privacy the following:

> This right is required to be guaranteed against all such interferences and attacks whether they emanate from State authorities or from natural or legal persons. The obligations imposed by this article require the State to adopt legislative and other measures to give effect to the prohibition against such interferences and attacks as well as to the protection of this right.[56]

Additionally, the general comment indicates,

> the gathering and holding of personal information on computers, data banks and other devices, whether by public authorities or private individuals or bodies, must be regulated by law.[57]

The legal provision of Article 17 differs from the wording of Article 19, paragraph 3, as it does not provide a clause regarding the elements on permitting restrictions. However the framework enables permissible limitations on the right to privacy where "(a) they are authorized by domestic law that is accessible and precise and that conforms to the requirements of the covenant, (b) they pursue a legitimate aim and (c) they meet the tests of necessity and proportionality."[58] In this digital age, legitimate restrictions on the right to privacy, including involving online security tools such as encryption or anonymity, must be described clearly by the law. This requirement applies to a publicly accessible law. Moreover, restrictive measures must accord with the legitimate objectives of the covenant such as to protect the rights of others, including children, and be necessary and proportionate to the precise circumstances for reaching that legitimate aim.[59] This prerequisite of accessibility of the law means that laws regulating any interference with the right to privacy must be published and sufficiently precise in detailing the specific circumstances and legitimate aims, nature, and duration of the surveillance powers permitted. In this way, persons who may be affected by the surveillance practice on communications may foresee its effects.[60] Otherwise, vague or broadly defined legal provisions represent a greater risk that governments will exercise arbitrary discretion powers beyond the bounds of the law. In this scenario, states would be at risk of enacting restriction measures that do not meet the test of lawfulness and effective protection to privacy under international human rights law. Consequently, states must respect and protect this fundamental human right to privacy in communications on the Internet de jure and de facto and ensure the strict observance of the principles of legality and necessity and proportionality for a legitimate purpose in accordance with their international human rights obligations.[61]

In 2019, UNICEF asserted that in the context of digital technologies, "laws should not encourage internet censorship and restrict the use of technology by young people in the effort to protect them from harm."[62] Thus, states cannot use the aim of child protection to justify limiting access or monitoring users' private communications online. Expressly, states must adopt and implement legal rules with reasonable clarity to ensure that restrictive measures regarding the Internet and other new ICTs conform to international human rights standards. Otherwise the essence of the rights to privacy and freedom of expression may be undermined. At the same time, states must ensure remedies provided by national law in cases of infringement of individual rights or unnecessary use of coercive powers.

This online problem demonstrates the intertwined nature of the rights to privacy and freedom of expression particularly in cases involving domestic and extraterritorial digital surveillance of personal communications, encryption, and anonymity. According to legal obligations under international human rights law, states must ensure, in law and practice, that restrictive measures do not go beyond the scope of the interference for reaching a legitimate aim. In this connection, the HRCttee highlights the need "to ensure that any interference with the right to privacy complies with the principles of legality, proportionality, and necessity regardless of the nationality or location of individuals whose communications are under direct surveillance."[63] This postulate relates to the principle of nondiscrimination (Article 26, ICCPR)[64] that when read with Article 17 and Article 2(1)[65] of the ICCPR ensures equal levels of human rights protection to foreigners and citizens within national security surveillance oversight regimes under the covenant.[66] UNGA Resolution 68/167 calls upon all nations "to respect and protect the right to privacy, including in the context of digital communication" and to ensure that their "relevant national legislation complies with their obligations under international human rights law."[67] International human rights law, a body of international law, provides the universal framework to ensure that interference with privacy is neither arbitrary nor unlawful. More specifically, the HRCttee, in General Comment no. 16 on Article 17, emphasizes the necessity of legal interference:

The term "unlawful" means that no interference can take place except in cases envisaged by the law. Interference authorized by States can only take place on the basis of law, which itself must comply with the provisions, aims and objectives of the covenant.[68]

Moreover, the HRCttee underscores,

> The expression "arbitrary interference" can also extend to interference provided for under the law. The introduction of the concept of arbitrariness is intended to guarantee that even interference provided for by law should be in accordance with the provisions, aims and objectives of the covenant and should be, in any event, reasonable in the particular circumstances.[69]

This interpretation of the concept of reasonableness indicates that "any interference with privacy must be proportional to the end sought and be necessary in the circumstances of any given case."[70] Thus, in conformity with international human rights standards when assessing the necessity of a measure limiting the right to privacy, states must uphold the principle of proportionality to avoid putting in jeopardy the right to freedom of expression and access to information that may affect all individuals, including children—not least because "widespread restrictions on the use of digital communications and censorship are not only unacceptable but also ineffective solutions to these concerns."[71] From a legal perspective, human rights norms offer guidance to states to achieve an appropriate balance between the effective implementation and execution of regulatory standards to protect children from harm and the protection of fundamental rights of both adults and children in the digital world. Therefore, these norms provide states with appropriate direction to avoid disproportionately restricting rights when achieving the goal of child protection.

The UN Convention on the Rights of the Child: Legal Standards to Balance Children's Fundamental Rights to Freedom of Expression, Access to Information, Privacy, and Protection

We have established that children are beneficiaries of the civil rights enshrined in the ICCPR.[72] In addition, the UNCRC focuses on the child as a rights holder. It provides a firm foundation for states to protect and promote children's rights and well-being, particularly when addressing online safety concerns. Thus, the UNCRC establishes a foundational basis for safeguarding children's rights and their inherent dignity while balancing restrictive measures to avoid disproportionately restricting their fundamental right to freedom of expression, access to information, and privacy. This legally binding instrument in Article 13, which shares aspects of Article 19 of the ICCPR, asserts the right of children to freedom of expression subject to restrictions for the sake only of protecting the rights of others or of public order.[73]

This legal provision can be read in conjunction with Article 12 on the right to be heard and Article 17 on the right to have access to information and material from a diversity of national and international sources. Together they provide human rights protections to children's freedom of expression analogous, if not more significant, to those that Article 19 of the ICCPR offers to individuals.[74] As they progressively mature and reach full autonomy, children can exercise the rights under the UNCRC, including the realization of their right to freedom of expression. While considering the principle of the evolving capacities of children, their parents and where applicable other persons legally responsible for them should provide appropriate direction and guidance to them by holding their best interest as the primary concern when they exercise their human rights.[75] States' restrictions on children's right to freedom of expression and access to information require a careful balance. They must be provided by law on the grounds established in the Article 13 cited at the end of the previous paragraph (paragraphs 2[a] and [b]) and in conformity with the strict test of proportionality—applying *mutatis mutandis* Article 19, paragraph 3, of the ICCPR to the right of children to freedom of expression.[76] Moreover, Article 17(e) of the UNCRC mandates that states develop "appropriate guidelines for the protection of the child from information and material injurious to his or her well-being" including that of a pornographic nature.[77] As children are vulnerable to sexual exploitation, states should implement proportional measures and policies to protect them in line with relevant international human rights standards.

The European Convention on Human Rights: Restrictions on Rights to Privacy and Freedom of Expression

While the sexual exploitation of children in cyberspace is a decidedly new phenomenon, many policy and legislative decisions have already been made at national and international levels. In Europe, binding case laws from the ECtHR demonstrate efforts to protect children from harm on the Internet. In these cases the court interprets the ECHR in light of changing conditions in modern societies, responding to any evolving convergence toward practical and effective protection of human rights. These situations include circumstances where individuals threaten a child victim's physical and moral welfare, which is a situation of greater importance.

In the ECHR, lawful types of interference usually fall to the rights enshrined in Articles 8 to 11. The justification of limitations on these articles is on the grounds of "public safety, the protection of the rights and freedoms (or reputations) of others, and the protection of health, morals or public order/ordre public (or the prevention of disorder)."[78] Thus, these specific purposes prescribed by law include Article 8, paragraph 2, of the convention regarding the right to respect for private and family life, home, and correspondence:

> There shall be no interference by a public authority with the exercise of this right except such as is in accordance with the law and is necessary in a democratic society in the interests of national security, public safety or the economic well-being of the country, for the prevention of disorder or crime, for the protection of health or morals, or for the protection of the rights and freedoms of others.[79]

There is a recognition that the exercise of this right may be subject to limited restrictions that (1) must be prescribed by or are in accordance with the law, (2) meet one or more of the legitimate purposes corresponding to the second paragraph, and (3) are necessary in a democratic society. When provided by law and necessary, such as for the prevention of crime and the protection of the fundamental rights of others, including children. These applicable standards and the scope of the rights involved are demonstrated in the following cases.

2017 Trabajo Rueda v. Spain

Trabajo Rueda took his computer to a technician at a computer shop to replace a defective data recorder. The technician replaced the part and did some tests by opening some files, which he noticed contained CSAM. The technician contacted the police who seized the computer and had its files examined by computer experts. Trabajo Rueda was arrested on his way to pick up his computer at the shop.

The ECtHR determined that there had been a violation of Article 8 (right to respect for private life). Specifically, the court noted that the interference was prescribed by law pursuing the legitimate aims of "prevention of crime" and "protection of the rights of others." The court also emphasized that "sexual abuse is unquestionably an abhorrent type of wrongdoing, with debilitating effects on its victims" and that "children and other vulnerable individuals are entitled to state protection." The court recognized that police had accessed the files of the computer without judicial authorization, which was not proportionate to the legitimate aims pursued and thus was not "necessary in a democratic society." Although it was difficult to determine the urgency of the police in seizing the files from the computer before judicial authorization, that authorization would have been relatively quick to obtain as the computer was already in the hands of police and doing so would not have impeded the course of the investigation.[80]

2008 K.U. v. Finland

A twelve-year-old boy was advertised on an Internet dating site without his knowledge, making him a target for pedophiles. The unidentified individual who posted the advertisement stated on it that "he was looking for an intimate relationship with a boy of his age or older 'to show him the way.'" As a result, one person responded to the dating advertisement by emailing the boy with an offer to meet and "then to see what you want." With this email, the boy found out about the posted advertisement.

Although the interested man was identified through his email address, the person responsible for posting the advertisement was not. This person's ISP refused to disclose his IP address on the grounds of confidentiality according to national legislation. Finnish courts endorsed this position, arguing that telecommunications identification data may not be released in malicious misrepresentation cases as determined at national jurisdictions. However the ECtHR held that there had been a violation of Article 8 of the convention (right to respect for private life). The court noted that posting an advertisement exposing a minor as a target for pedophiles on the Internet is a criminal act. At the same time, it found that the state failed to protect the child victim by not taking effective steps to identify, investigate, and prosecute the offender (the person who placed the advertisement) due to the overriding requirement of confidentiality.

The court determined that although the state must respect online users' rights to privacy and freedom of expression, such guarantees cannot be absolute and must sometimes yield to other legitimate imperatives. Thus, the legislature should have provided a framework for reconciling the confidentiality of Internet services with the prevention of disorder or crime, or the protection of the rights and freedoms of others, particularly of children and vulnerable individuals. Consequently the court recognized that states are required to protect children from sexual abuse through the Internet.[81]

Jurisprudence from the ECtHR reflects legal developments regarding protecting children's human rights in cyberspace concerning sexual exploitation. Pertaining to Article 8 (respect for private life), the court in *Dudgeon v. the United Kingdom* highlighted that this right deals with the "most intimate aspect of private life."[82] Furthermore, in *DP & J.C. v. the United Kingdom*, the court held that "Article 8 of the Convention may impose positive obligations to protect the physical and moral integrity of an individual from other persons."[83] The positive duty of the state to safeguard the child, including from sexual abuse, implies that limitations of a specific right or rights should be according to the law. In this regard, the law should meet the accessibility requirement. The court reasoned in the *Sunday Times v. the United Kingdom* case that the legal provision is accessible to citizens in the sense that they "must be able to have an indication that is adequate in the circumstances of the legal rules applicable to a given case."[84] The law must be sufficiently precise to enable citizens to reasonably foresee the consequences a given act may entail. On the grounds of a legitimate purpose, the law should provide adequate safeguards to protect the substantive scope of the rights invoked in a manner consistent with the legal system of the country in question and the object of the ECHR. Additionally, governments should ensure that the interference serves the needs of democracy. This condition refers to the requirement of "necessary in a democratic society," which the court in *Silver v. the United Kingdom* summarized in certain principles of its jurisprudence.[85]

Within the European human rights legal culture, states' effective measures with respect to the needs of democracy may include efforts of criminalization and require that domestic laws are "proportionate to the legitimate aims pursued."[86] The court has developed such an approach since the 1968 *Belgian Linguistic* Case (no. 2) on Article 14—prohibition of discrimination—when it affirmed, "Article 14 is likewise violated when it is clearly established that there is no reasonable relationship of proportionality between the means employed and the aim sought to be realised."[87] For instance, when considering the nature of democratic necessity, the court held in *Handyside v. the United Kingdom* that freedom of expression is one of its "essential foundations" and, consequently, within the framework set in Article 10, paragraph 2, mentioned below, the legitimate aims must be narrowly construed.[88] Article 10, paragraph 2, on the right to freedom of expression states,

> The exercise of these freedoms, since it carries with it duties and responsibilities, may be subject to such formalities, conditions, restrictions or penalties as are prescribed by law and are necessary in a democratic society, in the interests of national security, territorial integrity or public safety, for the prevention of disorder or crime, for the protection of health or morals, for the protection of the reputation or rights of others, for preventing the disclosure of information received in confidence, or for maintaining the authority and impartiality of the judiciary.[89]

This legal provision references the "duties and responsibilities" of individuals connected to the right of expression, which may vary depending on the circumstances.[90] States' actions of interference must be proportionate to and offer adequate protection to avoid the occurrence of possible abuses by infringing the rights of others. In the pursuit of one or more of the legitimate aims stated, the principle of proportionality is essential to assess whether, and if so to what extent, lawful interference with a right to the use of technology may be "necessary in a democratic society." With regard to freedom of expression, the court held in *Handyside v. the United Kingdom* that according to Article 10, paragraph 2, the notion of "necessity" implies that a "pressing social need" exists.[91] In conformity with the CoE's standards, the doctrine of margin of appreciation in Strasbourg case law gives national authorities discretion in assessing in any given case that the law and measures of restrictions are in accordance with the rights protected by the convention. The court explained that this permitted discretionary power of appreciation "goes hand in hand with a European supervision. Such supervision concerns both the aim of the measure challenged and its 'necessity'; it covers not only the basic legislation but also the decision applying it." It follows that the court's supervisory function is not to "take the place of the competent national courts but rather to review under Article 10 the decisions they delivered in the exercise of their power of appreciation."[92] The court must determine that the respondent state acted reasonably, carefully, and in good faith and must ascertain that the interference was proportionate and based on relevant and sufficient reasons for justification. Restrictive measures may require that states apply a domestic margin of appreciation.

Wealth

Policy-oriented jurisprudence describes the human value of wealth as the "production, distribution and consumption of goods and services" or "control of resources."[93] The value of wealth in an Internet context would necessarily refer to the management and availability of technological resources worldwide. The Internet is a universal tool that can promote the development of individuals around the world.[94] For this reason, wealth (including the ability to access the Internet) should not be impeded because such access to global information is a crucial element of prosperity, contributing to states' human capital and the promotion of democratic values.

Considering this value of wealth, general cybertrafficking policies to address child sexual exploitation should not limit access to or use of the Internet more than is necessary for achieving the goal of child protection. On the contrary, states should promote broad availability of the Internet for the benefit of the global community so that everyone can enjoy their freedom to connect online and enjoy the benefits of it, including (but not limited to) gaining knowledge, exposure to new ideas, and a sense of community. This premise is essential because the Internet can play a positive role in preventing certain types of cyberoffenses by serving as a tool to educate the public, including children, about the potential risk of cybertraffickers and exploiters who may reach out to them. Thus, the Internet can and should be used to work toward eliminating online child sexual exploitation practices to help protect potential and actual victims and to aid in prosecuting perpetrators.[95] Overall, the Internet is at the service of the entire world so policies should not limit Internet use or access based on broad approaches or ambiguous laws.

Enlightenment

"Enlightenment" in this context refers to the result of the processes of "gathering, disseminating, and enjoyment of information and knowledge." The realization of this value may include the expression in individuals' freedom in the giving and receiving of knowledge and information.[96] This interpretation is a recognition that encompasses Article 19 of the ICCPR, which asserts that "everyone shall have the right to hold opinions without interference. Everyone shall have the right to freedom of expression; this right shall include freedom to seek, receive and impart information and ideas of all kinds, regardless of frontiers."[97] This same right is also in Article 19 of the UDHR.[98] The Internet has emerged as a unique and central means through which individuals exercise their right to free expression and opinion. In this regard, the HRCttee in General Comment no. 34 regarding the right to freedom of expression over the Internet, affirms that

> States parties should take account of the extent to which developments in information and communication technologies, such as internet and mobile based electronic information dissemination systems, have substantially changed communication practices around the world. There is now a global network for exchanging ideas and opinions that does not necessarily rely on the traditional mass media intermediaries. States parties should take all necessary steps to foster the independence of these new media and to ensure access of individuals thereto.[99]

This freedom of expression in cyberspace also has limits. Restrictions should be as provided by law and when necessary for the respect of the rights of others—for the respect of the human rights and the human dignity of children online. For example, distribution, downloading, or viewing of child pornography constitutes legitimate reasons for restricting access to these images based on children's right to protection.[100] Thus, the value of enlightenment serves as a reminder that policies—including those dealing with cybercrime and online child sexual exploitation—are inseparably linked to disseminating information and promoting cyber-risk-reduction education. In the global war against cybertrafficking, enlightenment thus refers to efforts in education and the promotion of antitrafficking awareness. Overall, in an anticybertrafficking context, the advancement of education for the benefit of children, including age-appropriate instruction on the dangers of the abuse of ICTs, should be a component of any well-drafted policy and strategy seeking to enhance children's online safety.

Well-Being

While the Internet brings many new opportunities to people across the globe, it also presents challenges to protecting human rights and fundamental freedoms. Well-being is related to "safety, health and comfort," and the UDHR refers to this value in recognizing all humans' right to "life, liberty and security of person" while condemning torture as well as cruel or inhuman treatment or punishment.[101] Safeguarding the well-being of children is a legitimate concern for governments because it is necessary for the promotion of social progress and the maintenance of public order. Regarding the value of well-being, the UDHR affirms in Article 25 that "motherhood and childhood are entitled to special care and assistance."[102] In addition, Article 24 of the ICCPR provides that each child is entitled to necessary "measures of protection as are required by his status as a minor, on the part of his family, society and the State."[103] This legal provision is a recognition of the right of children to special protection.

The preamble of the UN "Declaration of the Rights of the Child" affirms that "the child, by reason of his physical and mental immaturity, needs special safeguards and care, including appropriate legal protection, before as well as after birth."[104] Furthermore, Principle 2 of the declaration specifies this legal protection:

> The child shall enjoy special protection, and shall be given opportunities and facilities, by law and by other means, to enable him to develop physically, mentally, morally, spiritually and socially in a healthy and normal manner and in conditions of freedom and dignity. In the enactment of laws for this purpose, the best interests of the child shall be the paramount consideration.[105]

These guiding principles centered on guarding the child's best interest appear across legal instruments on children's rights.[106] The overwhelming support for the UNCRC demonstrates states' unwavering commitment to promoting and protecting children's rights and acknowledges they deserve special protection under international law. Specifically, Article 3(2) of the UNCRC mandates states parties to ensure for children "such protection and care as is necessary for his or her well-being" and to "take all appropriate legislative and administrative measures" to accomplish this.[107] In the context of human rights, it should be a priority of all states worldwide to promote children's well-being in cyberspace to ensure their ability to fulfill their aspirations and live a life unencumbered by the threat of cybercrimes, specifically sex trafficking. Based on the principle of nonpunishment of trafficked persons, children sexually exploited online are not criminals. Therefore, states should not subject them to criminal proceedings that link directly to their exploitation.[108] They are victims of human rights violations and, consequently, they are entitled to protection, services, and appropriate care.

The 2003 WSIS "Declaration of Principles and Plan of Action" (i.e., the Geneva Phase) also recognized the promotion of efforts to protect children and young people in information and telecommunication technologies. Specifically, the declaration, which established the principles on which the information society has been founded, states a commitment to ensure that the development of ICTs, applications, and operation of services respects and protects children's rights and well-being.[109] Furthermore, the plan of action, in which world leaders propose a means of realizing the vision of an inclusive and equitable information society, affirms that as part of an ethical dimension of ICTs, "the Information Society should be subject to universally held values and promote the common good and to prevent abusive uses of ICTs . . . such as . . . all forms of child abuse, including paedophilia and child pornography, and trafficking in, and exploitation of, human beings."[110] Thus, outcomes of the world summit reflect a solid international commitment to the protection of children online from all harm including sexual exploitation.

Skill

Global progress has often been fostered by technological innovation and increases in its accessibility to more individuals and populations. The technologies and information-sharing capacities of cyberspace have increased the pace of progress.[111] The remarkable advances in Internet technology are evidence of the human value of skill, which promotes "the utilization of technological know-how for the development of our global civilization."[112] The human value of skill can promote a better world order and facilitate the protection of human dignity. While Internet technology has served criminal communities in making it easier to commit cybercrimes, including sex and trafficking crimes, its power must also be harnessed in the context of international laws to develop innovative antitrafficking methods. This process can be especially effective if authorities collaborate and partner with the business sector, particularly with the Internet industry, to prevent and combat violations of children's rights and provide timely solutions to this growing concern.[113] Thus, when states develop anticybertrafficking policies with this value in mind, they promote and strengthen multistakeholder initiatives and partnerships. Different stakeholders, including technology companies, can help establish best practices in identifying, investigating, and interrupting potential online child sexual exploitation cases. Additionally, technology can facilitate reporting, confidential counseling, and assistance for child victims. Overall, the dissemination of resources and skills leads to purposeful changes for working toward realizing human dignity goals.

Affection

The human value of affection highlights a positive, inclusive approach that requires the Internet and its policies benefit the online community as a whole.[114] This human value refers to the dialogue and engagement of governments with all relevant actors in decision-making processes. For example, the multistakeholder model of the Internet Corporation for Assigned Names and Numbers (ICANN) echoes this value. This model recognizes the importance of promoting meaningful participation and cooperation among all stakeholders in policy development processes.[115] ICANN has a mandate to manage the Internet's naming system, which allows computers on the Internet to find one another and plays a crucial role in keeping the global Internet secure, stable, and interoperable.[116] This work reminds us that decentralization is one of the primary elements of the Internet's success.[117] ICANN makes the Internet accessible to human beings by promoting the global public interest of the Internet without controlling online content or online access.[118] Thus, through its policies and procedures, ICANN contributes to Internet governance and impacts the evolution of the Internet and rights and freedoms of Internet users by protecting freedom of expression and freedom of association. It operates for the benefit of the whole Internet community. ICANN's decisions and operations should consider human rights considerations to strengthen transparency and accountability in the Internet governance arena while improving its ability to serve the public interest.

Furthermore, the preamble to the UN charter is another example that relates to this value. It asserts that one of the UN's goals is "to unite our strength to maintain international peace and security," affirming the importance of cooperation among nations via treaties to achieve common purposes. Overall, mechanisms for international cooperation in protecting children's human rights and dignity in cyberspace include "mutual legal assistance treaties, direct law enforcement cooperation, multi-agency partnerships, forums for information-sharing, and informal direct law enforcement cooperation."[119] Public-private partnerships also play a key role with more than 50 percent of responding states having reported that they had established such partnerships to prevent and combat cybercrime.[120] In a human rights–based approach aimed at maximizing the value of affection to combat child exploitation in cyberspace, it is essential that the efforts of states are unified with those of all relevant key actors, including those in the private sector. Collective and collaborative work between governments and relevant key actors can help prevent these crimes, enhance techniques for the investigation of alleged cyberoffenses, prosecute cybercriminals, and help identify and rescue child victims.

Respect

The Internet was not initially designed to handle the level of sensitive data and activity that it carries now. The Internet has expanded considerably in both its sophistication and usage, growing from a user population of "just over 6 per cent of the world's population in 2000 to 43 per cent in 2015," or 3.2 billion people.[121] As of March 31, 2021, there were approximately 5,168,780,607 Internet users across the world.[122] Within this massive network of individuals and organizations, the human value of respect should be the core of Internet activities as human beings "reciprocally recognize and honor each other's freedom of choice about participation in other value processes."[123] All individuals are entitled to effectively participate in all community value processes. For example, the ICCPR recognizes "the inherent dignity and of the equal and inalienable rights of all members of the human family."[124] In the same way, Article 1 of the UDHR affirms that "all human beings are born free and equal in dignity and right."[125] Thus, the human value of respect entails recognizing human dignity and equal and inalienable rights and the freedom of all human beings without distinction of any kind.

In an anticybertrafficking context, respect recognizes the value of the participation and contributions of all stakeholders, including the private sector (e.g., owners of online products), NGOs, and academia in the development of tools, measures, and policies for the prevention and combat of cybertrafficking.[126] UNGA Resolution 65/230, unanimously adopted at the Twelfth UN Congress on Crime Prevention and Criminal Justice, endorses the Salvador Declaration, which underlines the importance of protecting human rights when preventing crime in the justice system.[127] This important document also recognizes the vulnerability of children and the importance of strengthening public-private partnerships and coordinated actions, calling upon the private sector to promote and support efforts to prevent the abuse and exploitation of children in cyberspace.

In 2011, the UN special representative of the secretary-general, John Ruggie, presented his final report, *Guiding Principles on Business and Human Rights: Implementing the United Nations "Protect, Respect and Remedy" Framework* for consideration by the HRC. He submitted these guiding principles to provide business enterprises with guidance on managing and reducing human rights–related risks that may involve them.[128] Fundamentally, this framework describes the state's primary duty to protect against human rights abuses by private actors.[129] The guiding principles define the responsibility of transnational corporations and other business enterprises to respect human rights, requiring that they take the following actions:

1. Avoid causing or contributing to adverse human rights impacts through their own activities, and address such impacts when they occur.
2. Seek to prevent or mitigate adverse human rights impacts that are directly linked to their operations, products or services by their business relationships, even if they have not contributed to those impacts.[130]

Therefore, companies should follow all applicable domestic laws and take the opportunity to promote policies and processes in harmony with universal human rights standards. In this regard, business enterprises should identify, prevent, and mitigate the risk of their involvement in adverse human rights impacts. These impacts may result from their own activities or be directly associated with their business relationships with other parties (e.g., operations, products, and services).[131] Consequently, the guiding principles consider businesses responsible for respecting human rights, implying their need to address potential and actual adverse human rights impacts that they may cause. Accordingly this basic responsibility of businesses requires adhering to human rights due diligence policies and processes to minimize the occurrence of human rights harm.[132] These actions refer to preventing adverse human rights impacts on children and may include developing efficient reporting and content-removal mechanisms to protect sexually abused and exploited minors.[133] At the same time, companies should support the realization of children's rights online.[134]

Corporate responsibility to respect children's rights exists independent of states' legal obligations.[135] In 2019, the CRC urged states parties of the OP-CRC-SC "to ensure that Internet service providers control, block and remove [sexually abusive imagery and videos] as soon as possible as part of their prevention measures."[136] When companies assume a commitment to respect human rights and, specifically, respect children's rights in cyberspace, they ensure that their policies take into account children's best interests. Companies should prevent individuals from misusing their operations, products, or services for criminal purposes such as causing harm to children. For example, they should prioritize severe acts or situations where a delayed response may have an irreparable effect on children's lives.[137] In doing so they will effectively contribute to ensuring children's well-being and safety in cyberspace while avoiding the risk of being implicated in an infringement of human rights by being perceived as an accomplice or beneficiary of a child's harm or abuse.[138]

Private entities or intermediaries constitute relevant stakeholders. They provide services and platforms to facilitate online communications and operations ranging from ISPs and search engine companies to blogging services and online community platforms.[139] In his report to the HRC, UN Special Rapporteur Frank La Rue affirmed that intermediary companies are responsible for respecting human rights and recommended they comply with international human rights standards through "clear and unambiguous services" showing respect for human rights.[140] Additionally, La Rue cautioned states about the importance of avoiding placing intermediaries in a position where they may be involved in human rights abuses that violate the rights of others.[141]

Based on a framework of corporate social responsibility and respect for the safety of children, ISPs should apply child protective strategies to prevent and mitigate the risk of the occurrence of these criminal activities in their infrastructures and services. At the same time, they should collaborate with law enforcement agencies to facilitate the detection and investigation of these crimes and provide mechanisms for online users to report incidents of possible child sexual abuse. The competent authorities, for their part, should take these acts seriously, keeping children's best interests (i.e., online safety) as their primary consideration. The strengthening of collaborative efforts between law enforcement authorities and ISPs should facilitate gathering information for investigation and prosecutorial purposes of suspected offenses.[142] Concomitantly, international cooperation is necessary to address these offenses expeditiously as they often transcend borders.

It should be clear that the transnational dimension of practices related to online sex trafficking poses significant new legal challenges for governments. Variations and a lack of appropriate legislation across countries demonstrate the need for a universal understanding to overcome the shortcomings of and impediments to successfully protecting children against these types of offenses over the Internet and facilitating international cooperation. Therefore, current developments and safeguards require government actions to obtain consensus on the most effective ways to protect children. Regulation and law enforcement activities related to the investigation and prosecution of this crime could be improved, for example, by enhancing interstate collaboration and coordination regarding evidence collection, the protection of child victims, and the removal of CSAM. National legal approaches or inconsistencies in legislative languages among countries otherwise create difficulties in identifying and locating offenders and protecting child victims when a crime of this nature is committed abroad.

Thus, anticybertrafficking policies informed by the value of respect recognize the equal dignity of human beings and involve the collaborative efforts of both public and private sectors and stakeholders across national borders. National legislation and policies should also seek to strengthen the role of families in protecting children against commercial and noncommercial forms of trafficking for the purpose of sexual exploitation both online and offline.

Rectitude

States have assumed a legal obligation to protect human rights under international law, which compels governments to respect, protect, and fulfill human rights.[143] "Rectitude" in the context requires that everyone act responsibly for the common good toward approximating a world public order in which the human dignity of children is better protected online. In the context of anticybertrafficking, the value of rectitude promotes cooperation among stakeholders to fulfill their duties to the community in order to achieve public order.[144] For example, at a strategic national level, collaborative efforts among countries have resulted in a common practice to combat trafficking in children. An example is the close collaboration between the U.S. Immigration and Customs Enforcement (ICE) and governments and NGOs in foreign countries to locate, investigate, gather evidence, and prosecute child sex tourists from the United States and to rescue their victims.[145] In addition, in 2004 the ICE Human Smuggling and Trafficking Center was created to prepare strategic assessments, coordinate trafficking initiatives, and exchange information with allies and partners including Interpol, Europol, and Frontex.[146]

Furthermore, since 2004 the Safer Internet Forum has been an excellent example of the EU's facilitation of sharing best practices and experiences among national stakeholders at a regional level in Europe. Using a multi-stakeholder approach, this annual international event has become a significant reference for raising awareness, promoting research, and facilitating policy efforts.[147] Overall, with the growing and changing threat of cybercrimes, it is necessary to ensure well-coordinated transnational investigations, enhanced public-private partnerships, and effective policy prevention measures to restore the public order to allow for the realization of human aspirations while eliminating the crime of online sex trafficking of children.

Coordinated and collaborative work by all key actors will facilitate dialogue toward a consistent global response to strengthen child safety online. The strengthening of collaboration is essential to the enhancement of prevention initiatives and protection measures. These efforts should include services for child victims of online sexual exploitation to help them recover and rebuild their lives. The Palermo Protocol notes that "policies, programmes and other measures . . . as appropriate, include cooperation with nongovernmental organizations, other relevant organizations and other elements of civil society."[148] Thus, it recognizes the importance of joint efforts among all stakeholders. The cooperation of all relevant actors including governments, the private sector, academia, NGOs, parents, educators, the children themselves, and the community at large will facilitate greater dissemination of information, better coordination, and improved responses to children. Moreover, the OHCHR's "Recommended Principles and Guidelines on Human Rights and

Human Trafficking" highlights the importance of collaboration. The guidelines insist that all states develop

> national plans of action to end trafficking. This process should be used to build links and partnerships between governmental institutions involved in combating trafficking and/or assisting trafficked persons and relevant sectors of civil society.[149]

Regarding cyberspace, the ECOSOC urges member states to promote a commitment to corporate social responsibility principles for ISPs and mobile phone companies to combat the sexual exploitation of children online.[150]

Thus, for durable and sustainable solutions, these collaborative efforts among relevant stakeholders are of utmost importance. Notably, the Internet industry is a critical player in maintaining a safe Internet, raising awareness, and empowering children against online risks related to sexual exploitation. For instance, a collaborative and coordinated response will facilitate interdisciplinary research to better understand these cyberoffenses and the factors that enable them, helping law enforcement better prevent and counter them.

CONCLUSION

States bear a primary responsibility to protect children and ensure their human rights in cyberspace. Each government's goal should be to exercise its power to protect the fundamental rights promised by the UDHR. Through a set of legal rules, states work to achieve specific objectives that safeguard individuals in their entire social context and, thus, act with the ultimate goal of achieving a public order of human dignity. Such a public order would afford full access by all and for all to enjoy all things valued by human beings in life. In this particular case, each state's ultimate goal is to promote a legal order that advances children's rights and well-being. Such a goal is in the common interest of a public order in which human dignity and well-being are enhanced in cyberspace.

States have the legal obligation to effectively protect children from abuse by third parties, including abuses facilitated by the digital space and considered cybertrafficking practices according to their obligations under international human rights law. In this way, states should take and strengthen action to prevent and combat child sexual exploitation online at the national and international levels. In this respect, by aiming to ensure respect for human dignity and protect the child's best interests, international human rights law standards can be applied in an online context, offering states a legal foundation to balance and defend the rights at issue.

Thus, governments play a fundamental role in enacting and implementing cybercrime legislative norms and frameworks to protect children online. Human rights protection can be applied to cyberspace context and communications via digital technologies and can guide governments in shaping fundamental conditions in law and policy to conform with the principles of legality and necessity and proportionality for achieving the legitimate aim of child protection.

Governments alone cannot effectively fight online child sexual exploitation. A comprehensive human rights approach to cybercrimes against children, specifically online child sex trafficking, requires multisectoral action by including the explicit criminalization of all forms of online child sexual exploitation and enhancing collaboration and coordinated responses among governments and the private sector, particularly the technology industry. By aiming to keep children safe online and support efforts by states, the guiding principles encourage technology companies to make human rights standards part of their policy to avoid human rights abuses in their platforms and services. Assessments of human rights impacts are necessary to identify, prevent, mitigate, and manage any adverse human rights impacts that involve children. Technology companies should commit to minimizing risk to children while expanding the online opportunities from which they can benefit.

The strengthening of public-private partnerships, according to the respective role and responsibility of each stakeholder, will lead to (1) increased research, (2) greater public awareness, (3) more-effective preventive measures, (4) awareness of digital citizen practices, (5) more effective identification and rescue of and support for victims, (6) establishment of online programs to aid and benefit victims (i.e., dissemination of information on victims' rights and facilitation of victims' report and self-identification into safe, supportive spaces), (7) increased gathering of digital evidence and cybertrafficking traces, (8) more-effective identification and prosecution of cybercriminals, and, perhaps most importantly, (9) a decrease in the number of online sexual predators—including traffickers and exploiters—who harm children and go unpunished.

This chapter mapped a landscape of legal and nonlegal recommendations and practical approaches to address one of the outstanding issues today. It established an anticybertrafficking framework that enshrines the values of human dignity as the beginning of a solution to gain insight into the direction of future policy decisions. These recommendations are in line with a holistic solution for enhancing the development of a comprehensive child protection response to make the Internet safer for children and improve their well-being online.

NOTES

1. The essence of this theory of law, often referred as the "New Haven School" or "policy-oriented jurisprudence," has been laid out in Harold D. Lasswell and Myres S. McDougal, *Jurisprudence for a Free Society: Studies in Law, Science and Policy*, vol. 1 (New Haven, CT: New Haven Press, 1992). See also Harold D. Lasswell and Myres S. McDougal, *Jurisprudence for a Free Society: Studies in Law, Science and Policy*, vol. 2 (New Haven, CT: New Haven Press, 1992).

2. McDougal and Lasswell define the term "world public order of human dignity" within the context of the New Haven School tradition. See Siegfried Wiessner, "The New Haven School of Jurisprudence: A Universal Toolkit for Understanding and Shaping the Law," *Asia Pacific Law Review* 81, no. 1 (2010): 51. In the New Haven nomenclature, the term "value" indicates preferred outcome. See Lasswell and Mcdougal, *Jurisprudence for a Free Society*, 1:336–338.

3. W. Michael Reisman et al., *International Law in Contemporary Perspective*, trans. G. D. H. Cole (New York: Foundation Press, 2004), 520–521.

4. Jean-Jacques Rousseau, *The Social Contract* (independently published, 2020), 10–13.

5. Ibid., 3.

6. Jean-Jacques Rousseau, *Rousseau: The Social Contract and Other Later Political Writings*, trans. and ed. Victor Gourevitch, 2nd ed. (Cambridge: Cambridge University Press, 2018), 41.

7. "Each of us puts his person and all his power in common under the supreme direction of the general will, and, in our corporate capacity, we receive each member as an indivisible part of the whole" (Rousseau, *The Social Contract*, 11).

8. U.S. Constitution, preamble.

9. Lasswell and Mcdougal, *Jurisprudence for a Free Society*, 1:30–31; Lasswell and Mcdougal, *Jurisprudence for a Free Society*, 2:737. See also Siegfried Wiessner and Andrew R. Willard, "Policy-Oriented Jurisprudence," *German Yearbook of International Law* 44 (2001): 96–112.

10. Siegfried Wiessner, "Law as a Means to a Public Order of Human Dignity: The Jurisprudence of Michael Reisman," *Yale Journal of International Law* 34, no. 2 (2009): 525–529. See generally W. Michael Reisman and Aaron M. Schreiber, *Jurisprudence: Understanding and Shaping Law* (New Haven, CT: New Haven Press, 1987).

11. Policy-oriented jurisprudence postulates dignity as a goal, with legal institutions part of the process of value shaping and sharing. See, generally, Myres S. McDougal and Harold D. Lasswell, "Jurisprudence in a Policy-Oriented Perspective," *Florida Law Review* 19 (1967): 486–500.

12. Myres S. McDougal, Harold D. Lasswell, and Lung-Chu Chen, *Human Rights and World Public Order: The Basic Policies of an International Law of Human Dignity*, 1st ed. (New Haven, CT: Yale University Press, 1980, 6.

13. W. Michael Reisman, "Legal Responses to Genocide and Other Massive Violations of Human Rights," *Law and Contemporary Problems* 59, no. 4 (1996): 75–76.

14. Mahnoush H. Arsanjani and W. Michael Reisman, "East African Piracy and the Defense of World Public Order," in *Law of the Sea in Dialogue*, ed. Holger Hestermeyer et al. (New York: Springer, 2011), 138.

15. Myres S. McDougal, "Perspectives for an International Law of Human Dignity," *Proceedings of the American Society for International Law* 53 (1959), 107.

16. ICCPR, preamble.

17. UDHR, art. 28 states, "Everyone is entitled to a social and international order in which the rights and freedoms set forth in this Declaration can be fully realized."

18. W. Michael Reisman, "Development and Nation-Building: A Framework for Policy-Oriented Inquiry," *Maine Law Review* 60, no. 2 (2008): 310–315.

19. McDougal, "Perspectives for an International Law of Human Dignity," 114.

20. Reisman, "Development and Nation-Building," 312.

21. Ibid., 310.

22. See UNGA, Resolution 71/177, Rights of the Child, A/RES/71/177 (January 30, 2017), para. 19 at 7.

23. United Nations Treaty Collection, "Status of Ratification: Protocol to Prevent, Suppress and Punish Trafficking in Persons, Especially Women and Children, Supplementing the United Nations Convention against Transnational Organized Crime," https://treaties.un.org/pages/ViewDetails.aspx?src=TREATY&mtdsg_no=XVIII-12-a&chapter=18&c.

24. Myres S. McDougal, W. Michael Reisman, and Andrew R. Willard, "The World Community: A Planetary Social Process," *UC Davis Law Review* 21 (1988): 900.

25. Europol, *Situation Report: Trafficking in Human Beings in the EU* (no. 765175) (The Hague: Europol, 2016), 12.

26. Valiant Richey, "Statement by OSCE Special Representative for Combating Trafficking in Human Beings on Need to Strengthen Anti-Trafficking Efforts in a Time of Crisis," OSCE, www.osce.org/secretariat/449554; UNODC, "COVID-19 Pandemic and Its Impact for Victims and Survivors of Trafficking in Persons," www.unodc.org/unodc/en/human-trafficking/Webstories2020/covid-19-pandemic-and-its-impact-for-victims-and-survivors-of-trafficking-in-persons.html.

27. Nicholas Tsagourias, "The Legal Status of Cyberspace," in *Research Handbook on International Law and Cyberspace*, ed. Nicholas Tsagourias and Russell Buchan (Camberley, UK: Edward Elgar, 2015), 13–29.

28. HRC, Resolution 20/8, "The Promotion, Protection and Enjoyment of Human Rights on the Internet," A/HRC/RES/20/8 (July 16, 2012), para. 1, at 2.

29. Ibid., para. 2, at 2.

30. Ibid., para. 3, at 2.

31. HRC, Resolution 26/13, "The Promotion, Protection and Enjoyment of Human Rights on the Internet," A/HRC/RES/26/13 (July 14, 2014), para. 1, at 2.

32. HRC, Resolution 32/13, "The Promotion, Protection and Enjoyment of Human Rights on the Internet," A/HRC/RES/32/13 (July 18, 2016), para. 1, at 3.

33. HRCttee, "General Comment no. 34, Article 19: Freedoms of Opinion and Expression," CCPR/C/GC/34, September 12, 2011, para. 15, at 4. For further reading, see Miloon Kothari, "The Sameness of Human Rights Online and Offline," in

Human Rights, Digital Society and the Law: A Research Companion, ed. Mart Susi (Abingdon, UK: Routledge, 2019), 28.

34. ICCPR, art. 2(1). See generally Eckart Klein, "The Duty to Protect and to Ensure Human Rights under the International Covenant on Civil and Political Rights," in *The Duty to Protect and to Ensure Human Rights*, ed. Eckart Klein (Berlin: Verlag A. Spitz, 2000), 295.

35. ICCPR, art. 2(1). See generally HRCttee, "General Comment no. 31[80]: The Nature of the General Legal Obligation Imposed on States Parties to the Covenant," CCPR/C/21/Rev.1/Add. 13, May 26, 2004, para. 10, at 4. See also the general non-discrimination provisions of Article 2(1) in HRCttee, "CCPR General Comment no. 18: Non-Discrimination," November 10, 1989, para. 1, at 1.

36. ICCPR, art. 2(3). See generally Eckart Klein, "Individual Reparation Claims under the International Covenant on Civil and Political Rights: The Practice of the Human Rights Committee," in *State Responsibility and the Individual, Reparation in Instances of Grave Violations of Human Rights*, ed. Albrecht Randelzhofer and Christian Tomuschat (The Hague: Martinus Nijhoff, 1999), 30.

37. OHCHR, "International Human Rights Law," www.ohchr.org/en/professionalinterest/pages/internationallaw.aspx.

38. W. Michael Reisman, Siegfried Wiessner, and Andrew R. Willard, "The New Haven School: A Brief Introduction," *Yale Journal of International Law* 32, no. 2 (2007): 575–582.

39. Klein, "The Duty to Protect and to Ensure," 297.

40. HRCttee, "General Comment no. 31[80]: The Nature of the General Legal Obligation Imposed on States Parties to the Covenant," para. 6, at 3.

41. ICCPR, art. 19(3).

42. Ibid.

43. HRCttee, "General Comment no. 34, Article 19," para. 22, at 6.

44. "The Application of Article 19 (3)" in HRCttee, "General Comment no. 34, Article 19," para. 21–36, at 5–9.

45. HRC, "Promotion and Protection of the Right to Freedom of Opinion and Expression, David Kaye," A/71/373, September 6, 2016, para. 57(a), at 23.

46. Klein, "The Duty to Protect and to Ensure," 295–302. See status of ratification, ICCPR, https://indicators.ohchr.org/.

47. VCLT, art. 26: "Pacta sunt servanda."

48. Ibid.

49. Ibid., art. 18: "Obligation Not to Defeat the Object and Purpose of a Treaty Prior to Its Entry into Force."

50. HRC, "Report of the Special Rapporteur on the Promotion and Protection of the Right to Freedom of Opinion and Expression, Frank La Rue," A/HRC/23/40, April 17, 2013, para. 79, at 20.

51. Ibid., para. 83, at 21.

52. UNGA, Resolution 68/167, "The Right to Privacy in the Digital Age," A/RES/68/167 (Jan. 21, 2014). See also HRC, "Report of the Special Rapporteur on the Promotion and Protection of Human Rights and Fundamental Freedoms While

Countering Terrorism, Martin Scheinin," A/HRC/13/37, December 28, 2009, para. 33–34, at 13.

53. HRC, Resolution 25/2, "Freedom of Opinion and Expression: Mandate of the Special Rapporteur on the Promotion and Protection of the Right to Freedom of Opinion and Expression," A/HRC/RES/25/2, April 9, 2014, at 1.

54. ICCPR, art. 17(1), (2).

55. UDHR, art. 12, states, "No one shall be subjected to arbitrary interference with his privacy, family, home or correspondence, nor to attacks upon his honour and reputation. Everyone has the right to the protection of the law against such interference or attacks."

56. HRCttee, "CCPR General Comment no. 16: Article 17 (Right to Privacy): The Right to Respect of Privacy, Family, Home and Correspondence, and Protection of Honour and Reputation," April 8, 1988, para. 1, at 1.

57. HRCttee, Ibid., para. 10, at 2.

58. HRC, "Report of the Special Rapporteur on the Promotion and Protection of Human Rights and Fundamental Freedoms While Countering Terrorism, Ben Emmerson," A/69/397, September 23, 2014, para. 30, at 12.

59. HRC, "Report of the Special Rapporteur on the Promotion and Protection of the Right to Freedom of Opinion and Expression, Frank La Rue," A/HRC/23/40, para. 29, at 8. See also, HRCttee, "General Comment no. 34, Article 19."

60. HRC, "The Right to Privacy in the Digital Age: Report of the Office of the United Nations High Commissioner for Human Rights," A/HRC/27/37, June 30, 2014, para. 28–30, at 10.

61. UNGA, Resolution 73/179, "The Right to Privacy in the Digital Age," A/RES/73/179 (January 21, 2019), para. 6, at 5. See generally HRC, "Surveillance and Human Rights: Report of the Special Rapporteur on the Promotion and Protection of the Right to Freedom of Opinion and Expression," A/HRC/41/35, May 28, 2019, para. 24, at 8.

62. UNICEF, *The Sale & Sexual Exploitation of Children: Digital Technology* (UNICEF Office of Research-Innocenti, 2019), 5.

63. HRCttee, "Concluding Observations on the Fourth Periodic Report of the United States of America," CCPR /C/USA/CO/4, April 23, 2014, para. 22(a), at 10.

64. ICCPR, art. 26.

65. ICCPR, art. 2(1).

66. HRC, "The Right to Privacy in the Digital Age," para. 35, at 12.

67. UNGA, Resolution 68/167, para. 4(b), at 2.

68. HRCttee, "CCPR General Comment no. 16: Article 17 (Right to Privacy)," para. 3, at 1.

69. Ibid., para. 4, at 1.

70. HRC, "The Right to Privacy in the Digital Age," para. 21, at 7.

71. HRC, "Promotion and Protection of the Right to Freedom of Opinion and Expression, Frank La Rue," A/69/335, August 21, 2014, para. 4, at 3.

72. Ibid., para. 10, at 4–5.

73. UNCRC, art. 13(2).

74. HRC, "Promotion and Protection of the Right to Freedom of Opinion and Expression, Frank La Rue," A/69/335, para 11, at 5.

75. UNCRC, art. 5

76. HRC, "Promotion and Protection of the Right to Freedom of Opinion and Expression, Frank La Rue," A/69/335, para 22, at 7; HRCttee, "General Comment no. 34, Article 19," para. 21, at 5–6.

77. HRC, "Promotion and Protection of the Right to Freedom of Opinion and Expression, Frank La Rue," A/69/335, para. 31, at 9.

78. Steven Greer, *Human Rights Files no. 15: The Exceptions to Articles 8 to 11 of the European Convention on Human Rights* (Strasbourg: Council of Europe, 1997), 6.

79. "European Convention on Human Rights, as amended by Protocols nos. 11, 14 and 15," signed November 4, 1950, C.E.T.S. 5, art. 8(2).

80. Author's summary of the case *Trabajo Rueda v. Spain*, ECHR (3rd sec.) [May 30, 2017], no. 32600/12. See the press release issued by the registrar of the EctHR: "Granting police access to computer files containing child pornography material without prior judicial authorisation, in a non-emergency situation, violated the owner's right to respect for his private life" (ECHR 171, May 30, 2017).

81. Author's summary of the case *K.U. v. Finland*, ECHR (4th sec.) [December 2, 2008], no. 2872/02; *Stubbings and Others v. the United Kingdom*, ECHR [October 22, 1996], 36–37/1995/542–543/628–629, § 64.

82. *Dudgeon v. the United Kingdom*, ECHR (Plenary) [October 22, 1981], no. 7525/76, para. 52, at 17.

83. *D.P. & J.C. v. the United Kingdom*, ECHR (1st sec.) [October 10, 2002], no. 38719/97, para. 118.

84. ECtHR (Plenary), *Sunday Times v. the United Kingdom* (no. 1), (Application no. 6538/74), 26 April 1979, para. 49.

85. *Silver and Others v. the United Kingdom*, ECHR (Chamber) [March 25, 1983], no. 5947/72; 6205/73; 7052/75; 7061/75; 7107/75; 7113/75; 7136/75, para. 97, at 32–33.

86. *Observer and Guardian v. the United Kingdom*, 14 EHRR 153 [October 24, 1991], 51/1990/242/313, para 40(c).

87. "Case Relating to Certain Aspects of the Laws on the Use of Languages in Education in *Belgium' v. Belgium (Merits)*," ECHR (Plenary) [July 23, 1968], no 1474/62; 1677/62; 1691/62; 1769/63; 1994/63; 2126/64, para. 10.

88. See Case of *Handyside v. the United Kingdom*, ECHR (Plenary) [December 7, 1976], no. 5493/72, para. 49, at 18.

89. "European Convention on Human Rights, as amended by Protocols nos. 11, 14 and 15," art. 10(2).

90. In *Handyside v. the United Kingdom*, para. 49, at 18–19, the court regarding the criteria of duties described in Article 10(2) states that "whoever exercises his freedom of expression undertakes 'duties and responsibilities' the scope of which depends on his situation and the technical means he uses."

91. Ibid., para. 48, at 18.

92. Ibid., para. 49–50, at 18–19.

93. Lasswell and Mcdougal, *Jurisprudence for a Free Society*, 1:31; Lasswell and Mcdougal, *Jurisprudence for a Free Society*, 2:38; Mcdougal, Lasswell, and Chen, *Human Rights and World Public Order*, 11.

94. Roy Balleste, "In Harm's Way: Harmonizing Security and Human Rights in the Internet Age," in *Cybersecurity and Human Rights in the Age of Cyberveillance*, ed. Joanna Kulesza and Roy Balleste (Lanham, MD: Rowman & Littlefield, 2015), 42.

95. Danah Boyd, Heather Casteel, Mitali Thakor, and Rane Johnson, "Human Trafficking and Technology: A Framework for Understanding the Role of Technology in the Commercial Sexual Exploitation of Children in the U.S.," www.microsoft.com/en-us/research/wp-content/uploads/2016/02/en-us-collaboration-focus-education-htframework-2011.pdf.

96. Mcdougal, Lasswell, and Chen, *Human Rights and World Public Order*, 9.

97. ICCPR, art. 19(1), (2).

98. UDHR, art. 19.

99. HRCttee, "General Comment no. 34, Article 19," para. 15, at 4.

100. HRC, "Report of the Special Rapporteur on the Sale of Children, Child Prostitution and Child Pornography, Maud de Boer-Buquicchio," A/HRC/28/56, December 22, 2014, para. 68, at 17.

101. Lasswell and Mcdougal, *Jurisprudence for a Free Society*, 2:738.

102. UDHR, art. 25(2).

103. ICCPR, art. 24.

104. UN, "Declaration of the Rights of the Child," preamble.

105. Ibid., principle 2.

106. The premise that "the best interest of the child shall be a primary consideration" can be found in UNCRC, art. 3(1); OP-CRC-SC, art. 8(3); and UNGA, "Optional Protocol to the Convention on the Rights of the Child on the Involvement of Children in Armed Conflict," entered into force February 12, 2002, U.N.T.S. 2173, preamble.

107. UNCRC, art. 3(2).

108. See chapter 6.

109. WSIS, "Declaration of Principles: Building the Information Society: A Global Challenge in the New Millennium," WSIS-03/GENEVA/DOC/4-E, December 12, 2003, para. 11.

110. WSIS, "Plan of Action," WSIS-03/GENEVA/DOC/5-E, December 12, 2003, C10 (25c).

111. For further reading, see William H. Dutton, "Internet Studies: The Foundations of a Transformative Field," in *The Oxford Handbook of Internet Studies*, ed. William H. Dutton (Oxford: Oxford University Press, 2014), 8–9.

112. Balleste, "In Harm's Way," 47. For more information on the human dignity value of skill, see Lasswell and Mcdougal, *Jurisprudence for a Free Society*, 2:31; Lasswell and Mcdougal, *Jurisprudence for a Free Society*, 2:738; and Mcdougal, Lasswell, and Chen, *Human Rights and World Public Order*, 12.

113. For example, the OP-CRC-SC explicitly mentions in its preamble "the importance of closer cooperation and partnership between Governments and the Internet industry" when addressing child pornography.

114. For information on the human dignity value of affection, see W. Michael Reisman, "A Policy-Oriented Approach to Development," *Journal of International and Comparative Law* 3, no. 1 (2016): 146; and Mcdougal, Lasswell, and Chen, *Human Rights and World Public Order*, 13.

115. ICANN, "Bylaws for Internet Corporation for Assigned Names and Numbers," art. 1, sec. 1.1, www.icann.org/resources/pages/governance/bylaws-en/#article1.

116. ICANN, "What Does ICANN Do?" www.icann.org/resources/pages/what-2012-02-25-en.

117. ICANN, "Affirmation of Commitments by the United States Department of Commerce and the Internet Corporation for Assigned Names and Numbers," para. 2, www.icann.org/resources/pages/affirmation-of-commitments-2009-09-30-en.

118. ICANN, "Bylaws for Internet Corporation," art. 1, sec. 1.2.

119. UNODC, *Comprehensive Study on Cybercrime* (New York: United Nations, 2013), xi.

120. UNODC, *Comprehensive Study on Cybercrime*, xxvii, 225. See also ECOSOC, Resolution 2011/33, "Prevention, Protection and International Cooperation against the Use of New Information Technologies to Abuse and/or Exploit Children," E/RES/2011/33 (July 28, 2011), 2; and HRC, Resolution 31/7, "Rights of the Child: Information and Communications Technologies and Child Sexual Exploitation," A/HRC/RES/31/7 (April 20, 2016), para 21, at 6.

121. UN, We Can End Poverty, "Goal 8: Develop a Global Partnership for Development," www.un.org/millenniumgoals/global.shtml.

122. Internet World Stats, "World Internet Usage and Population Statistics: 2021— Q1 Estimates," www.internetworldstats.com/stats.htm.

123. Mcdougal, Lasswell, and Chen, *Human Rights and World Public Order*, 7.

124. ICCPR, preamble.

125. UDHR, art. 1.

126. A similar collaborative approach is promoted to effectively combat the global phenomenon of trafficking. See OHCHR, "Recommended Principles and Guidelines on Human Rights and Human Trafficking," Guideline 11, at 16: "Encouraging and Facilitating Cooperation between Nongovernmental Organizations and Other Civil Society Organizations in Countries of Origin, Transit and Destination."

127. UNGA, Resolution 65/230, "Twelfth United Nations Congress on Crime Prevention and Criminal Justice," A/RES/65/230 (April 1, 2011). See generally "Salvador Declaration on Comprehensive Strategies for Global Challenges: Crime Prevention and Criminal Justice Systems and Their Development in a Changing World" in UNGA, Resolution 65/230, "Twelfth United Nations Congress on Crime Prevention and Criminal Justice," para. 40, at 10.

128. HRC, "Report of the Special Representative of the Secretary-General on the Issue of Human Rights and Transnational Corporations and Other Business Enterprises, John Ruggie," A/HRC/17/31, March 21, 2011, para 16, at 5.

129. HRC, "Report of the Special Representative of the Secretary-General on the Issue of Human Rights and Transnational Corporations and Other Business Enterprises, John Ruggie," A/HRC/17/31, March 21, 2011, para A(1), at 6.

130. Ibid., A(13), at 14.

131. Ibid., 15 (also see A(13), at 14 for definitions of "activities" and "relationships").

132. Ibid., A(17), at 16.

133. See generally UNICEF and the Guardian, *Children's Rights and the Internet from Guidelines to Practice* (UNICEF and the Guardian, 2016), 22–24.

134. ITU, *Guidelines for Industry on Child Online Protection* (Geneva: International Telecommunication Union Publications, 2020), 2.

135. HRC, "Report of the Special Representative of the Secretary-General on the Issue of Human Rights and Transnational Corporations and Other Business Enterprises, John Ruggie," A/HRC/14/27, April 9, 2010, para. 65, at 14.

136. OP-CRC-SC Guidelines, para. 41, at 10.

137. Operational Principle 24, stating that "where it is necessary to prioritize actions to address actual and potential adverse human rights impacts, business enterprises should first seek to prevent and mitigate those that are most severe or where delayed response would make them irremediable." See HRC, "Report of the Special Representative of the Secretary-General on the Issue of Human Rights and Transnational Corporations and Other Business Enterprises, John Ruggie," A/HRC/17/31, 21.

138. For information on the concepts of sphere of influence and complicity in a corporate responsibility discourse, see HRC, "Clarifying the Concepts of 'Sphere of Influence' and 'Complicity'" in "Report of the Special Representative of the Secretary-General on the Issue of Human Rights and Transnational Corporations and Other Business Enterprises, John Ruggie," A/HRC/8/16, May 15, 2008, para. 30, at 9.

139. HRC, "Report of the Special Rapporteur on the Promotion and Protection of the Right to Freedom of Opinion and Expression, Frank La Rue," A/HRC/17/27, May 16, 2011, para. 38, at 11.

140. Ibid., para. 48, at 14.

141. Ibid., para. 44, at 13.

142. UNGA, Resolution 74/174, Resolution adopted by the General Assembly on 18 December 2019, A/RES/74/174 (December 18, 2019), para. 5, at 4; The Commission on Crime Prevention and Criminal Justice, Resolution 16/2, "Effective Crime Prevention and Criminal Justice Responses to Combat Sexual Exploitation of Children," (2008), para. 16, at 4.

143. States assume human rights obligations under treaties they have ratified. See Olivier De Schutter, "Part III The Mechanisms of Protection," in *International Human Rights Law, Cases, Materials, Commentary*, 3rd ed. (Cambridge: Cambridge University Press, 2019), 809.

144. Balleste, "In Harm's Way," 47; Reisman, "A Policy-Oriented Approach to Development," 146.

145. ICE, "Operation Predator: Targeting Child Exploitation and Sexual Crimes," www.ice.gov/factsheets/predator.

146. ICE, "Human Smuggling and Trafficking Center," www.ice.gov/human-smuggling-trafficking-center.

147. Better Internet for Kids, "Safer Internet Forum 2021," www.betterinternetforkids.eu/en-GB/policy/safer-internet-forum.

148. Palermo Protocol, art. 9(3).

149. OHCHR, "Recommended Principles and Guidelines on Human Rights and Human Trafficking," Guideline 1(3), at 3.

150. ECOSOC, Resolution 2011/33, "Prevention, Protection and International Cooperation against the Use of New Information Technologies to Abuse and/or Exploit Children," para. 14, at 4.

Chapter 8

Recommendations for Expanding the International Policy for Cyberspace

International law mandates that states take legislative measures and other actions needed to protect children's human rights and dignity.[1] Promoting a public order that supports such norms in cyberspace is an essential aspect of this protection. This chapter argues that adherence to international law, and establishing national norms, should provide the basis for it. This chapter discusses strategic developments to protect children from online sexual exploitation and trafficking in circumstances in which perpetrators can exercise powers of ownership over a child in cyberspace. It further provides an analysis of the role of international law in the formation and evolution of norms pertaining to these online activities, with attention to the sources of international law from which arise states' legal obligation to better protect children from online exploitation. Finally, the chapter proposes an internationally binding instrument that considers the unique legal challenges of cyberspace and a human rights–based approach to future decisions to ensure a more effective global response to this form of crime against children.

LEGAL OBLIGATIONS OF STATES

As established in previous chapters, the nature of the Internet poses specific challenges for states charged with two simultaneous responsibilities: protecting individuals from crime online, and ensuring human rights protections. International human rights norms are applicable in cyberspace: states' traditional international obligations emerging from conventional treaties or customary international law pertain also in the virtual world.[2] Therefore, the duty of states to protect children's human rights and human dignity derives from sources of international law. The International Court of Justice (ICJ) acts as the principal judicial organ of the UN, and the statute of the ICJ notes the following sources of international law:

- international treaties establishing rules expressly accepted by the states parties
- international customs evidencing a general practice among the international community of states accepted as law
- general principles of law
- judicial decisions and teachings of the most highly qualified publicists, as subsidiary means for determining rules of law[3]

For the determination of legal rules in international disputes, the ICJ applies the sources above to decide cases among states.[4] By virtue of Article 93 of the UN charter, member states of the organization are ipso facto parties of the statute of the ICJ, and nonmember states of the UN can also become a party to the statute.[5] This policy reflects a universal consensus among states on the sources of international law. Although the drafters did not express the sources' hierarchy, they highlighted an order for them. In practice, international conventions and international customs are most significant. International conventions prevail because they specifically establish obligatory character rules for states parties. According to international customs, treaties and customary international law may overlap such as in cases where treaties reiterate rules of customary international law.[6] Moreover, a treaty provision may be displaced by a rule of customary international law if the provision contradicts a peremptory norm of international law.[7] Therefore, it is impossible to make divisions using this order in all cases.

This set of norms in the international law framework also applies in cyberspace and contributes to the governing of online activities.[8] However, the international community must build consensus and common understanding on how it does so as this domain challenges how international legal Internet norms emerge, are interpreted, and evolve. Nevertheless the legal structure that shapes these rules does not vary. One example is the ongoing work of the UN Group of Governmental Experts (GGE), "Advancing Responsible State Behavior in Cyberspace in the Context of International Security" (2010, 2013, and 2015 reports transmitted by the secretary-general).[9] The GGE reports were drafted by experts seeking to cull emerging state norms for international peace, security, and cyberspace stability. In 2013 the GGE affirmed that "international law, and in particular the Charter of the UN, is applicable and is essential to maintaining peace and stability and promoting an open, secure, peaceful and accessible ICT environment."[10] Additionally, the GGE agreed on a substantive consensus on norms, rules, and principles of responsible behavior of states in the cybersphere and the applicability of international law to ICTs.[11] This report of the GGE reflects a landmark consensus among experts from twenty nations that existing international law should guide states to engage in normative legal development in cyberspace. These norms play a vital role in implementing states' responsible behaviors. The GGE's 2015 report further affirms compliance with the rules and principles of international law as essential to improve global security and promote an open and accessible cyberspace. In fact, the UNGA adopted resolution 70/237 in December 2015, unanimously calling upon member states to align their ICT use frameworks with the 2015 GGE report.[12]

As the principal actors in international law and the primary bearers of international obligations, states play a crucial role when creating, interpreting, executing, and enforcing most international rules. Arguably, the classic doctrine of the law of state responsibility is vis-à-vis states. "Vis-à-vis" pertains to interstate relations, that is, between injured states and wrong-doing states. In 1947, the UNGA established the International Law Commission (ILC), which provides important work on the understanding of international law. This commission is responsible for developing and codifying rules, including Draft Articles on State Responsibility, that codify state practice and operate primarily under the traditional doctrine parameters. In Article 1, the doctrine confirms the general rule that "every internationally wrongful act of a State entails the international responsibility of that State."[13] Thus a state breaches an international obligation when an internationally wrongful act (e.g., states' actions or omissions of one or more organs or agents) is attributable to that state under international law.[14] Additionally, the ICJ made an important note that states by virtue of their membership in the international community have obligations toward the international community as a whole (*erga omnes* obligations).[15] For example, in modern international law these obligations may arise from protecting human beings from slavery and racial discrimination wherein all states possess a legal interest in realizing these crucial obligations as they benefit all human beings.

States parties bound by a human rights treaty have an international legal obligation to promote and protect human rights and fundamental freedoms set out therein so that everyone in the state may enjoy them. However, as Eckert Klein points out,

> the traditional law of state responsibility only envisages entitlements of the injured State or States, and even the draft of the International Law Commission maintains this attitude. This limited approach has rightly been criticized because it does not take into account at all a whole category of international treaties, namely that of human rights treaties, thus neglecting important modern developments.[16]

Therefore, in the field of human rights, taking into account contemporary developments in international law, a broader approach to international state responsibility is necessary. Under international law, states have undertaken duties, such as carrying out the UN charter and various international instruments, to protect fundamental human rights. States parties of human rights treaties acquire explicit obligations to effect each treaty's provisions, acting in conformity with the principle of *pacta sunt servanda*.[17] In other words, when a state breaches a treaty-based international human rights obligation, the consequences may include the obligation of providing an effective remedy to victims by a competent domestic tribunal for human rights violations.[18]

Children are afforded special protection within international law.[19] The international community of states has recognized children's vulnerability to sexual abuse and exploitation, including in online realms.[20] The ratification of the UNCRC by 196 states parties (the most of any international convention) is reliable evidence of the universal importance of the human rights of children and exemplifies the intention of states to take the protection of children seriously.[21] At the same time, this broad acceptance indicates that the UNCRC's relevant provisions have also crystallized as expressions of customary international law because the state practice is articulated with a sense of obligation (*opinio juris*).[22] The UNCRC conveys that indifference toward children and their well-being, including their freedom from all forms of economic and sexual exploitation, is no longer tolerated globally. This consensus relies in part on a shared understanding that children's still incomplete development (physical, emotional, and cognitive) and limited knowledge and experience prevents them from being able to perceive and make decisions in their own best interest.[23] Such an understanding would help ensure the inclusion by the UNCRC and the Palermo Protocol of special provisions for children that protect them from harm.

There is a normative consensus that each child's best interests should be a primary consideration for states in all actions concerning them.[24] This principle presumes that the promotion and enhancement of children's well-being is a priority in states' national and international agendas. Under international law, states can be held responsible for wrongful acts committed by private persons or nonstate actors in cyberspace.[25] Failure of a state in its duty to protect the rights of children in its territory or under its jurisdiction can relate to a failure to take appropriate measures to prevent child exploitation by abusers (nonstate actors) and, when a criminal act has occurred, to respond to human rights violations in cyberspace.[26] In the context of the general obligations of states in the field of human rights, even if the state does not itself commit the violation it can be responsible for its own acts or omissions that breach an international legal obligation (e.g., if it fails to investigate a situation or prosecute and punish the perpetrators).[27] Therefore, the state's duty to protect includes providing special legal measures for victim protection, support, and access to redress while facilitating special procedures to investigate cases of exploitation or trafficking as part of its national response.[28] In compliance with the international legal standard of due diligence, states are mandated to such behaviors to prevent and respond to human rights violations of children, such as, inter alia, exploitation.

Under this human rights guidance, protecting children's human rights should be a central and prevalent concern in states' legislation.[29] Although the UNCRC does not directly address child sexual exploitation in cyberspace, it requires its states parties to apply a holistic approach to protect children's rights and asks them to consider all relevant areas of children's lives. This mandate includes fighting against all forms of sexual exploitation.[30] The UNCRC recognizes children as rights holders and considers their particular needs and rights.[31] Under international law, the state as protector should make combating all forms of online child sexual exploitation an integral part of its governmental policy. At the same time, the promotion of international security and stability in cyberspace requires the responsible behavior of states to strengthen standards and procedures on child protection.

Consequently, states have an imperative to penalize by legal means these illicit online activities. This obligation requires that national legislation, law enforcement, and prosecutorial and judicial bodies work to eliminate these forms of cybercriminality in the shortest possible time frame.[32] At the same time, states must secure justice for child victims. With this imperative in mind, the next section analyzes the state's legal obligations in light of international law's primary sources. This section examines whether states have accepted the practice of prohibiting online child exploitation as law through the lens of customary international law.

THE PROHIBITION OF ONLINE CHILD EXPLOITATION AS AN EMERGING CUSTOMARY LAW NORM

According to the statute of the ICJ, customary international law includes "general practice[s] accepted as law."[33] This postulate means that in order for customary law norms to come into existence, states must have the confluence of two elements: (1) a belief, subjective element of *opinio juris sive necessitates*,[34] that the state practice is rendered obligatory, and (2) the objective element, the repeated behavior of states (*diuturnitas*), with a substantial uniformity in practice to show a general recognition that a rule of law or a legal obligation is involved. For example, the ICJ in the Asylum Case between Colombia and Peru, relying on Article 38 of its statute regarding the requirements of custom in international law, specified the following:

The party which relies on custom . . . must prove that this custom is established in such a manner that it has become binding on the other party . . . that the rule invoked . . . is in accordance with a constant and uniform usage practiced by the States in question, and that this usage is the expression of a right pertaining to the State . . . and a duty incumbent on [the other State].[35]

Therefore, emerging legal norms could have the nature of customary international law recognized as an international law source. These norms bind states and result from an informal process that occurs over time. In this regard, states' conduct influences the formation, modification, or termination of a customary norm (customary process).[36] In other words, the state must believe—manifestations of *opinio juris*—that its actions are required by international law together with the practice of other states. However, new technological developments have shown the rapid formation of customary rules in cases involving technology. In the *North Sea Continental Shelf* case of 1969, the ICJ noted, regarding the status of emerging customs, "The passage of only a short period of time is not necessarily, or of itself, a bar to the formation of a new rule of customary international law."[37] Indeed, Judge Manfred Lachs and Judge Sørensen even in their dissenting opinions in this case confirmed the need to recognize a possibility for the expeditious development of customary international law in contexts of technological development where practice frequently precedes codification.[38] The development of new norms of space law demonstrates the relatively rapid consolidation of contemporary international laws in some cases (as Judge Lachs noted).[39] For example, the UNGA in 1963 unanimously adopted "Declaration of Legal Principles Governing the Activities of States in the Exploration and Use of Outer Space," which constituted customary international law in the assessment of outer space activities.[40] The principles enshrined in this declaration were recognized as a response to new technological developments despite their rapid emergence and short duration of practice. The rapid emergence of customary law norms in cyberspace does, however, necessitate discussion of the objective and subjective elements of general customary international law rules required to evidence an emerging norm of customary law.

The Objective Element: Uniform and Consistent State Practice

State practice does not need to have a universal application by the entire community of nations to identify general customary international law rules. Instead, the practice must be sufficiently widespread.[41] Although there is no specific requirement for the number of states that must engage in a practice before a custom emerges, the greater the number of engaged states, the greater the evidence that a norm has been formed.[42] Regardless, once a customary rule of general application has formed, it applies to all states including those who did not participate in the relevant practice that led to its establishment.[43] Significantly, customary international law rules can be general, binding all states, or particular, such as regional or local, and apply to a limited number of states, for instance, in a specific geographic area[44] or connected by a clear mutual interest or activity.[45]

It would be difficult to assess the relevant practice of all countries around the world and their corresponding legal views to determine whether a general customary norm on the prohibition of online child sexual exploitation has emerged. Moreover, some nations' conduct may reflect inaction, which would create difficulties for establishing the existence of the practice and the state's conviction on whether the practice may be legally compelled. However, the actual practice of individual states may be relevant for determining whether a consistent state practice exists and whether this practice is accepted as law (accompanied by *opinio juris*). In the international arena, acts of states by national authorities, such as the executive, legislative, and judicial branches, and others by which states exercise their powers can manifest their current conduct and legal position regarding a practice in question.[46] Therefore, state practice through national legislation, national courts' decisions, ratified treaty provisions, acts before international organizations, and international collaborations among law enforcement agencies—law in action—may be linked to this reasoning as a common cause. Such forms of relevant behavior by state authorities may reflect their conduct and potentially contribute to weighing the legality of this relevant practice.

Established National Laws

Australia

Australian legislation criminalizes any person "using a carriage service to procure persons under 16 years of age."[47] Thus any sender who uses a carriage service[48] to transmit communication to a person under sixteen (recipient) with the intent of procuring that person to engage in sexual activity commits a crime. Even without a detailed description, this provision may help address the recruitment of persons under sixteen for sexual exploitation (e.g., sex trafficking).[49]

China

According to Chinese legislation, ISPs must remove and report suspected online criminal activities and content as intended to pursue the purpose of ensuring information security and safeguarding the legitimate interests of individuals on China's computer network. Specifically, the "Decision of the Standing Committee of the National People's Congress on Preserving Computer Network Security" stipulates,

> Any unit that engages in the computer network business shall carry out activi-
> ties in accordance with law and, when it discovers illegal or criminal acts or
> harmful information on the computer network, shall take measures to suspend
> transmission of harmful information and report the matter to the relevant author-
> ity without delay.[50]

This legal provision can connect with "Implementation Measures Relating to the Temporary Provisions for the Management of Computer Information Networks in the People's Republic of China That Take Part in International Internetworks." This regulation prohibits the use of international Internetworks[51] to engage in criminal activities and produce or disseminate pernicious information, including pornographic materials. Once an ISP knows of the presence of this material, it must report it to the competent authorities promptly and take adequate measures to prevent the spread of the information.[52]

EU Member States

Online Grooming of Children for the
Purposes of Sexual Exploitation

Directive 2011/93/EU aims to harmonize national legislation among EU member states and enhance legal solutions to sexual abuse and sexual exploitation of children. This directive provides legal protection to children primarily from online grooming.[53] Therefore, this normativity may help criminalize elements that link to various forms of exploitation, such as sexual extortion of children. However, this protective measure may leave children above the age of sexual consent, as defined in national law, without protection.[54]

Concerning the implementation of this directive in some countries, the explanatory memorandum of Ireland's Criminal Law (Child Grooming) Bill 2014 highlights the importance of criminalizing both online and offline child grooming perpetrators. It notes that noncontact sexual abuse can occur even without a face-to-face meeting, and it may be too late to protect the child in question once grooming has already happened.[55] However, the bill admits the child's age as a possible defense, for example, if the child was seventeen years old at the time that the alleged crime was committed.[56]

Spain transposed this union law into national legislation by introducing a criminal code reform in 2015.[57] The newly added section 2 in Article 183 ter of the Spanish criminal code seeks to punish any person who uses an ICT, including the Internet, to contact a minor under sixteen years of age. The offender's intention must be to trick that child into providing or showing pornographic material of a minor.[58] Therefore, this provision in the Spanish criminal law system protects minors under the age of sexual consent—sixteen years old—from grooming involving pornographic images on the Internet.

In summary, member states are fitting their domestic criminal law to comply with community commitments, particularly about legal harmonization, to more appropriately respond to new criminal offenses, including the online sexual exploitation of minors. These progressive achievements of states are strengthening the child protection framework and digital security. Today most member states and the United Kingdom have taken the necessary measures to integrate this EU law into national law.[59] This transposition of the directive means states must introduce or adapt their criminal law to include ICTs in provisions protecting the fundamental rights and well-being of children.

Regulation on Data Retention

In 2016, the EU Parliament approved the General Data Protection Regulation (GDPR) to harmonize data privacy laws across Europe.[60] Although this legally binding regulation applies directly to EU countries, they were mandated to implement such provisions into national legislation by May 25, 2018.[61]

The GDPR requires the processing of personal data "by competent authorities for the purposes of the prevention, investigation, detection or prosecution of criminal offences or the execution of criminal penalties, including the safeguarding against and the prevention of threats to public security."[62] This regulation can be applied to combat Internet-facilitated child sex trafficking; specifically, the GDPR mentions that the permission of "processing of personal data relating to criminal convictions and offences" is granted on the basis of lawful processing, including "under the control of official authority or when the processing is authorised by Union or Member State law providing for appropriate safeguards for the rights and freedoms of data subjects."[63] In addition, the GDPR stipulates a principle regarding storage limitation, saying that personal data can be kept "for no longer than is necessary for the purposes for which the personal data are processed."[64] This principle can be read in conjunction with Directive (EU) 2016/680 that gives member states the power to "provide for appropriate time limits to be established for the erasure of personal data or for a periodic review of the need for the storage of personal data."[65] From a practical perspective, countries setting time limits on retention periods may reduce the risk of storing personal data longer than needed. Thus this regulation may help clarify technology companies' obligations concerning data preservation in the context of child protection online. In particular, criminal investigations and prosecutions of crimes, including those likely associated with online sex trafficking, should strike a balance between the need to secure data and the need for law enforcement to access information for child protection purposes. However, the fact that the GDPR does not explicitly address periods for data retention may lead to inconsistencies of time between countries' jurisdictions to preserve users' data that law enforcement can use in investigations.

This new data protection framework aligns with domestic legislation in EU member states and the United Kingdom.[66] Furthermore, these data protection standards may have a global impact as countries such as Argentina, Brazil, Canada, Colombia, Japan, and South Africa have adopted or are introducing data privacy laws aligned with the GDPR.[67]

Republic of the Philippines

Republic Act no. 9208, also known as the Anti-Trafficking in Persons Act of 2003, penalizes acts that

> advertise, publish, print, broadcast or distribute, or cause the advertisement, publication, printing, broadcasting or distribution by any means, including the use of information technology and the internet, of any brochure, flyer, or any propaganda material that promotes trafficking in persons.[68]

Therefore, the Philippines legislation penalizes actions that promote or facilitate trafficking in persons, including via digital technology.

South Africa

Prevention and Combating of Trafficking in Persons Act 2013 aims to prevent and address human trafficking in terms of the country's obligations acquired via international agreements. This law mandates that electronic communications service providers "take all reasonable steps to prevent the use of its service for the hosting of information" that promotes trafficking in persons.[69] Additionally, it mandates electronic communications service providers to identify any electronic communications containing such information stored or transmitted over its electronic communications system and to expeditiously report it to the South African Police Service.[70] Any electronic communications service provider that fails to comply with such provision is guilty of an offense.[71]

United States

Under U.S. federal law, statutes address the following offenses related to child sexual exploitation in the digital space.

Promotion or Facilitation of Prostitution and Reckless Disregard of Sex Trafficking

According to 18 USC § 2421A, any person who "owns, manages, or operates an interactive computer service, or conspires or attempts to do so, with the intent to promote or facilitate the prostitution of another person" commits a federal criminal offense.[72] This statute creates an exception to providers from the immunity granted by section 230 of the Communications Decency Act.[73] It can be considered an effort to curb online sex trafficking, particularly child exploitation content and the advertisement of commercial sexual services via websites with the intent to engage persons, including children, in forms of sexual exploitation (e.g., forced and child prostitution). For example, in 2018 the FBI seized www.backpage.com and affiliated websites using provisions of the Allow States and Victims to Fight Online Sex Trafficking Act of 2017 (FOSTA) legislation, which includes the Stop Enabling Sex Traffickers Act of 2017 (SESTA). FOSTA-SESTA allows law enforcement action against individuals and businesses, thus preventing sex trafficking victims, such as young girls, from being sold via online advertisements for sexual services.

Online Enticement of Children for Sexual Activity

According to 18 USC § 2422, it is a crime under federal law to knowingly induce, entice, or coerce a child—any person under eighteen years of age—to engage in prostitution or in any sexual activity.

Child Pornography

The following major penal statutes are related to online activities concerning CSAM:

1. 18 USC § 2251 regards offenses directly related to the production of child pornography. It bans any individual from persuading, inducing, enticing, or coercing any minor to engage in sexually explicit conduct in order to produce or transmit any visual depiction of that conduct. In addition, this statute criminalizes offenders who engage in advertising for minors with the intent to participate in child pornography (18 USC § 2251(d)(1)(B)) and advertising child pornography itself (18 USC § 2251(d)(1)(A)).
2. 18 USC § 2251A addresses the selling or buying of children for the purpose of producing pornography. Federal law prohibits any person, including any parent or legal guardian, from selling or transferring custody or control of a minor with the intent to engage the minor to produce visual depictions of sexually explicit conduct (child pornography).

3. 18 USC § 2252 prohibits any individual from knowingly possessing, receiving, or distributing any visual depiction that involves a minor engaging in sexually explicit conduct. Therefore, this description refers to nonproduction offenses.

4. 18 USC § 2252A penalizes any individual who knowingly receives or distributes child pornography (2252A(a)(2), (a)(3), (a)(4), and (a)(6)). Moreover, this section punishes any person who knowingly advertises or promotes child pornography (18 USC § 2252A(a)(3)). Violations under federal jurisdiction may occur by any means, including computer, and may include interstate or international commerce. Additionally, this statutory provision in subsection (a)(5) proscribes knowingly accessing with the intent to view any material that contains an image of child pornography on the Internet. Furthermore, an offense is committed under federal law if one "knowingly produces with intent to distribute, or distributes, by any means, including a computer . . . child pornography that is an adapted or modified depiction of an identifiable minor" (18 USC § 2256(7)). Notably, the provisions above (sections 2252 and 2252A) ban any person who knowingly sells any child pornographic material regardless of the intention to profit from the distribution.

5. 18 USC § 2256 defines child pornography as any visual depiction involving the use of a minor engaging in sexually explicit conduct. These explicit visual depictions include an actual minor engaged in sexually explicit conduct, a digital representation indistinguishable from an actual minor,[74] or an identifiable minor[75] (18 USC § 2256(8) (a)(b)(c)). According to legal definitions, "sexually explicit conduct" includes sexual intercourse, masturbation, bestiality, sadistic or masochistic abuse, or lascivious exhibition of the genitals or pubic area (18 USC § 2256(2)). This explanation means that a visual depiction of a child who is nude or partially clothed, and without the need to be portrayed engaging in sexual activity, may still be sexually suggestive to the point of qualifying as a child pornography offense under the federal law.[76] Notably, once a minor—any person under eighteen years of age—is exploited in child pornography, this constitutes a violation under federal law regardless of the age of sexual consent in a given state (18 USC § 2256).[77] In addition, visual depictions of child pornography materials include undeveloped film and videotape and digitally stored data capable of conversion into a visual image. This stipulation may set applicability in many cases to the federal jurisdiction for violations committed through the use of computers and the Internet when a visual image is transmitted, downloaded, or stored in a permanent format (18 USC § 2256(5)).

6. 18 USC § 2260 prohibits the production of visual depictions involving a minor in sexually explicit conduct for importation or transmission into the United States (18 USC § 2260(a)). Additionally, section 2260(b) makes it unlawful to possess with the intent to distribute child pornography material in the United States.

All these federal statutes include the penalization of attempted acts and conspiracies to commit such criminal acts, with severity of punishment scaling according to severity of crime.[78] For example, under 18 USC § 2251, a person can be fined and face a period of fifteen years (minimum) to thirty years (maximum) in prison. These circumstances can vary if the person has had previous incidents with the law or if the offense occurred in violent or aggravated situations (e.g., if the visual depictions are masochistic or sadistic, or involve sexual abuse). These situations can be aggravating factors that may, under certain circumstances, lead an offender to face life imprisonment.[79] Importantly, offenders' prosecution may be under federal or state law (or both) on child pornography offenses.

Responsibility of ISPs to Report Offenses

Per the mandate of 18 USC § 2258A, ISPs are required to report to the CyberTipline of the NCMEC when they obtain "actual knowledge of any facts or circumstances" about an apparent violation that involves child pornography activities. This means knowledge of websites or individuals producing any visual depiction involving the use of a minor engaging in sexually explicit conduct, selling or buying children, possessing or distributing child pornography, and deceiving children into viewing obscene material. The NCMEC forwards the report to the appropriate law enforcement agency to investigate. Therefore, this federal provision provides a legal reporting obligation of ISPs once they know or suspect incidents involving CSAM and child sex trafficking have occurred through their networks.

Global Initiatives: Law in Action

States must execute legally sound strategies to prevent child sexual abuse, protect victims, and investigate, criminalize, and prosecute cyberoffenders. Strategies to protect children in cyberspace may be revealed as states develop and strengthen national legislation and practices through international partnerships and alliances to share expertise, expand capabilities, and build collaborations with the private sector. The success of the following partnerships and law enforcement operations around the world demonstrate concerted efforts that have led to better protection of children online.

The WeProtect Global Alliance Model National Response

The WeProtect Global Alliance (WPGA) is a multistakeholder movement that brings together 98 countries and 123 organizations (53 companies, 61 civil society organizations, and 9 international institutions) to unite efforts and raise common standards to more effectively combat online child sexual exploitation.[80] In 2015, the alliance agreed to establish a coordinated response to this form of cybercrime. The WPGA Model National Response aims to provide guidance and support to governments, building and improving their response to this global problem. It aims to unite forces to penalize criminals and reduce this problem. This response identifies select capabilities that states must have in place for a complete national response, including further concrete action and partnership with technology companies and civil society.

For example, capability 3 identifies the need to criminalize all forms of child sexual exploitation (online and offline), identify perpetrators, and protect child victims. For adequate responses to apprehend offenders and protect child victims, a dedicated law enforcement capability is needed to conduct investigations and equip officers with the requisite knowledge, skills, tools, and resources (capability 4). Capability 21 refers to the need for universally agreed-on terminology to ensure a consistency of understanding in the context of online child sexual exploitation. Furthermore, capability 19 articulates the need for technology companies to bring attention to this issue voluntarily, following corporate social responsibility in their business practices. This capability aims to ensure company policy measures to appropriately identify, prevent, and mitigate child sexual exploitation activities or any violations concerning children's safety.

Some countries address this online problem as part of a successful strategy to enhance the security of their computer networks. For example, "the United Kingdom takes a lead on cross-border cybersecurity challenges through initiatives such as the WeProtect Global Alliance."[81] In this regard, when countries develop capabilities and strengthen international cooperation to deal with cybersecurity, combating this form of cybercrime comes to be seen as a critical aspect of national security.

Law Enforcement Investigative Techniques and Peer-to-Peer Operations

Law enforcement's role in detecting, investigating, and prosecuting these crimes is an essential aspect of the legal response. There are several outstanding international cooperation efforts by law enforcement agencies, including some with specialized units, to further investigations and prosecutions of crimes related to online child sexual exploitation. Joint and coordinated law enforcement action to protect children may involve Europol, Interpol, the FBI, the VGT, and others.

Europol
Europol identifies the use of anonymity tools (e.g., Tor) and the modality of the crime of livestreaming of child sexual abuse as critical threats against children in cyberspace.[82] Notably, Europol's priority crime areas (between the 2018–2021 and 2022–2025 EU policy cycles—EMPACT [European Multidisciplinary Platform Against Criminal Threats]) include the fight against online child sexual exploitation as a modality of cybercrime.[83]

Interpol
Interpol's ICSE database is a tool of intelligence and investigation that allows specialists to share data on child sexual abuse cases worldwide. Specifically, it uses sophisticated software to analyze and compare the visual and audio content of images and videos found on the Internet and other computer networks and seized devices to locate child victims and offenders across the world. Today it has helped investigators identify 23,564 child victims globally and holds more than 2.7 million images and videos of child sexual abuse.[84] A formal mutual legal assistance request via the Interpol National Central Bureau or through informal police-to-police cooperation requests facilitates access to this information for international investigations.[85]

The FBI
The FBI's Operation Pacifier (2015) and Operation Torpedo (2011) represent efforts to fight online child sexual exploitation via hidden services sites. Agents used network investigative techniques to access suspected websites and identify IP addresses linked to these sites' activities.[86] This information has helped lead to the arrest of anonymous viewers and possessors of CSAM on the Darknet and the rescue of sexually exploited children worldwide. In 2017, two years after taking down the Playpen website as a result of Operation Pacifier, the FBI's accomplishments included 350 arrests in the United States, the prosecution of 25 producers of child pornography in the United States, the prosecution of 51 hands-on abusers in the United States, the identification or rescue of 55 children in the United States, the arrest of 548 individuals internationally, and the identification or rescue of 296 children internationally.[87] According to information from the FBI, its field offices and international collaboration actions with countries and international agencies—including Europol, Israel, Turkey, Peru, Malaysia, Chile, Ukraine, CNCPO Polizia Postale e Comunicazioni of Italian State Police, the United Kingdom's National Crime Agency, and New Zealand's Department of Internal Affairs—contributed to the success of Operation Pacifier.

In practice, law enforcement authorities face significant challenges due to differences between countries' jurisdictions. Consequently, considering the transnational dimension of cybercrime and the volatile nature of electronic evidence, these challenges point to the need for a common approach between countries to overcome obstacles to the criminalization of online child exploitation offenses with an urgent area of focus being the prosecution of offenders and the safeguarding of child victims worldwide.

The VGT

The VGT works to establish an international coalition of law enforcement agencies that work together to effectively protect children from abuse online.[88] Since its establishment in 2003, the VGT has identified and investigated more than one thousand potential suspects and located and rescued hundreds of child victims worldwide. The VGT builds international partnerships and shares best practices among law enforcement colleagues to develop a collaborative approach, engaging all country members in this fight and channeling their efforts in the same direction. The VGT prepares current and future member countries with crucial and advanced resources to address online child sexual exploitation. Their work has substantially facilitated cross-jurisdictional investigations and information sharing through practitioner-level collaboration. Examples of VGT peer-to-peer operations include Operation Globe in 2016, Operation Atlas in 2015, Operation Endeavour in 2014, Operation Rescue in 2011, and Operation Basket in 2010.[89] Additionally, members of the VGT have highlighted the importance of a law enforcement framework for coordinating undercover operations on the Darknet and sharing security intelligence among law enforcement agencies to combat the sexual exploitation of children via livestreaming.[90] Involving state-level initiatives will likely augment the effectiveness of such transnational crime-fighting efforts, leading to faster criminalization of all aspects of online child sexual exploitation.

Digital Forensics and Emerging Technologies

Digital forensics examiners are concerned with the recovery and investigation of electronic material, whether stored or transient, that may have evidential value. In investigations, forensics tools that help ensure the integrity of the evidence collected include hash values. This analysis tool compares files to identify CSAM in a fast and accurate manner. It creates cryptographic algorithms (hashes) of an image to match it with a group list of child exploitation material (a hash database) to detect similar content without altering the data. Microsoft's PhotoDNA is an example of this innovative technology. This technology allows technology companies such as ISPs to identify and remove online child sexual exploitation images on their platforms and more efficiently report them to law enforcement or the NCMEC. Other countries have also implemented this forensic tool such as the IWF in the UK.[91]

However, it is essential to remember that this technique may not have the same efficacy when websites and applications use more robust encryption technologies. Although security enhancements protect users' privacy rights, including the security of children's data (messages and content) transmitted over their systems, they may hinder law enforcement's ability to lawfully access individuals' communications for detecting child exploitation imagery and activity.[92] For the practice of law enforcement, this scenario requires, after appropriate legal authorization, first decrypting the contents of communications and then searching for material to investigate a child sexual exploitation case.

Indeed, while enhanced encryption mechanisms may benefit users' privacy, they can also impede law enforcement actions to find and prosecute offenders. In 2016, Facebook launched Secret Conversations[93] in Messenger to protect users' privacy using end-to-end encrypted communications. However, the software may also increase risks for children because it may protect offenders by impeding actions from law enforcement to identify and locate them. In 2020, Facebook reported a total of 20,307,216 suspected online exploitation incidents (i.e., potential cases of CSAM, child sex trafficking, and online solicitation or grooming of children) to the NCMEC's CyberTipline. While Facebook information is not categorized according to various platforms and apps, this reported number was 94.7 percent of the total number of reports that CyberTipline received from these providers (21,447,786).[94]

In 2019, Facebook announced the implementation of end-to-end encryption for all private communications across its network, including Instagram and WhatsApp. Specifically, Mark Zuckerberg, Facebook CEO, outlined the company's vision and principles around developing its privacy-focused social network proposal, which would increase the privacy and security protections of users' data.[95] This approach concerns the future of the Internet and may help accomplish some objectives regarding personal data protection. However, there would be a trade-off that could imply an increased risk of serious crimes, including child sexual exploitation.[96] This proposed Facebook approach would limit information sharing and the facilitation of collaborative responses with law enforcement because it could cover child exploitation criminals' tracks and thus undermine efforts to bring exploiters to justice and to safeguard victimized children.

WhatsApp is a privacy-focused platform. WhatsApp offers an encrypted messaging service that protects all private content and does not store data or encryption keys. This service may pose additional challenges for law enforcement authorities particularly for data retention and preservation for criminal investigation of an offender and for the safeguarding and support of a child victim.[97] The absence of computer data or communication contents may bring difficulties for law enforcement in detecting and prosecuting offenders, obtaining evidence of digital traces for investigations (IP addresses), and identifying child victims' locations.

Reflection on State Practice

At the international level, these examples of practice by states and their competent authorities (e.g., national legislation, policies, and practices) describe states' particular behavior individually and jointly with others. Hence, these legislative and law enforcement responses and measures help determine the existence of consistent practice and states' actual positions regarding the prohibition of online child sexual exploitation. In the current global legislative landscape, states have demonstrated national progress toward achieving the goal of child protection. Countries seem to be moving to a more effective way of combating online child sexual exploitation practices. Some states are making ongoing efforts, and others are strengthening their measures and good practices to prevent and fight virtual child sexual exploitation activities.

There is some consensus among states on the criminalization of this area of cybercrime. In the last decade, online forms of child sexual exploitation have become a new challenge of globalization. Evidence indicates that countries can enhance international networks and coordination against these abuses committed against children in the online world. Arguably, states wish to continue improving legislation and other measures to prevent and address this problem. Even though countries' practices can reflect divergent approaches to online child sexual exploitation, with different concepts and definitions in their legal systems, these practices demonstrate a relatively uniform intention overall. The growing global trend of countries making progressive steps toward best practices for this fight is a crucial development in the context of customary international law. As noted above, neither absolute consistency nor any specific duration is required for the presence of a customary law to be inferable. At present, countries are consistently moving toward appropriate legislation and more robust measures to protect children from such exploitative acts. There is thus a usage (*usus*) that describes the existence of a practice of state authorities regarding a particular behavior. The consistent conduct of states may also reflect a special and prevalent consideration of the principle of the child's best interests in cyberspace.

The Subjective Element: *Opinio Juris* (Acceptance as Law)

The second component required to evidence the presence of a customary law is *opinio juris*. The conduct of states in their international relations reveals a consistent opposition to online child exploitation and consistent development to better protect children from being targeted and victimized by offenders in cyberspace. Nevertheless, states' own free will manifested in the practice of prohibiting online child sexual exploitation does not reflect their conviction in the existence of a new rule of law.[98] Therefore, the current practice of states prohibiting such online predatory behaviors may not necessarily evidence a corresponding *opinio juris*. There is no sign that states operate with a constant or uniform practice as accepted as law. Globally, national legislation and responses from states prohibiting online activities of this kind reflect discrepancies in legal definitions, offenses, and human rights safeguards. In addition, some countries show poor implementation or enforcement of needed practices and others may not have any legal provisions to protect children online.[99]

States' sovereign consent does not reflect that such particular behavior, depicted in the customary practice, is recognized by other states as having the force of law.[100] Consequently, states' activity must depend on a perception of a legal obligation, which would create a customary law norm. It may be argued that this is an emerging customary law norm that may develop over a short period of time via the two mandatory requirements. Currently, a consistent practice of states arguably exists to condemn online criminal activities with the intent to sexually exploit children—the element of uniform state practice—which contributes to the rapid emergence of this new cyberspecific customary law. Additionally, consistent state practice continues to strengthen with measures to fulfill this particular obligation of penalizing child sexual exploitation in cyberspace. However, the element of *opinio juris* could still be considered to be in formation. In this instance the state practice of prohibiting online child exploitation may not imply that states perform such practice in a manner that reflects their belief or causes other states to believe that a new obligation has emerged. In other words, there may not be such a belief of states articulating *opinio juris*, and it manifests in their conviction as legally obligating them to undertake this relevant practice as if in compliance with a new norm of customary international law.

To summarize the points thus far on *opinio juris* regarding this topic, states recognize the vulnerability of children, and some are promulgating or strengthening appropriate legislation and other measures to adequately protect children from sexual abuse and exploitation online. Moreover, many countries are enhancing international cooperation efforts to curb abuses against children in the online world. However, this practice of countries on the prohibition of such acts may not yet reflect states' positive acceptance of a legally obligatory rule. Consequently, there may be cases of noncompliance of states with such a rule that may not manifest that their behavior would violate international law. However, a legally binding custom in this matter may have an accelerated formation compared with historical precedents. It can still be considered in an evolutionary process of norm creation as there is a lack of *opinio juris* of states helping to generate a binding legal rule accepted as law and, in this sense, establish customary international law. Unlike a treaty with written norms, once a relatively consistent practice of states operated in conjunction with their affirmative consent and even over a short period of time, this new cyberspecific customary norm on the prohibition of online child sexual exploitation would come into existence and, therefore, legally bind them to act. Once this occurred, if most states agreed that such a new norm of customary international law prohibiting online child exploitation has emerged, then special protections for children as a vulnerable group would crystalize in cyberspace. One primary implication of the emergence of a general custom as a rule of law is that this new status of a particular cybercrime would raise the possibility of its use in court decisions. For example, it could be used in domestic or municipal courts as appropriate once adopted under the national legislative process. Therefore, this development would create international case law requiring states to take specific measures to fulfill their legal obligation under international law.

Today, international regulations and norms in this matter are still developing. In addition, the obligation of states to exercise due diligence to prevent, investigate, and punish offenders and to protect and assist child victims may contribute to the process of generating *opinio juris*, engaging nations in the practice of prohibiting cyberspace-related child sexual exploitation with a sense of legal obligation and thus finding themselves contributing to the development of a rule of customary international law. State authorities must continue to improve responses toward the comprehensive protection of society's most vulnerable members by ensuring the cover of all these offenses under their penal law. Furthermore, states must ensure the investigation of all such suspected crimes for the purpose of sexual exploitation through cyberspace. All countries must make more progress and be more comprehensive primarily to ensure shared understandings to reduce legislative discrepancies and facilitate the prosecution and punishment of perpetrators worldwide. States must adapt their national legislation to the challenges new technology brings in this matter. However, regulation has yet to become a general rule of customary international law and to thereby bind states generally.

POLICING ONLINE CHILD SEXUAL EXPLOITATION

Developing an Effective Legal Protection Framework

International law mandates states to promote and respect human rights and fundamental freedoms enshrined in the charter of the UN and underscored in the International Bill of Rights. States are obliged to prohibit activities likely associated with online sex trafficking by private actors. Overall, states must protect legitimate interests and achieve child protection goals consistent with international human rights law. This obligation includes the prevention of such activities, the identification and apprehension of child sexual exploitation offenders, and the protection of child victims with full respect for individual rights on the Internet. States must ensure compliance with their obligations under international law to strengthen the fight against this form of cybercrime. States must provide a secure cyberspace for children by increasing their resources, national capacities, international coordination and cooperation mechanisms, and response systems to better protect children in the digital environment.

The treaties discussed in previous chapters, such as the Palermo Protocol and the OP-CRC-SC, while applicable to cybercrime, were not intended for cyberspace. At the time of their adoption in 2000, communications technologies were not as widespread and developed as they are now, so drafters were not focused on crimes in the online environment. The extraordinary change in the nature of these crimes has complicated these Protocols' interpretation and highlights the need for a seperate binding instrument. States should ensure children in their territories do not become targets and victims of cybercriminals who intend to exploit them. Gaps in policies and procedures need to be bridged to improve antitrafficking responses online and may require national and international responses.

States' international commitments play an essential role in the promotion of international policy. The global dimension of child sexual exploitation in cyberspace affects all countries without distinction, and the lack of a common approach among them represents significant legislative challenges for effective crime prevention and criminal justice response. These challenges, inter alia, include the following:

1. Differences in legal approaches may reveal a lack of relevant legislation on these crimes at the domestic level, overlapping roles among responsible governmental bodies, delays or imprecision of law enforcement in detection, and different levels of protection for child victims.[101] Notably, different legal approaches lead to various responses among all other relevant stakeholders such as private industry. Therefore, the industry

may be developing business practices on the same issue with different standards in place (e.g., risk assessment plans and processes dealing with online content, revisions and reports to law enforcement agencies).

2. The lack of alignment with international standards may present difficulties that are primarily visible in transnational cases. These cases may require cooperation in investigative measures such as collecting electronic evidence and prosecution across national boundaries. Globally, divergences in the scope of collaboration and procedures among countries will create difficulties in combating this cybercrime and in dealing with the computer forensics issues that arise. For example, states' discrepancies in legal definitions (such as the age of consent), misunderstandings or confusion in response time obligations, and variance in safeguards among jurisdictions may present obstacles to the prosecution of offenders, preservation of data, authorization in getting access to electronic data when necessary for a specific investigation, and searches and seizures across borders. For these reasons, common safeguards need to be in place for international cooperation with precise communication mechanisms at the interstate level, including effective communication among states on police cooperation and coordination for the expedited preservation of computer data. These measures will facilitate law enforcement's extraterritorial evidence gathering that may require timely responses and specialized investigative procedures to prosecute an offender and better fight this Internet-related crime.

3. Due to the lack of a common framework, there are deficiencies in official data collection and analysis. For example, data on the extent of this cybercrime, encompassing forms and the modus operandi of exploitation mechanisms and the number of child victims identified and offending perpetrators, may be inaccurate or misleading.

This problem highlights the urgent need for a harmonized and international legal response such as a human rights treaty for cyberspace—one that would protect children from activities that begin offline but continue online as well as those that start and end online. The objective of this new treaty would be to harmonize child protection measures in domestic legislation with uniform legal norms geared at safeguarding the dignity and integrity of children in the online environment.

With due respect to human rights in the information society, an international legally binding agreement would boost efficiency in the global fight against online trafficking. It would impose legal obligations on countries to strengthen their policies and practices to protect children in the digital space. This solution would include the criminalization of all forms of activity associated with online sex trafficking and necessary measures for ensuring that investigation, prosecution, and content removal across jurisdictions occur more efficiently.

The challenge in the borderless realm of cyberspace requires a legally binding instrument in line with current international standards to provide states parties with a legal basis for ensuring an appropriate balance between access for legitimate crime prevention and control purposes on the one hand, and on the other, respect for the rights and freedoms of individuals online, particularly the rights to freedom of expression and to privacy. To this end, when law enforcement authorities exercise investigative powers according to law, these must be necessary and proportional to the stated aim to achieve the goal of child protection. Lawful restrictions must comply with state obligations under international human rights law, meaning they must be the least intrusive possible and should not adversely affect the established rights of children or others. All persons must be able to use and enjoy ICTs, which can be essential tools for exercising human rights and accelerating progress and prosperity in society.[102] In this respect, human rights safeguards are necessary to avoid the negative impact on users' rights that may occur as a result of arbitrary practices such as censorship or restricted access in an effort to accomplish children's right to protection.

States parties to this proposed treaty would create legal obligations based on their consent to be bound and, therefore, perform the treaty precepts in good faith. Under this scenario, according to the fundamental international law principle of *pacta sunt servanda*, once states ratify a uniform treaty, states parties cannot invoke national law to justify a failure to fulfill the treaty. Instead, they acquire the legal obligation to put in force the provisions of the treaty at the domestic level.

Considering that treaties constitute one primary source of international law, states' adoption of a legally binding instrument addressing cyberexploitation practices would go some way toward filling the existing normative lacuna at the domestic level. Implementing a legally binding instrument to harmonize national policies and procedures and promote cooperation among nations would complement international standards. It would enhance preventive measures against these criminal activities and improve investigations and prosecution through a cooperative process across governments. Such an instrument must consider the particular nature of electronic evidence, victim protection provisions—for example, recovery and reparation—and mechanisms for collaboration with key stakeholders. In this manner, the process would promote a multisectoral response for safe and positive childhood experiences on digital platforms.

The enactment of a treaty explicitly dealing with the use of cyberspace in trafficking children for the purpose of sexual exploitation would establish a legal framework to criminalize these activities. It would also establish measures to optimize the response capacity of states in this type of borderless crime. A new international legally binding agreement would further guide states to the achievement of uniformity in national criminal legislation and procedures by adopting common standards in norms at the national level. More specifically, with the guidance of international human rights law, a new treaty would (1) help to enhance the protection and safety of children online by reducing criminality gaps that may create safe havens for offenders globally, (2) improve international cooperation mechanisms among governments for timely preservation and supply of digital evidence (criminal investigative measures), (3) intensify capacity building for law enforcement and criminal justice officials, including prosecutors and judges at the national level, and (4) foster public-private partnerships and collaboration to more effectively address this realm of online crime. In this way, legislation at the national level mirroring an international legal instrument would translate into a comprehensive and more straightforward legal framework for achieving the goal of child protection. In particular, this binding agreement would help states in adopting or improving national legislation and practices, including criminal law provisions, with a consistent understanding of universally agreed terminology. It would ensure a more robust law enforcement machinery, including a dedicated and specialized capacity to investigate and prosecute cases with due diligence and improve international cooperation to advance information-sharing and procedural tools involving electronic evidence across borders.

Regarding the private sector, this international agreement would facilitate multistakeholder collaboration among relevant key players. Finally, based on principles set out in the UNCRC, this treaty could encourage child participation in policy and practices in a matter that concerns them directly. Children's and young people's voices and views could be heard in the decision-making process.

In light of states' international human rights obligations, a new legally binding agreement would require states parties to enact more robust measures to fulfill their duty to protect children from harm. Central components of a complete national response combat—through detection, investigation, and prosecution—cyberperpetrators of trafficking-related exploitation, including those who operate across borders. A comprehensive response would also protect child victims by responding to them in a victim-centered framework and preventing future abuse online.

Furthermore, states would potentially engage in a dialogue among the negotiating states parties and collaborate in drafting provisions as state practice has already demonstrated engagement in the prevention and combat of online child sexual exploitation through national legislation and other measures. This progress of states toward more appropriate responses would promote a less intensive negotiation process of the treaty. Based on current developments, during the negotiating process concluding this potential uniform legally binding cyberspecific child-protective treaty, governments would dialogue on current practices, collaborations, and possible future commitments, which would help them achieve consensus during the preparatory work of this online child protection framework convention. In particular, this treaty would require states to adequately address legislative gaps to penalize all forms of online sex trafficking, protect child victims, and prevent offenders from evading prosecution. At the same time, it would supplement states' current responses to child sex trafficking and exploitation.

The Relationship between a Potential Treaty and the Crystallization of an Emerging Customary Law Rule

The adoption of a treaty, particularly if it secures a higher level of ratification from states, crystallizing this emerging customary rule on prohibiting online child sexual exploitation as gaining acceptance of this state practice as law among individual nations—affirmative international consensus (*opinio juris* existence)—would form a cybercustom.[103] States would undertake this relevant practice with the sense of a legal obligation, and as such it would reach the status of customary law, giving the practice a binding character. In this scenario, the practice would acquire the authority of a general rule of international law, requiring states to treat it as a matter of law. As the ICJ has noted, multilateral conventions can play an important role "in recording and defining rules deriving from custom, or indeed in developing them."[104]

The practice of nonparties in this treaty in their interstate relations, when in conformity with conventional provisions, may demonstrate their legal inclination (acceptance as law) to this relevant practice. Therefore, state behavior would establish the rule as a rule of customary international law.[105] Consequently, if a general rule on this matter were to emerge, it would help to fill the treaty's legal gaps or any ambiguities that may require outside reference or interpretation. At the same time, if a state is not part of the treaty, in some circumstances that state may nevertheless be bound by a norm of customary law embodied in the agreement.[106] Therefore, if states engage in this practice as outlined in the treaty or a new norm of customary international law, this scenario would help define the actions needed against perpetrators.

The Challenge for the Adoption of an International Legislative Framework: Verifying Compliance

Within this approach, one primary challenge to overcome in adopting a treaty in a cybertrafficking context would be the general absence of a compulsory enforcement mechanism to verify states parties' compliance with the treaty's terms and implementation. Although a monitoring mechanism does not guarantee that states parties fully comply with their assumed legal obligations as a party to a treaty, establishing a monitoring mechanism contributes to greater compliance by states parties to a treaty. Thus a monitoring mechanism would help states meet the objectives of a treaty that they have already agreed to on paper, making it effective in practice.

To this end, a monitoring body of experts would be responsible for supervising and monitoring the implementation of the treaty obligations by states parties in a way similar to the monitoring of core international human rights instruments.[107] For example, the ICCPR, one of the essential instruments for the protection of civil and political rights, created and dictated a clear mandate to the HRCttee for monitoring regarding governments' compliance with the treaty's obligations.[108] In the ambit of human rights protection, the power of the HRCttee is one of authority to ensure that governments are accountable for the performance (e.g., actions and omissions) of their legal obligations and meeting the desired expectation of the specific rights and treaty-based standards contained in the ICCPR in good faith. Accordingly, in a similar process and based on a treaty mandate, states parties would assume the obligation to submit regular reports to the monitoring body on the steps they have taken to incorporate the treaty's provisions at the domestic level. The monitoring body would examine the reports and provide observations to states parties discussing concerns and recommendations.[109] In addition, as part of this monitoring function, the body would elaborate in general comments on selected provisions of the treaty to aid states parties in better interpreting and applying these provisions. Once the new treaty established a committee of independent experts—acting in their personal capacity and serving with these critical functions to monitor compliance—this committee would guide states parties to achieve the ultimate objectives of the convention.

A UN General Declaration as a Precursor to an International Legally Binding Instrument

The fact that this area of cybercrime is of common interest to governments would likely lend urgency and force to the formation of collaborations and cooperative efforts to combat child exploitation in cyberspace. The relative uniformity of attitudes among nations toward protecting children may facilitate a UN general declaration that would reflect current developments and help clarify evolving and emerging international customary law.[110] The declaration drafting process would occur with the formation of a consultative committee to oversee the elaboration of this declaratory instrument. The declaration would serve as a standard of reference for states and directly influence their practice of protecting the dignity and well-being of children online. If the UNGA adopted a general declaration in this regard, it would offer an important insight into the emerging and collective opinion of member states. At the same time, a UN general declaration could enable a gradual transition to the drafting and implementation of a treaty in which states would acquire legally binding obligations.

An important precedent is the UDHR, an example of a declaration whose ideas galvanized support and were transformed into legally binding instruments. In 1948, the new UN Commission on Human Rights, charged with creating an international bill of rights, initiated its work by preparing a draft declaration and concluded its task by drafting two treaties instead of one. After a protracted negotiation process among states, the UNGA adopted them by consensus in 1966. These treaties are the ICCPR and the ICESCR.[111] According to this precedent, although a potential UN general declaration would have a non–legally binding character, it would reflect the commitment of member states to safeguard the human rights of children and promote the rule of law in cyberspace. This UN general declaration would provide recommendations to states on this particular international issue, taking into account the child's best interests as a primary consideration in the online realm. Consequently, this soft-law instrument (i.e., non–legally binding to states) would promote fundamental principles for child protection in the digital space. Once adopted, it would have the effect of advancing relevant conduct for states by prohibiting online practices that have the intent of sexual exploitation of children, and it would therefore be the first step to beginning the process of creating a treaty.

Normative Guidance for a Global Online Child Protection Policy

In a holistic global approach, international law, including international human rights law, guides states in building global legal frameworks. According to international human rights law, children require special protection by law. Based on the principle of sovereignty of states, which applies in cyberspace, states should take measures that include the prevention, prohibition, and criminalization of these practices by nonstate (private) actors in the online domain according to their obligations under international law. States should pursue responses to strengthen the fight against this form of cybercrime and its proliferation globally. Currently, there is no specific international binding agreement addressing Internet-related sexual abuse of children.[112] To eliminate safe havens for perpetrators, a human rights treaty addressing trafficking of minors for the purpose of sexual exploitation in an area of criminality not covered by existing legislative instruments would harmonize core elements of online offenses against children that states would translate into national laws.

The international community of states needs to strengthen responses to cybercriminal offenses within national legal systems by following international law standards. A potential international legally binding instrument would ensure that certain types of online activities are considered criminal offenses under national legal systems. Such an instrument could help states adjust or introduce appropriate national laws to combat these cybercrimes by improving crime prevention strategies and criminal justice responses. In light of criteria established by international law, a legislative framework would provide states with clear guidance on the criminalization of these behaviors and, thereby, strengthen online child protection measures in cyberspace. This international legislative framework would establish uniformity in states' legal obligations, including human rights guarantees. The guidance of these clear rules and procedures would help states take action according to the principles of legality, necessity, and proportionality. Therefore, this international legislative framework, under a comprehensive human rights–based approach consistent with international standards and norms, would help countries holistically combat this form of cybercrime by guiding them in the following aspects.

Harmonization of National Laws

This would be the primary purpose of a uniform cyberspecific treaty. The transnational nature of these online offenses necessitates creating an international solution that implements common policy norms covering substantive criminal law, procedures, and international cooperation rules. Therefore, this treaty would provide a legal basis and a practical framework for implementing adequate legislation. This shared understanding of states would include the penalization of offenses related to commercial and noncommercial sex trafficking of minors committed or facilitated through the use of computer systems—online sex trafficking of children—at the national level. Acts and activities related to these criminal activities would include

- grooming or enticing children for purposes of exploitation online or offline
- recruiting, using, procuring, or offering a child—advertising and selling—in electronic form for sexual exploitation purposes in the virtual or physical world
- arranging services and purchase (buying and selling) and related offenses for the specific purpose of exploitation of a child
- possessing pornographic materials, including imagery and videos of a child for extortion purposes of that child online or offline
- producing, transmitting, or knowingly accessing with the intent to view performances of child abuse and exploitation through livestreaming
- committing offenses related to CSAM

Including Acts Related to CSAM

The problem of CSAM remains significant worldwide. This treaty should provide legal standards to countries to criminalize visual representations, including depictions that may be sexually suggestive (i.e., associated with provoking a sexual response from the observer), which have the intention to sexually exploit children. In addition, it must also criminalize audio recordings intended to incite sexual excitement or gratification in the listener, which is also for child sexual exploitation purposes. Moreover, the prohibition of producing, offering or making available, distributing or transmitting, procuring, accessing with intent to view, or possessing regardless of an intent of distribution must be explicit, without leaving the criminalization of any of those acts to the discretion of states. The penalization of such exploitative acts must be applied regardless of whether the person engaged in the sexually explicit conduct is a minor, a person who looks like a minor, or a realistic image of a nonexistent child.

Children's Consent Should Be Irrelevant in Online Sex Trafficking–Related Practices

The consent of a child—any person under eighteen years of age—who has been recruited, bought, sold, or maintained for exploitative practices through cyberspace should be rendered irrelevant. At the same time, offenders should not use it as a defense.[113] Such offenders' actions demonstrate their effective control over a child with the intent of their sexual exploitation. For example, an offender can engage a child in forms of commercial or commodified sexual activities such as commodified relationships. As described in chapter 4, these relationships often link to exchange for remuneration or other forms of consideration to the child through the digital space.[114] Modern practices that reflect trafficking elements such as exploitation of the child (e.g., as a sexual object or commodity) are prohibited under international human rights law.

Identifying and Prosecuting All Online Child Sexual Exploitation Offenders

In the online trafficking context, the investigation and prosecution of all activities likely associated with online sex trafficking may involve various criminals. The fight against these online activities includes identifying and bringing to justice individuals who commit noncontact child offenses for the purpose of sexual exploitation regardless of any intent to meet a child offline. That said, all offenders who abuse cyberspace, including the Internet, to commit, facilitate, or otherwise promote the sexual exploitation of children would be accountable. In addition, this postulate aligns with current international standards such as Article 9(5) of the OP-CRC-SC, which mandates to states parties the criminalization of the promotion of sexual exploitation of children.[115]

This construction includes the prosecution of offenders who seek financial gain, preferential access to exploitative child material online, or sexual gratification from a child. Therefore, this criminalization would apply to individuals who disseminate information to support, encourage, or facilitate virtual or physical child-exploitative acts and activities. Examples include individuals who interact with other like-minded individuals who may be anonymous contacts in groups or forums on the Darknet to discuss countries or places with flexible laws or weak law enforcement to access children or to identify those more vulnerable to abuse to engage them in sexual acts offline.

Protecting and Supporting Child Victims: A Victim-Centered Approach in Cyberspace

Legal norms concerning the pursuit of a common criminal policy should also uphold an approach to the protection and support of children. Protection measures for victimized children should make the child's best interests a primary consideration, including assessing their needs and helping them rebuild their lives. This postulate includes implementing measures for child victims' recovery and the possibility of making available appropriate remedies. Assistance, treatment, and care for child victims, specifically meeting children's special needs, is essential in the fight against online exploitation. As these criminal acts cause harm to the well-being, health, and safety of children, countries should provide support and assistance to child victims, including psychological assistance, in cooperation with civil society organizations such as NGOs to cover all children's needs.[116]

Improving International Cooperation

Given that forms of crime linked to online sex trafficking often transcend state borders, eliminating or reducing them requires facilitating international cooperation. A comprehensive and aligned global framework is critical to improving state strategy at the domestic level primarily to ensure investigation and prosecution of offenders and the protection of child victims who may live in another jurisdiction.

In light of this, enhanced, practical, international cooperation mechanisms are needed among governments for accessing, preserving, and securing digital evidence with clear international standards. This will make it possible to achieve consensus among countries to improve elements of international cooperation to combat the online trafficking of children especially in circumstances where there may be an immediate threat of harm that requires a prompt response across jurisdictions and borders. States should address issues that may relate to international collaboration associated with this criminal matter of online exploitation of children as one of the highest priorities.

Training Law Enforcement and Other Relevant Authorities

Training and technical assistance are essential components to effectively combat this growing international problem. States' efforts should include training for law enforcement (both specialized and nonspecialized personnel) and the judiciary at the national level. Training should cover prevention and exchange of good practices to better fight this crime. For example, training should include discussions on the importance of fostering a multistakeholder approach with technology companies, NGOs, academia, and other elements of civil society.

Effectively Engaging States with Relevant Stakeholders (Partnerships and Collaborations)

This treaty would set solid foundations for strengthening a multiactor or multistakeholder collaboration approach. Considering that "everyone has duties to the community," as recognized by the UDHR,[117] the involvement of governments with other stakeholders, according to their roles and responsibilities, is necessary to effectively eradicate illegal sexual content of children and fight against online sex trafficking. In this respect, as part of a coordinated response, public and private sector efforts would include private-sector actors (including ISPs), child protection services, NGOs, academic institutions, and other key stakeholders.

Better delineating the role of the private sector in preventing and combating these practices in line with international standards will lead to the implementation of programs and procedures on digital child safety, including terms of use, rules of conduct, and codes of ethics and self-regulation, increasing responsibility in preventing and mitigating the potential and actual harmful effects of digital technology on children.

This legal instrument will promote better engagement of the technology industry and encourage more robust and transparent corporate policies and sound child-protection practices in compliance with international human rights law. Business action can support government efforts through mandatory standards and initiatives such as the promotion of human rights and digital security through cybercrime prevention strategies, child digital literacy, digital citizenship practices, accessible reporting tools, and positive Internet use for children. Consequently, business actions countering this growing threat against children connect to human rights due diligence processes to identify, prevent, mitigate, and manage risks related to online child sexual exploitation. At the same time, these processes will help foster trust and security in the digital space.

Corporate self-regulatory initiatives will lead to better assessment, risk prioritization, and concrete action plans when addressing any business impact on human rights regarding child sexual exploitation. Based on human rights standards, company commitments will contribute to eradicating these practices in balance with the need to ensure data security and privacy. In addition, company initiatives will help build an awareness of risk and educate children and other users on this issue, helping minimize risks to children online. Furthermore, it is essential that companies enforce more robust identification and takedown processes to remove or block access to CSAM, which will help reduce both the further distribution of content and revictimization of child victims.

Additionally, with the help of the technology industry and as part of a collaborative, multisectoral approach, law enforcement personnel must increase their skills and knowledge related to ICTs. A collaborative effort will allow law enforcement to become skilled in the field of trafficking and the technology that offenders, including cybertraffickers and their accomplices, misuse.

When appropriate, child protection services, NGOs, and other relevant organizations can help provide psychological counseling and assistance to online child victims. In addition, academic institutions can further the research in this area. Overall, the participation and engagement of all citizens and sectors of civil society is vital to effectively prevent and combat the online sex trafficking of children.

Overall, there is a need for various stakeholders to be involved in ending online sex trafficking and related offenses. Prevention measures will include education for children according to their age and maturity on how to safely use the Internet, the risks and traumatic consequences associated with sexual exploitation, and how to obtain help and support. For example, it is essential that children know that once their images or videos are shared with others online, they lose control over these images and the images never really disappear as they can remain on the Internet permanently. In addition, children should know that anyone who asks a child to engage in sexual activity online must be reported to their parents or a trusted person and the police. Protecting children against the practices associated with online sex trafficking is everyone's job.

Summary of Current Needs

States are mandated to respect international law in cyberspace. The applicability of international human rights law in cyberspace implies a necessity to protect human rights and fundamental freedoms online. Currently, governments must strengthen their efforts and measures to fight cybercrime against children. Based on international consensus, a cyberspecific treaty would provide specific degrees of uniformity in national criminal legislation and policies in a comprehensive, human rights–centered approach. In this case, states would address substantive criminal law aspects, prevention, and child protection related to online trafficking activities for sexual purposes. Consequently, this treaty will promote harmonized national laws and treaty-based protections in particular vis-à-vis the limits of human rights online such as the rights to freedom of expression and to privacy.

At the international level, the application of a legally binding instrument will serve governments by helping them fulfill their duty to protect children and strengthen legislation, policies, and practices that address these criminal misuses of information technologies. This normative framework will also promote the responsible behavior of states in cyberspace. This legally binding international instrument will provide common protection standards to national authorities and a basis to strengthen each state's capacity to address this problem in cyberspace. In particular, this treaty would aim to enhance prevention, detection, and response mechanisms. Additionally, under this human rights approach, the establishment of an international legislative framework will promote a multistakeholder collaboration within the respective roles and responsibilities of nonstate actors. In particular, it will call for more involvement of the private sector as an essential partner in government efforts to prevent and combat child sexual exploitation through the use of ICTs. The following section proposes a draft of a treaty and analyzes its potential contributions toward implementing a future legal regime that will effectively improve the global community response for protecting children against sexual exploitation in cyberspace.

Sample of a Draft Treaty

To codify a harmonizing core of offenses to fight the phenomenon of online sex trafficking of children, the Palermo Protocol, the UNCRC, the OP-CRC-SC, and the CoE Convention on Cybercrime should serve as standards of reference for a new draft binding international agreement that will prohibit the use of cyberspace to victimize minors for the purpose of sexual exploitation. Thus this treaty should have, as its primary purpose, the establishment of a common criminal policy addressing these digital offenses. It should contain, at a minimum, the twenty-three articles included in the following draft.

* * *

*Draft Treaty on the Prevention, Prohibition, and Penalization
of Online Activity for the Purpose of the Sexual Exploitation
of Children—Online Sex Trafficking of Children*[118]

PREAMBLE

The States Parties to this Treaty,

Recognizing that the Universal Declaration of Human Rights and the
International Covenants on Human Rights have proclaimed that everyone is
entitled to all the rights and freedoms set forth therein, without distinction
of any kind;

Bearing in mind that the Universal Declaration of Human Rights and the
UN have proclaimed that childhood is entitled to special protection, especially against all forms of cruelty and exploitation;

Recalling the provision of the Declaration of the Rights of the Child:
"The child, by reason of his physical and mental immaturity, needs special
safeguards and care, including appropriate legal protection, before as well as
after birth";

Conscious of the growing challenges that the development of information
technologies, globalization of computer systems bring and the importance of
protecting society, including children, against cybercrime;

Concerned by the risk that computer systems may be used for committing
criminal offenses concerning trafficking in children for the purpose of sexual
exploitation and that the evidence relating to such offenses may be stored and
transferred via computer systems;

Conscious of the need to protect children from being sexually exploited or
bought and sold as a commodity through cyberspace;

Convinced that the best interests of the child shall be a primary consideration even in cyberspace;

Convinced of the need to pursue, as a matter of priority, an international,
comprehensive, and legal common criminal policy to criminalize cybercrime,
inter alia, for trafficking in children for the purpose of sexual exploitation;

Taking into account the fact that despite the existence of a variety of
international instruments containing rules and practical measures to combat
exploitation, there is no universal instrument that addresses all relevant areas
of child exploitation when it is facilitated or committed through information
and communication technologies;

Concerned that in the absence of such an instrument, and bearing in mind the vulnerability of children to exploitation, children will not be sufficiently protected in cyberspace;

Convinced that the elimination of child sex trafficking will be facilitated by adopting a comprehensive approach addressing child exploitation in cyberspace;

Believing in the need for the present Convention to deter cyberpractices for the purpose of sexual exploitation of children, including in pornographic performances and materials, prostitution, commodified sexual activities, in the travel and tourism industry, or otherwise exploiting a child for such purposes;

Mindful of the need to protect the rights of the child by implementing appropriate legislation and fast and reliable cooperation mechanisms between States to facilitate the detection, investigation, and prosecution of criminal offenses;

Recognizing the need to ensure a proper balance between effectively combating cybercrime and protecting legitimate interests and due respect for and adequate protection of fundamental human rights and liberties in cyberspace, including the right to freedom of expression and privacy;

Considering the 2000 Protocol to Prevent, Suppress and Punish Trafficking in Persons, Especially Women and Children, Supplementing the UN Convention against Transnational Organized Crime; the 1989 UN Convention on the Rights of the Child; the 2000 Optional Protocol to the Convention on the Rights of the Child on the Sale of Children, Child Prostitution and Child Pornography; the 1999 International Labour Organization's Worst Forms of Child Labour Convention; and the Stockholm Declaration and Agenda for Action, adopted at the First World Congress against Commercial Sexual Exploitation of Children (August 1996);

Believing in the value of fostering international cooperation with other States Parties to this convention in that it facilitates a coordinated response at domestic and international levels;

Recognizing the need for closer cooperation and partnership between governments and the private sector, especially with the technology industry, in accordance with their responsibilities to prevent and combat cybercrime, including child exploitation, and the need to protect the human dignity of children via information and communication technologies;

Have agreed as follows:

I. GENERAL PROVISIONS

Article 1

The provisions of the present Convention shall complement the legal child protection standards and be interpreted on the basis of the meaning set forth in the UN Optional Protocol to the Convention on the Rights of the Child on the Sale of Children, Child Prostitution and Child Pornography, the UN Protocol to Prevent, Suppress and Punish Trafficking in Persons, Especially Women and Children, and the International Labour Organization Convention No. 182 (1999) concerning the Prohibition and Immediate Action for the Elimination of the Worst Forms of Child Labour.

Article 2

The purposes of this Convention are:

 a. To prevent and combat the use of computer systems for the purpose of child sex trafficking and exploitation;
 b. To protect and assist child victims, with full respect for their human rights;
 c. To foster cooperation among States Parties in order to meet those objectives.

Article 3

For the purposes of this Convention:

 a. "Computer system" means any device or group of interconnected devices that share a central system operating independently with the ability to connect with other related devices and to perform the automatic processing of data.
 b. "Computer data" means any display of information, facts, or concepts in a manner appropriate for computer system processing, including in the form of programs that enable a computer system to execute a function.
 c. "Service provider" means:
    i. Any entity, either public or private, that enables its users to communicate via a computer system, and
    ii. Any entity that processes or stores computer data for these communication service providers or their users.
 d. "Traffic data" means any computer data processed or stored by a computer system that relates to a communication and that may indicate the

origin, destination, route, time, date, size, duration, or any other type of information that is part of the process of the communication.

e. "Online sex trafficking of children" means:

The use of computer systems, networks, and computer data to engage in the recruitment, solicitation, offering, advertisement, transportation, sale, transfer, harboring, or receipt of a child for the purpose of sexual exploitation regardless of the child's consent. Sexual exploitation shall include, at a minimum, the sexual exploitation of children in prostitution or other forms of sexual exploitation, sexual services, slavery or practices similar to slavery, or sexual servitude.

For the purposes of the present article, it shall be considered online sex trafficking of children with or without the use of means of the threat or the use of coercion, fraud, deception, the abuse of power or a position of vulnerability, or the giving or receiving of payments or benefits to achieve the consent of a person having control over a child for the purpose of sexual exploitation.[119]

Article 4

The consent of the child is irrelevant in practices concerning online sex trafficking. It shall be considered online sex trafficking in children when a child is involved for the purpose of his or her sexual exploitation.

Article 5

A child means every human being below the age of 18 years.

II. PREVENTIVE MEASURES

Article 6

States Parties shall protect children from cybertrafficking activities. For this purpose, States Parties shall take all appropriate policies, programs, and other measures to prevent the use of computer systems, networks, and computer data for:

a. The sale of children for the purpose of sexual exploitation;
b. The trafficking of children for the purpose of sexual exploitation;
c. The exploitative use of children for sexual purposes;
d. The facilitation of any of the above actions.

III. CRIMINALIZATION

States Parties shall ensure that, at a minimum, the following activities in cyberspace are fully covered under their domestic criminal law when committed intentionally, whether such offenses are committed on an individual basis or via organized groups and whether intended for commercial or non-commercial purposes.

Article 7: Offenses regarding child sexual abuse material (child pornography)

States Parties shall prohibit the production, distribution, procurement, access with intent to view, or possession of any visual depiction, audiovisual and audio recordings, whether transmitted, made available, or produced by electronic means, that involve the use of a minor engaging in sexually explicit conduct or intended for sexual purposes, which includes material that represents an actual minor or an individual who appears to be a minor or a realistic depiction of a minor.

Article 8: The facilitation of the sexual exploitation of children in prostitution

States Parties shall prohibit the use of a child in sexual activities where a transaction in cash or in kind to the child or to one or more third parties is given, promised, or remunerated.

For the purposes of the present article, the use of a child in sexual exploitation in prostitution shall include:

a. Committing cyberthreats or other forms of coercion, fraud, or any means of inducing a child to engage in commodified sexual acts;
b. Luring or recruiting a child for the purpose of sexual exploitation of the child in the commercial sex trade;
c. Promoting, offering, advertising, obtaining, buying, or selling a child for sexual services;
d. Arranging the sexual services of a child;
e. Conducting transactions, such as money transfers, with the intent to sexually exploit a child.

Article 9: The facilitation of the sexual exploitation of children in travel and tourism (child sex tourism)

States Parties shall prohibit the use of a child for the purpose of sexual exploitation in travel and tourism.

For the purposes of the present article, "the use of a child for the purpose of sexual exploitation in travel and tourism" shall mean:

a. Promoting, offering, advertising, obtaining, buying, or selling a child for sexual purposes in a destination place;
b. Arranging travel with the intent to engage the child in the sex trade or other forms of sexual exploitation.

Article 10: The facilitation of online child sexual abuse via livestreaming

States Parties shall prohibit the use of a child to participate in pornographic performances through livestreaming, regardless of distribution for profit or any other form of consideration, and shall include the criminalization of the following acts:

a. Coercing or recruiting a child for the purpose of the exploitation of that child through pornographic performances through livestreaming;
b. Producing live sexual interactive content of a child for the purpose of transmitting such performances;
c. Knowingly accessing with the intent to view sexual interactive content of a child through livestreaming.

Article 11: The facilitation of sexual extortion of children

States Parties shall prohibit the luring or coercing of a child with the intent to acquire sexual abuse material from the child for the purpose of extorting the child to perform sexual acts or obtaining sexual materials, money, or any other benefit from the child based on that sexual material or imagery possession.

Article 12: The solicitation of children for sexual purposes (grooming)

States Parties shall prohibit the process of luring or coercing a child in order to establish a relationship with the child with the intent of soliciting that child for sexual purposes, which includes viewing and engaging in exploitative sexual practices, whether in person or through a computer system.

Article 13: The facilitation of the sale of children for noncommercial sexual exploitation

States Parties shall prohibit the sale of a child for the purpose of noncommercial sexual exploitation facilitated via computer systems. For the purposes of the present article, the term the "sale of a child for the purpose of noncommercial sexual exploitation" shall include:

   a. The facilitation of child marriage, which includes offering or advertising a child, for the purpose of exploitation.
   b. The facilitation of illegal adoption, which includes offering or advertising a child, for the purpose of exploitation.

Article 14: Attempt and aiding or abetting

1. States Parties shall apply the same measures to an attempt or conspiracy to commit any of the said acts, complicit participation in any of the said acts, or organizing or directing others to commit any of the said acts through a computer system, network, or computer data.
2. States Parties shall undertake measures to make such offenses against children punishable by appropriate penalties in the national law, considering their grave nature.

IV. PROCEDURAL LAW

Article 15: Powers and limitations

States Parties shall ensure that the powers and procedures established in this section are subject to conditions and safeguards according to their domestic laws, providing adequate protection of human rights and liberties, including obligations arising pursuant to the 1966 UN International Covenant on Civil and Political Rights and applicable international human rights instruments, including the principle of proportionality.

For the purposes of the present article, the application and implementation of powers and limitations for the protection of human rights under a State's domestic law shall include, inter alia, judicial or other independent supervision in view to ensure safeguards and the scope and duration of such procedures.

V. COMPUTER DATA

Article 16: Expedited preservation of stored computer data

Each State Party shall take such measures as may be necessary to enable its competent authorities to order or similarly obtain the expeditious preservation of specified computer data, including traffic data or data that has been stored on a computer system, especially when there is reasonable ground to believe that the computer data is vulnerable to being deleted or modified.

Article 17: Real-time collection or recording of traffic data

Each State Party shall take such measures as may be necessary to enable its competent authorities to collect or record real-time traffic data related to specified communications transmitted or made available in its territory or in cooperation with a service provider, in accordance with its technical capabilities on the territory of that Party, for such purposes in consistency with the powers and limitations set forth in Article 15.

Article 18: Seizure and access to computer data

Each State Party shall take such measures as may be necessary to enable its competent authorities to seize or similarly secure a specific computer system or part of it, or the computer data therein, from the offenses in Articles 7 to 13, with adequate safeguards, in consistency with the powers and limitations set forth in Article 15.

VI. JURISDICTION

Article 19: Jurisdiction

1. Each State Party undertakes to adopt such measures as may be necessary to establish jurisdiction over offenses established in accordance with Articles 7 to 13 when the offense is committed in its territory or onboard a ship flying the flag of that Party or on an aircraft registered under the laws of that State Party.
2. Each State Party undertakes to adopt such measures as may be necessary to establish jurisdiction over offenses established in accordance with Articles 7 to 13 in the following cases:
   a. When the alleged offender is a national of the State Party, if the offense is punishable under criminal law where it was committed,

or if the offense is committed outside the territorial jurisdiction of
any State;

b. When the alleged offender is present in the territory of the State
Party and it does not extradite him or her to another Party solely on
the basis of his or her nationality after a request for extradition;

c. The present Convention does not exclude any criminal jurisdiction
exercised in accordance with domestic law.

3. When more than one State Party claims jurisdiction over an alleged
offense established in this Convention, the States Parties involved shall,
where appropriate, consult with a goal to define the most appropriate
jurisdiction for prosecution.

VII. INTERNATIONAL COOPERATION

Article 20: International cooperation

The States Parties undertake cooperation with each other in accordance with
this Convention and through the application of relevant international instruments on international cooperation in criminal matters. This cooperation
will be to the broadest extent possible for the purposes of investigations or
proceedings concerning trafficking offenses related to the Internet and other
computer networks or for the collection of evidence in electronic form of a
trafficking offense.

VIII. COOPERATION WITH RELEVANT
ORGANIZATIONS AND CIVIL SOCIETY

Article 21: Cooperation measures

States Parties shall establish policies and programs, as appropriate, to cooperate with nongovernmental organizations, relevant organizations, and other
elements of civil society. These measures include the technology industry,
including service providers to prevent and combat online sex trafficking,
protect child victims, and strengthen measures including but not limited to
education and awareness-raising toward an effective fight against all forms
of online child sexual exploitation.

IX. PROTECTION OF CHILD VICTIMS OF ONLINE SEX TRAFFICKING

Article 22: Protection of child victims of online sex trafficking

a. In appropriate cases and to the extent possible under domestic law, States Parties shall protect the privacy and identity of child victims of online sex trafficking, including, inter alia, by making legal proceedings confidential.

b. States Parties shall ensure that their domestic law contains measures that can assist child victims in their psychological and social recovery and diminish the risk of revictimization online, including in appropriate cases cooperation with nongovernmental organizations and civil society.

c. States Parties shall ensure that their domestic legal systems contain measures that offer to minor victims of online sex trafficking the possibility of obtaining compensation for damage suffered.

d. States Parties shall ensure that their domestic legal systems contain measures that offer to minor victims of online sex trafficking protection from prosecution or the imposition of penalties for being subjected to any criminal offense set forth in Articles 7 to 13.

X. INFORMATION EXCHANGE AND TRAINING

Article 23: Information exchange

Law enforcement, immigration, or other competent authorities of States Parties shall, as appropriate, cooperate by exchanging information according to their domestic laws to enable them to prevent, detect, investigate, and penalize the commission of offenses established in accordance with Section III of this Convention.

Article 24: Training

States Parties shall undertake measures to provide or strengthen training for law enforcement, immigration, and other relevant state authorities to address the criminal misuse of computer systems, networks, and computer data in the abuse and exploitation of children, considering children's special protection and gender-sensitive issues.

* * *

IMPLICATIONS FOR COMPREHENSIVE
POLICY AND STRATEGY

As the Internet and the use of mobile telephone communications technologies grow at unprecedented rates, both children and perpetrators are increasingly becoming users of digital spaces. The Internet can be a powerful facilitating tool to victimize persons, including children. Online sex trafficking practices constitute an evolving phenomenon as advances in digital technology are ongoing, providing new ways for this form of cybercrime to be committed. States must provide legal protection to children from online activities through which they can be sexually exploited or bought and sold as sexual objects through the use of cyberspace. I have argued that crimes that evidence the commodification of children for the purpose of sexual exploitation may represent modern slavery in the digital sphere. New forms of online activities concerning sex trafficking in children constitute a growing concern due to a changing social reality. For example, in 2020, Interpol reported that offenses relating to online sexual exploitation represented an increased threat for children during the COVID-19 pandemic with offenders taking advantage of lockdown measures and the increased time children were spending online to target and commit offenses across the globe.[120] It is essential that countries enhance their understanding of these online activities, which constitute severe forms of crime against the human person of the child. They should take all the actions needed to combat human trafficking and its venues, including cyberspace.

Countries should address shortcomings or deviations in their criminal laws in relation to the sexual exploitation of minors in the virtual world and ensure criminalization of all such new types of offenses. Because no nation is immune from this new type of Internet-related crime against children, this problem requires a coordinated global response from states. An international response through which governments implement and enforce appropriate national legislation and measures is essential to adequately protect children against such exploitation practices facilitated or committed online. Such a response would work toward enhancing (1) prevention of offenses, (2) detection of offenses, (3) investigation of offenses, (4) law enforcement response to offenses, including the proactive prosecution of such offenses, and (5) identification and protection of victimized children in a victim-focused approach. In this way, under a human rights–centered approach that takes into account the state's obligation to respect, protect, and fulfill human rights, an internationally binding instrument would help countries, in law and practice, address this new issue by overcoming significant legal challenges, including those related to (1) legislative definitions and offenses, (2) prevention, (3) jurisdictions, (4) international cooperation, (5) protection and responses to child victims that include access to redress, and (6) public-private partnerships. Therefore, states would acquire international obligations consistent with human rights norms and standards to adopt appropriate legislation and more adequate measures to prohibit and combat online content and activity for the purpose of sexual exploitation of children at domestic levels.

States' implementation of cyberspecific legislation with clear definitions and a more robust law enforcement capacity would connect to the pillars of the rule of law. States must protect children under their jurisdiction from human rights violations committed or facilitated online by third parties.[121] At the same time, states must ensure a proper balance between this need to protect children from harm and the need to protect the individual rights of children and other users in cyberspace, including the rights to privacy and freedom of expression and association.[122] In this context, national laws should not allow undue restrictions regarding access to information or surveillance and monitoring activities on the Internet under the premise of protecting children from unlawful content and practices. Such actions could enable human rights abuses and, thus, undermine democracy and the rule of law. Therefore, this proposed international legal framework could reinforce the human rights obligations of states in cyberspace.

Furthermore, forms of crimes likely associated with online sex trafficking represent common challenges for government authorities and various stakeholders across civil society sectors, including the private sector. It is of utmost importance to strengthen private-public partnerships and collaboration with a better articulation of the responsibilities of the technology industry for respecting human rights.[123] The goal of states to make the digital environment safer for children within their jurisdictions requires them to adopt concrete policies and strategies coordinated and aligned with the involvement of the private sector. States cannot overcome this crime alone. This binding international agreement would encourage partnerships and cross-sector collaboration with various stakeholders, including the technology industry.

Multistakeholder collaboration is a component of a holistic response to reduce and eliminate this form of cybercrime against children and to promote child safety online. States' implementation of international legal norms will encourage the adoption of codes of conduct and internal rules for private sector actors based on corporate social responsibility. The use of technological innovation in this area of child protection online will help to better detect child victimization and disrupt networks. Additionally, the private sector may provide education and awareness resources that are vital to better respond to children online.

CONCLUSION

This chapter seeks to improve protection measures that ensure children's well-being and a safer Internet based on international human rights law as a source of obligations for states. It promotes the Internet as an essential means that offers a space for the exercise of fundamental human rights, particularly the rights to privacy and freedom of opinion and expression. However, states have obligations to address the threat to children of exploitation and enhance online child safety. Internet-related offenses may involve subjecting a child to acts such as recruitment, enticement, or advertising of the child for the purpose of sexual exploitation. In addition, in some circumstances, children can be made the object of a transaction (e.g., payments sent or received for services) for their sexual exploitation. These exploitative scenarios can expose elements of trafficking. They may also reflect the exercise of one or more powers attached to the right of ownership over the person of a child as the child receives treatment as an exploitative sexual commodity. Thus, virtual exploitative practices to engage a child in commercial or commodified sexual activities amount to forms of slavery or slavery-like practices. There is an urgent need for states to take action to punish these practices. As a vulnerable group, children require immediate protection from these exploitative activities against them via cyberspace.

This chapter has addressed the challenges involved in the fight against modern forms of slavery and exploitation related to the online forms of victimization likely associated with the online sex trafficking of children. I have argued that these practices constitute human rights violations online. They directly affect the human person of a child and represent a growing international problem as they are increasingly occurring on the Internet and Darknet platforms. Because these offenses bring new legislative challenges for governments, a comprehensive, coordinated, and consistent international response is needed to combat this form of cybercrime holistically. A common understanding among states on the sexual exploitation of children on the Internet is required to strengthen the protection of their rights and dignity in this digital era. It is essential that countries improve child safety efforts by implementing legal and policy responses to more adequately protect children against the evolving nature of these crimes based on universal standards.

I have argued that a legally binding instrument for online activities presents a potential legal solution to achieve legal harmonization at the international level. This new instrument would provide a comprehensive legal framework for states to develop new and more robust laws and policies to prohibit forms of crime likely associated with online sex trafficking. In this way, it could aid the fight against all forms of child sexual exploitation and keep children safer online. Overall, it would promote the adequate protection of human dignity and children's rights in the digital world. When national laws and policies are in compliance with human rights norms and principles, states will ensure the complete protection of children with regard to forms of online sexual exploitation in a way that promotes or facilitates the realization of free expression and human rights in cyberspace.

A human rights framework with a view to protect children in cyberspace would establish that states must ensure criminalization of sexually exploitative activities against children; promote the likelihood of successful prosecution of perpetrators, particularly by guaranteeing guidance on practical coordination for obtaining stored and real-time data without delay; hasten identification and assistance of online child victims; and promote faster identification and effective blocking and removal of CSEM online at the source country. These aspects would work toward building a better coordinated and more aligned global fight against online child sex trafficking and related exploitation.

Importantly, states can integrate the combat of these crimes as part of digital security strategies. This approach may promote access to and use of the Internet and ICTs in a safe way for all, including children. In this way, countries can combat this area of cybercrime as part of a holistic action to strengthen cybersecurity capabilities to promote an open, accessible, and secure Internet. Intending to promote global security, the proposed international instrument is designed to create better protection of children against this form of Internet-related crime and also to encourage the need to preserve the free flow of information and respect for human rights and fundamental freedoms.

I believe that online activities related to the sex trafficking of children can be effectively addressed and reduced if there is a genuine commitment of states to the elimination of such behaviors and a common legislative framework in place among them. Based on states' human rights obligations, they have a direct responsibility to prevent and combat these online acts perpetrated by nonstate actors with the intent to sexually exploit children. Online trafficking of children represents new legislative challenges to governments. Under a human rights–based approach to combating these online exploitation acts, states should strengthen the normative responses and appropriate measures in their national legal systems and practice. A solid human rights framework for online child protection would help states more effectively deter offenders, significantly increase enforcement capacity, and improve global efforts in a sustainable, long-term response to the trafficking and sexual exploitation of children in cyberspace.

In addition, because these virtual activities represent a complex phenomenon, the involvement of various stakeholders is essential in their prevention and effective eradication. States should ensure the free flow of information in the digital environment and promote multistakeholder collaboration, including the technology industry, to benefit from the effective use of technological tools, including raising awareness and promoting digital literacy. The foregoing discussion and proposed treaty aspire to help build an order based on law whereby everyone can thrive and reach their full potential in an order of human dignity.

NOTES

1. For example, HRC, Resolution 31/7, Resolution on 23 March 2016, A/HRC/RES/31/7 (Apr. 20, 2016), para. 4, at 4.

2. VCLT, art. 26.

3. UN, "Statute of the International Court of Justice," adopted on June 26, 1945, T.S. 993, art. 38(1).

4. Ibid., art. 34(1), 36(2).

5. UN, "Charter of the United Nations," signed June 26, 1945, ch. XIV, art. 93(1), (2).

6. See generally, Malcolm N. Shaw, *International Law*, 7th ed. (Cambridge: Cambridge University Press, 2014), 50.

7. James R. Crawford, *Brownlie's Principles of Public International Law*, 8th ed. (Oxford: Oxford University Press, 2012), 22–23.

8. For further reading see Harold H. Koh, "International Law in Cyberspace," *Harvard International Law Journal* 54 (2012), 2–3.

9. Formerly "Developments in the Field of Information and Telecommunications in the Context of International Security." See UNGA, "Group of Governmental Experts on Developments in the Field of Information and Telecommunications in the Context of International Security," A/65/201, July 30, 2010; UNGA, "Group of Governmental Experts on Developments in the Field of Information and Telecommunications in the Context of International Security," A/68/98*, June 24, 2013; and UNGA, "Group of Governmental Experts on Developments in the Field of Information and Telecommunications in the Context of International Security," A/70/174, July 22, 2015.

10. UNGA, "Group of Governmental Experts on Developments in the Field of Information and Telecommunications in the Context of International Security," A/68/98*, 8.

11. UNGA, "Group of Governmental Experts on Developments in the Field of Information and Telecommunications in the Context of International Security," A/70/174.

12. UNGA, Resolution 70/237, "Developments in the Field of Information and Telecommunications in the Context of International Security," A/RES/70/237 (December 30, 2015).

13. ILC, "Draft Articles on Responsibility of States for Internationally Wrongful Acts, with Commentaries 2001," A/56/10, art. 1, at 32.

14. ILC, "Draft Articles on Responsibility of States for Internationally Wrongful Acts," A/56/10, art. 2, at 34.

15. *Barcelona Traction, Light and Power Company, Limited (Belgium v. Spain)*, Second Phase, ICJ 32, (February 5, 1970), para. 33.

16. Eckart Klein, "Individual Reparation Claims under the International Covenant on Civil and Political Rights: The Practice of the Human Rights Committee," in *State Responsibility and the Individual, Reparation in Instances of Grave Violations of Human Rights*, ed. Albrecht Randelzhofer and Christian Tomuschat (The Hague: Martinus Nijhoff, 1999), 27–28.

17. VCLT, art. 26.

18. ICCPR, art. 2. See generally HRCttee, "General Comment no. 31 [80]: The Nature of the General Legal Obligation Imposed on States Parties to the Covenant," CCPR/C/21/Rev.1/Add.13, May 26, 2004, para. 8, at 3.

19. For example, UNCRC, art. 34, 35. See generally OP-CRC-SC, art. 1–3. See also Palermo Protocol, art. 3(c).

20. CoE, "Convention on Cybercrime," signed November 23, 2001, E.T.S. 185, art. 9.

21. UN, "Status of Treaties: Convention on the Rights of the Child," https://treaties.un.org/Pages/ViewDetails.aspx?src=IND&mtdsg_no=IV-11&chapter=4&clang=_en.

22. *Prosecutor v. Sam Hinga Norman*—Decision on Preliminary Motion Based on Lack of Jurisdiction (Child Recruitment), Special Court for Sierra Leone, no. SCSL-2004–14-AR72(E), (May 31, 2004), para. 17–20.

23. Jean D'Cunha, "Trafficking in Persons: A Gender and Rights Perspective," EGM/TRAF/2002/EP.8, November 8, 2002, 10.

24. UNCRC, art. 3(1).

25. Such an act of a state can be characterized as internationally wrongful if it constitutes a breach of an international obligations of that state. See ILC, "Draft Articles on Responsibility of States for Internationally Wrongful Acts," A/56/10, art. 3.

26. For example, in the context of human rights, the ICCPR provides universal parameters regarding the extent of legal duties of states.

27. For example, the obligation of the state hinged on such a consideration in the case of *Rantsev v. Cyprus and Russia* (discussed in chapter 1), para. 286, at 70.

28. Palermo Protocol, art. 5.

29. For example, CoE, "Convention on Cybercrime," preamble, art. 9. For a thorough discussion on the best interests of the child as primary consideration, see chapter 6.

30. UNCRC, art. 34(b), (c).

31. Ibid., art. 3(1). See generally CRC, "General Comment no. 13 (2011): The Right of the Child to Freedom From All Forms of Violence," CRC/C/GC/13, April 18, 2011, para. 3(f), at 3, observing the fundamental premise that "the right of children to have their best interests be a primary consideration in all matters involving or affecting them must be respected, especially when they are victims of violence, as well as in all measures of prevention."

32. For example, UNGA, Resolution 70/1, "Transforming Our World: The 2030 Agenda for Sustainable Development," A/RES/70/1 (Oct. 21, 2015), SDG 16.2, at 25.

33. UN, "Statute of the International Court of Justice," art. 38(1)(b).

34. Crawford, *Brownlie's Principles*, 25.

35. *Asylum Case: Colombia v. Peru*, Judgment, ICJ 276, (Nov. 20, 1950).

36. Tullio Treves, "Customary International Law," in *Oxford Public International Law: Max Planck Encyclopedia of Public International Law* (New York: Oxford University Press, 2006), 3.

37. *North Sea Continental Shelf* (Federal Republic of Germany/Denmark; Federal Republic of Germany/Netherlands), Judgment, ICJ 43 (Feb. 20, 1969), para 74, at 44.

38. *North Sea Continental Shelf* (Dissenting Opinion of Judge Lachs), Judgment, ICJ 230 (1969); *North Sea Continental Shelf* (Dissenting Opinion of Judge Sørensen), Judgment, ICJ 244 (1969).

39. *North Sea Continental Shelf* (Dissenting Opinion of Judge Lachs), 230.

40. Bin Cheng, "United Nations Resolutions on Outer Space: 'Instant' International Customary Law?" in *Studies in International Space Law* (Oxford: Clarendon Press, 1997).

41. UNGA, "Second Report on Identification of Customary International Law, by Special Rapporteur Michael Wood," A/CN.4/672*, May 22, 2014, para. 52, at 34.

42. UNGA, "Second Report on Identification of Customary International Law, by Special Rapporteur Michael Wood," para. 53, at 35.

43. For example, *Prosecutor v. Sam Hinga Norman—Decision on Preliminary Motion Based on Lack of Jurisdiction (Child Recruitment)*, para. 51, at 26; and *Case Concerning Sovereignty over Pedra Branca/Pulau Batu Puteh, Middle Rocks and South Ledge* (Malaysia/Singapore), Judgment, ICJ 50–51 (May 23, 2008), para. 121.

44. For example, in *Asylum Case: Colombia v. Peru*, the ICJ observed that the Colombian Government did not prove the existence of a regional or local custom of Latin American states concerning to the right to the state granting unilateral and definitive asylum.

45. For example, ILC, "Draft Conclusions on Identification of Customary International Law, with Commentaries," A/73/10, 2018, draft conclusion 16(1), para. 5, at 154–155.

46. UNGA, "Identification of Customary International Law: Ways and Means for Making the Evidence of Customary International Law More Readily Available: Memorandum by the Secretariat," A/CN.4/710*, January 12, 2018, draft conclusion 6, at 18.

47. *Criminal Code Act 1995* (Cth), sec. 474.26.

48. "*Carriage service* refers to a service for carrying communications by means of guided or unguided electromagnetic energy," Telecommunications Act 1997, no. 47, part 1(7).

49. ICMEC, *Studies in Child Protection: Technology-Facilitated Child Sex Trafficking* (Alexandria, VA: ICMEC, 2018), 34.

50. "Decision of the Standing Committee of the National People's Congress on Preserving Computer Network Security," Chinese Government's Official Web Portal, para. 7, http://english1.english.gov.cn/laws/2005-09/22/content_68771.htm.

51. Federation of American Scientists, "The Implementation Measures Relating to the Temporary Provisions for the Management of Computer Information Networks in the People's Republic of China That Take Part in International Internetworks," art. 3(1), https://fas.org/irp/world/china/docs/980306-internet.htm.

52. Ibid., art. 20.

53. Directive 2011/93/EU, art. 6(2).

54. Ibid.

55. Criminal Law (Child Grooming) Bill 2014: Explanatory Memorandum, no. 89.

56. Ibid., sec. 1(2C), at 4.

57. Ley Orgánica 1/2015, de 30 de marzo, por la que se modifica la Ley Orgánica 10/1995, de 23 de noviembre, del Código Penal, BOE-A-2015-3439 (2015).

58. Ibid., art. 183 ter (2).

59. Currently, Denmark is the only member state that has not formally notified national transposition measures pertaining to this EU law; see EU Law, "National Transpositions by Member States," https://eur-lex.europa.eu/legal-content/EN/NIM/?uri=CELEX:32011L0093.

60. EU Law, "EU Regulation 2016/679 of the European Parliament and of the Council of 27 April 2016 on the Protection of Natural Persons with Regard to the Processing of Personal Data and on the Free Movement of Such Data, and Repealing Directive 95/46/EC (General Data Protection Regulation)," *Official Journal of the European Union* 119 (2016): 1–88.

61. Intersoft Consulting, "General Data Protection Regulation (GDPR)," https://gdpr-info.eu/.

62. EU Law, "EU Regulation 2016/679," art. 2(2)(d).

63. Ibid., art. 10, 6(1).

64. Ibid., art. 5(1)(e).

65. EU Law, "Directive (EU) 2016/680 of the European Parliament and of the Council of 27 April 2016 on the Protection of Natural Persons with Regard to the Processing of Personal Data by Competent Authorities for the Purposes of the Prevention, Investigation, Detection or Prosecution of Criminal Offences or the Execution of Criminal Penalties, and on the Free Movement of Such Data, and Repealing Council Framework Decision 2008/977/JHA," *Official Journal of the European Union* 119 (2016): art. 5.

66. European Commission, "EU Member States Notifications to the European Commission under the GDPR," https://ec.europa.eu/info/law/law-topic/data-protection/data-protection-eu/eu-countries-gdpr-specific-notifications_en.

67. ICMEC, *Child Sexual Abuse Material: Model Legislation & Global Review*, 9th ed. (Alexandria, VA: International Centre for Missing and Exploited Children, 2018), 19.

68. Republic Act no. 9208, Congress of the Philippines, 12th Cong. (2003), sec. 5(c).

69. Act no. 7: Prevention and Combating of Trafficking in Persons Act 2013, no. 36715, *Government Gazette* 577 (July 29, 2013): art. 8(2)(a).

70. Act no. 7: Prevention and Combating, art. 8(2)(b).

71. Ibid. Art. 8(3), (4) further states, "Nothing in this section places a general obligation on an electronic communications service provider to—(a) monitor the data which it transmits or stores; or (b) actively seek facts or circumstances indicating an unlawful activity."

72. 18 USC § 2421A.

73. 47 USC § 230.

74. The term "indistinguishable" is defined at 18 USC § 2256(11).

75. For definition of the term "identifiable minor" see 18 USC § 2256(9).

76. The court pointed out factors that may be relevant to determining the presence of "lascivious exhibition of the genitals or pubic area" in *United States v. Dost*, 636 F. Supp. 828 (S.D. Cal. 1986).

77. See U.S. Department of Justice, "Citizen's Guide to U.S Federal Law on Child Pornography," www.justice.gov/criminal-ceos/ citizens-guide-us-federal-law-child-pornography.

78. For example, 18 U.S.C. §§ 2251(e), 2252(b), 2252A(b), 2260(c).

79. For example, 18 U.S.C. § 3559(e).

80. WPGA, "The Alliance," www.weprotect.org/members.

81. UNGA, "Report of the Secretary-General: Developments in the Field of Information and Telecommunications in the Context of International Security," July 19, 2016, A/71/172, 24.

82. Europol, "Child Sexual Exploitation," www.europol.europa.eu/ crime-areas-and-trends/crime-areas/child-sexual-exploitation.

83. Europol, "EU Policy Cycle-Empact," www.europol.europa.eu/ crime-areas-and-trends/eu-policy-cycle-empact.

84. Interpol, "International Child Sexual Exploitation Database," www.interpol.int/ Crimes/Crimes-against-children/International-Child-Sexual-Exploitation-database.

85. Interpol, "Databases," www.interpol.int/en/How-we-work/Databases.

86. See Operation Torpedo in U.S. Attorney's Office, *2015 Annual Report* (Omaha, NE: U.S. Attorney's Office, 2015), 21; U.S. Federal Bureau of Investigation, "Playpen Creator Sentenced to 30 Years," www.fbi.gov/news/stories/ playpen-creator-sentenced-to-30-years.

87. U.S. Federal Bureau of Investigation, "Playpen Creator."

88. See VGT, "Member Countries," http://virtualglobaltaskforce.com/member-countries/; and VGT, "Private Sector Partners," http://virtualglobaltaskforce.com/ private-sector-partners/.

89. For a list of VGT Operations, see VGT, "Operations," http://virtualglobaltaskforce. com/operations/.

90. VGT, "VGT Announce 20 Arrests in 6 Months from Operation Globe," http://virtualglobaltaskforce.com/vgt-announce-20-arrests-in-6-months-from-operation-globe/.

91. IWF, www.iwf.org.uk/our-services/hash-list.

92. Ethel Quayle, "Prevention, Disruption and Deterrence of Online Child Sexual Exploitation," *ERA Forum* 21 (2020): 429–447.

93. Facebook, "Secret Conversations," www.facebook.com/help/ messenger-app/1084673321594605.

94. NCMEC, *2020 Reports by Electronic Service Providers* (Alexandria, VA: National Center for Missing and Exploited Children, 2020).

95. Mark Zuckerberg, "A Privacy-Focused Vision for Social Networking," Facebook, www.facebook.com/notes/mark-zuckerberg/a-privacy-focused-vision-for-social-net working/10156700570096634/.

96. See governmental response from ministers, Priti Patel et al., "Open Letter: Facebook's 'Privacy First' Proposals," U.S. Department of Justice, www.justice.gov/opa/press-release/file/1207081/download.

97. "In the ordinary course of providing our service, WhatsApp does not store messages once they are delivered or transaction logs of such delivered messages, and undelivered messages are deleted from our servers after 30 days. WhatsApp offers end-to-end encryption for our services, which is always activated" (WhatsApp, "Information for Law Enforcement Authorities," https://faq.whatsapp.com/general/security-and-privacy/information-for-law-enforcement-authorities).

98. See *Asylum Case: Colombia v. Peru,* 277, 286; and *Case Concerning Right of Passage over Indian Territory (Portugal v. India)*, Judgment, ICJ 42–43 (1960).

99. ICMEC, *Child Sexual Abuse Material: Model Legislation & Global Review,* at 36.

100. *Case Concerning Right of Passage over Indian Territory (Portugal v. India)*, Judgment, ICJ 42–43 (1960).

101. WPGA, "Capability 21: Universal Terminology," in *Preventing and Tackling Child Sexual Exploitation and Abuse (CSEA): A Model National Response* (2016).

102. HRC, Resolution 38/7, "The Promotion, Protection and Enjoyment of Human Rights on the Internet," A/HRC/RES/38/7 (July 17, 2018).

103. *Lex ferenda* means "law that ought to be made," that is, developing law; *lex lata* means "law that has been made," that is, positive law. In the present context, a custom in a late stage of development (*lex ferenda*) is made positive law (*lex lata*) through its crystallization in a treaty.

104. *Case Concerning the Continental Shelf (Libyan Arab Jamahiriya/Malta)*, Judgment, ICJ 29–30 (1985), para. 27.

105. ILC, "Draft Conclusions on Identification of Customary International Law, with Commentaries," conclusion 9, (4) at 139.

106. For example, VCLT, art. 38, asserting that "a rule set forth in a treaty from becoming binding upon a third State as a customary rule of international law, recognized as such."

107. OHCHR "The Core International Human Rights Instruments and Their Monitoring Bodies," www.ohchr.org/EN/ProfessionalInterest/Pages/CoreInstruments.aspx.

108. ICCPR, art. 28.

109. Ibid., art. 40(4).

110. ILC, "Draft Conclusions on Identification of Customary International Law, with Commentaries," conclusion 12, at 147.

111. UNGA, Resolution 543(VI), "Preparation of Two Draft International Covenants on Human Rights," A/RES/543(VI), (February 4, 1952).

112. UNICEF, *The Sale & Sexual Exploitation of Children: Digital Technology*, 3.

113. UNODC, *Legislative Guides for the Implementation of the UN Convention against Transnational Organized Crime and the Protocols Thereto* (New York: United Nations, 2004), para. 38, at 270.

114. For example, OP-CRC-SC Guidelines, para. 58, at 12.

115. OP-CRC-SC, art. 9(5) states that "States Parties shall take appropriate measures aimed at effectively prohibiting the production and dissemination of material advertising the offences described in the present Protocol."

116. For example, Palermo Protocol, art. 6, para. 3, 4.

117. UDHR, art. 29.

118. Author's draft treaty based on the Palermo Protocol, the UNCRC, the OP-CRC-SC, and the CoE Convention on Cybercrime.

119. Author's definition of "online sex trafficking of children."

120. Interpol, *Threats and Trends Child Sexual Exploitation and Abuse: Covid-19 Impact* (2020).

121. HRCttee, "General Comment no. 31 [80]," para. 8, at 3.

122. For example, UNGA, Resolution 68/167, "The Right to Privacy in the Digital Age," A/RES/68/167 (January 21, 2014), para. 3, at 2; HRC, Resolution 20/8, "The Promotion, Protection and Enjoyment of Human Rights on the Internet," A/HRC/RES/20/8 (July 16, 2012), para. 2, at 2; HRC, "Report of the Special Rapporteur on the Promotion and Protection of the Right to Freedom of Opinion and Expression, David Kaye," A/HRC/29/32, May 22, 2015, para. 11, at 5; HRC, "Report of the Special Rapporteur on the Promotion and Protection of Human Rights and Fundamental Freedoms While Countering Terrorism, Martin Scheinin," A/HRC/13/37, December 28, 2009.

123. HRC, "Report of the Special Representative of the Secretary-General on the Issue of Human Rights and Transnational Corporations and Other Business Enterprises, John Ruggie," A/HRC/17/31, March 21, 2011, Chapter II, at 13.

Bibliography

Allain, Jean. "Bellagio-Harvard Guidelines on the Legal Parameters of Slavery." In *The Law and Slavery*, 555–563. Leiden: Brill/Nijhoff, 2015. https://doi.org/10.1163/9789004279896_030.

Balleste, Roy. "In Harm's Way: Harmonizing Security and Human Rights in the Internet Age." In *Cybersecurity and Human Rights in the Age of Cyberveillance*, edited by Joanna Kulesza and Roy Balleste, 39–62. Lanham, MD: Rowman & Littlefield, 2015.

Bergman, Michael K. "White Paper: The Deep Web: Surfacing Hidden Value." *Journal of Electronic Publishing* 7, no. 1 (2001), https://doi.org/10.3998/3336451.0007.104.

Bossler, Adam M., Kathryn Seigfried-Spellar, and Thomas J. Holt. *Cybercrime and Digital Forensics: An Introduction*, 2nd ed. Abingdon, UK: Routledge, 2017.

Bossuyt, Marc. *Guide to the* Travaux Préparatoires *of the International Covenant on Civil and Political Rights*. New York: Springer, 1987.

Bourke, Michael L. "The Myth of the Harmless Hands-Off Offender." In *The NetClean Report 2016*. NetClean, www.netclean.com/wp-content/uploads/sites/2/2017/06/NetClean_Report_2016_English_print.pdf, 34–35.

Busch-Armendariz, Noël B., Maura Nsonwu, and Laurie C. Heffron. *Human Trafficking: Applying Research, Theory and Case Studies*. New York: Sage Publications, 2018.

Canadian Centre for Child Protection. *Survivors' Survey: Full Report*. Winnipeg: Canadian Centre for Child Protection, 2017.

Carozza, Paolo G. "Human Dignity." In *The Oxford Handbook of International Human Rights Law*, edited by Dinah Shelton, 345–359. Oxford: Oxford University Press, 2013.

Clayton, Ellen W., Richard D. Krugman, and Patti Simon, eds. *Confronting Commercial Sexual Exploitation and Sex Trafficking of Minors in the United States*. Washington, DC: National Academies Press, 2013.

Clough, Jonathan. *Principles of Cybercrime*, 2nd ed. Cambridge: Cambridge University Press, 2015.

Cockbain, Ella. *Offender and Victim Networks in Human Trafficking*. Abingdon, UK: Routledge, 2018.

Council of Europe. "Convention on Cybercrime." November 23, 2001. ETS 185.

————. "Convention on the Protection of Children against Sexual Exploitation and Sexual Abuse." October 25, 2007. CETS 201.

————. "Council of Europe Convention on Action against Trafficking in Human Beings." May 16, 2005. CETS 197.

————. "Directive 2011/36/EU of the European Parliament and of the Council of 5 April 2011 on Preventing and Combating Trafficking in Human Beings and Protecting Its Victims, and Replacing Council Framework Decision 2002/629/JHA." *Official Journal of the European Union* 101 (2011): 1–11.

————. "Explanatory Report to the Convention on Cybercrime." November 23, 2001. ETS 185.

————. "Explanatory Report to the Council of Europe Convention on Action against Trafficking in Human Beings." May 16, 2005. CETS 197.

————. "Explanatory Report to the Council of Europe Convention on the Protection of Children against Sexual Exploitation and Sexual Abuse." October 25, 2007. CETS 201.

Crawford, James R. *Brownlie's Principles of Public International Law*, 8th ed. Oxford: Oxford University Press, 2012.

Devine, Carol, Carol Rae Hansen, Ralph Wilde, Daan Bronkhorst, Frederic A. Moritz, Baptiste Rolle, and Rebecca Sherman. *Human Rights: The Essential Reference*, edited by Carol Devine and Hilary Poole. Phoenix, AZ: Oryx Press, 1999.

Doek, Jaap E. "The Human Rights of Children: An Introduction." In *International Human Rights of Children*, edited by Ursula Kilkelly and Ton Liefaard, 3–29. New York: Springer, 2019.

Dutton, William H. "Internet Studies: The Foundations of a Transformative Field." In *The Oxford Handbook of Internet Studies*, edited by William H. Dutton, 1–26. Oxford: Oxford University Press, 2014.

Düwell, Marcus, Jens Braarvig, Roger Brownsword, and Dietmar Mieth. "Why a Handbook on Human Dignity?" In *The Cambridge Handbook of Human Dignity, Interdisciplinary Perspectives*, edited by Marcus Düwell, Jens Braarvig, Roger Brownsword, and Dietmar Mieth. Cambridge: Cambridge University Press, 2014.

ECPAT International. *Online Child Sexual Exploitation: An Analysis of Emerging and Selected Issues*. Bangkok: ECPAT International, 2017.

————. *Trends in Online Child Sexual Abuse Material*. Bangkok: ECPAT International, 2018.

European Cybercrime Centre.

Internet Organised Crime Threat Assessment. The Hague: Europol, 2019.

————. *Internet Organised Crime Threat Assessment*. The Hague: Europol, 2018.

————. *Internet Organised Crime Threat Assessment*. The Hague: Europol, 2020.

————. *Online Sexual Coercion and Extortion as a Form of Crime Affecting Children: Law Enforcement Perspective*. The Hague: Europol, 2017.

European Committee of Social Rights. "Decision on the Merits of the Complaint: *Federation of Catholic Family Associations in Europe (FAFCE) v. Ireland*." no. 89/2013. September 12, 2014.

European Union Law. "Directive (EU) 2016/680 of the European Parliament and of the Council of 27 April 2016 on the Protection of Natural Persons with Regard to the Processing of Personal Data by Competent Authorities for the Purposes of the Prevention, Investigation, Detection or Prosecution of Criminal Offences or the Execution of Criminal Penalties, and on the Free Movement of Such Data, and Repealing Council Framework Decision 2008/977/JHA." *Official Journal of the European Union* 119 (2016): 89–131.

———. "Directive 2011/93/EU of the European Parliament and of the Council of 13 December 2011 on Combating the Sexual Abuse and Sexual Exploitation of Children and Child Pornography, and Replacing Council Framework Decision 2004/68/JHA." *Official Journal of the European Union* 335 (2011): 1–14.

———. "EU Regulation 2016/679 of the European Parliament and of the Council of 27 April 2016 on the Protection of Natural Persons with Regard to the Processing of Personal Data and on the Free Movement of Such Data, and Repealing Directive 95/46/EC (General Data Protection Regulation)." *Official Journal of the European Union* 119 (2016): 1–88.

Feehs, Kyleigh, and Alyssa Currier Wheeler. *2020 Federal Human Trafficking Report.* Fairfax, VA: Human Trafficking Institute, 2020.

Frank, Michael J., and G. Zachary Terwilliger. "Gang-Controlled Sex Trafficking." *Virginia Journal of Criminal Law* 3, no. 2 (2015): 342–434.

Gallagher, Anne T. *The International Law of Human Trafficking.* Cambridge: Cambridge University Press, 2012.

Greiman, V., and C. Bain. "The Emergence of Cyber Activity as a Gateway to Human Trafficking." *Journal of Information Warfare* 12, no. 2 (2013): 41–49.

Hughes, Donna M. "Trafficking in Human Beings in the European Union: Gender, Sexual Exploitation, and Digital Communication Technologies." *SAGE Open* (2014): 1–8. https://doi.org/10.1177/2158244014553585.

Inter-Agency Coordination Group against Trafficking of Persons. *Issue Brief 8: Non-Punishment of Victims of Trafficking.* Vienna: Inter-Agency Coordination Group against Trafficking of Persons, 2020.

International Centre for Missing and Exploited Children. *Child Sexual Abuse Material: Model Legislation & Global Review*, 9th ed. Alexandria, VA: ICMEC, 2018.

———. *Online Grooming of Children for Sexual Purposes: Model Legislation & Global Review*, 1st ed. Alexandria, VA: ICMEC, 2017.

———. *Studies in Child Protection: Technology-Facilitated Child Sex Trafficking.* Alexandria, VA: ICMEC, 2018.

International Labour Organization. *Global Estimates of Modern Slavery: Forced Labour and Forced Marriage.* Geneva: International Labour Organization, 2017.

International Law Commission. "Draft Articles on Responsibility of States for Internationally Wrongful Acts, with Commentaries 2001." A/56/10. 2008.

———. "Draft Conclusions on Identification of Customary International Law, with Commentaries." A/73/10. 2018.

International Telecommunication Union. *Global Cybersecurity Index 2018.* Geneva: International Telecommunication Union Publications, 2019.

———. *Guidelines for Industry on Child Online Protection.* Geneva: International Telecommunication Union Publications, 2020.

———. *Measuring Digital Development: Facts and Figures.* Geneva: International Telecommunication Union Publications, 2021.

Internet Watch Foundation. *Annual Report 2017.* Cambridge: Internet Watch Foundation, 2018.

———. *Annual Report 2018.* Cambridge: Internet Watch Foundation, 2019.

———. *Annual Report 2019.* Cambridge: Internet Watch Foundation, 2020.

———. *Trends in Online Child Sexual Exploitation: Examining the Distribution of Captures of Live-Streamed Child Sexual Abuse.* Cambridge: Internet Watch Foundation, 2018.

Interpol. *Threats and Trends Child Sexual Exploitation and Abuse: Covid-19 Impact.* Lyon: Interpol, 2020.

Interpol and ECPAT. *Towards a Global Indicator on Unidentified Victims in Child Sexual Exploitation Material: Technical Report.* Bangkok: ECPAT International, 2018.

Kälin, Walter, and Jörg Künzli. *The Law of International Human Rights Protection,* 2nd ed. Oxford: Oxford University Press, 2019.

Kendall, Virginia M., and T. Markus Funk. *Child Exploitation and Trafficking: Examining the Global Challenges and U.S. Responses.* New York: Rowman & Littlefield, 2011.

Klein, Eckart. "The Duty to Protect and to Ensure Human Rights under the International Covenant on Civil and Political Rights." In *The Duty to Protect and to Ensure Human Rights,* edited by Eckart Klein. Berlin: Verlag A. Spitz, 2000.

Koh, Harold H. "International Law in Cyberspace." *Harvard International Law Journal* 54 (2012): 1–12.

Kothari, Miloon. "The Sameness of Human Rights Online and Offline." In *Human Rights, Digital Society and the Law*: *A Research Companion,* edited by Mart Susi, 15–30. London: Routledge, 2019.

Lanzarote Committee. *First Implementation Report: Protection of Children against Sexual Abuse in the Circle of Trust: The Framework.* Strasbourg: Council of Europe, 2015.

———. *Opinion on Article 23 of the Lanzarote Convention and Its Explanatory Note.* Strasbourg: Council of Europe, 2015.

Lasswell, Harold D., and Myres S. McDougal. *Jurisprudence for a Free Society: Studies in Law, Science and Policy,* volumes 1–2. New Haven, CT: New Haven Press, 1992.

League of Nations, "Slavery Convention." March 9, 1927. U.N.T.S. 2861.

Livingstone, Sonia, Julia Davidson, Joanne Bryce, Saqba Batool, Ciaran Haughton, and Anulekha Nandi. *Children's Online Activities, Risks and Safety: A Literature Review by the UKCCIS Evidence Group.* London: LSE Consulting, 2017.

Lööfs, Lars. "Sexual Behaviour, Adolescents and Problematic Content." In *Understanding and Preventing Online Sexual Exploitation of Children,* edited by Ethel Quayle and Kurt M. Ribisl. Abingdon, UK: Routledge, 2012.

Martellozzo, Elena. *Online Child Sexual Abuse: Grooming, Policing and Child Protection in a Multi-Media World.* Oxfordshire, UK: Routledge, 2012.

McAlinden, Anne-Marie. *"Grooming" and the Sexual Abuse of Children: Institutional, Internet, and Familial Dimensions*. Oxford: Oxford University Press, 2012.

McDougal, Myres S., Harold D. Lasswell, and Lung-Chu Chen. *Human Rights and World Public Order: The Basic Policies of an International Law of Human Dignity*, 1st ed. New Haven, CT: Yale University Press, 1980.

National Center for Missing & Exploited Children. *Trends Identified in Cybertipline Sextortion Report*. Alexandria, VA: National Center for Missing & Exploited Children, 2016.

———. *2020 Reports by Electronic Service Providers*. Alexandria, VA: National Center for Missing & Exploited Children, 2021.

Neverauskaitė, Justė. *In the Shadows of the Internet: Child Sexual Abuse Material in the Darknets*. Brussels: ECPAT Belgium, 2015.

Office of the United Nations High Commissioner for Human Rights. "Recommended Principles and Guidelines on Human Rights and Human Trafficking." E/2002/68/Add.1. May 20, 2002.

Olson, Eric, and Jonathan Tomek. *Cryptocurrency and the BlockChain: Technical Overview and Potential Impact on Commercial Child Sexual Exploitation*. LookingGlass, 2017.

Ost, Suzanne. *Child Pornography and Sexual Grooming, Legal and Societal Responses*. Cambridge: Cambridge University Press, 2009.

Owen, Gareth, and Nick Savage. *Paper Series: no. 20—September 2015: The Tor Dark Net*. Centre for International Governance Innovation, Royal Institute of International Affairs, 2015.

Pati, Roza. "Rights and Their Limits: The Constitution for Europe in International and Comparative Legal Perspective." *Berkeley Journal of International Law* 23, no. 1 (2005): 223–229.

———. "Trafficking in Human Beings: The Convergence of Criminal Law and Human Rights." In *The SAGE Handbook of Human Trafficking and Modern-Day Slavery*, edited by Jennifer B. Clark and Sasha Poucki. London: Sage Publications, 2019.

Protection Project. "Model Law on Combating Child Sex Tourism." In *International Child Sex Tourism: Scope of the Problem and Comparative Case Studies*, 187–188. Washington, DC: John Hopkins University / The Paul H. Nitze School of Advanced International Studies, 2007.

Quayle, Ethel. "Prevention, Disruption and Deterrence of Online Child Sexual Exploitation." *ERA Forum* 21 (2020): 429–447. https://doi.org/10.1007/s12027-020-00625-7.

Reisman, Michael W. "Development and Nation-Building: A Framework for Policy-Oriented Inquiry." *Maine Law Review* 60, no. 2 (2008): 310–15.

———. "A Policy-Oriented Approach to Development." *Journal of International and Comparative Law* 3, no. 1 (2016): 141–148.

Reisman, Michael W., Siegfried Wiessner, and Andrew R. Willard, "The New Haven School: A Brief Introduction," *Yale Journal of International Law* 32, no. 2 (2007): 575–582.

Schutter, Olivier D. "The United Nations Human Rights Treaties System." In *International Human Rights Law, Cases, Materials, Commentary*, 3rd ed., 869–942. Cambridge: Cambridge University Press, 2019.

Shaw, Malcolm N. *International Law*, 7th ed. Cambridge: Cambridge University Press, 2014.

Thomas, Stephen B., and Erica Casper. "The Burdens of Race and History on Black People's Health 400 Years after Jamestown." *American Journal of Public Health* 109, no. 10 (2019): 1346–1347. https://doi.org/10.2105/AJPH.2019.305290.

Thorn Digital Defenders of Children and Vanessa Bouché. *A Report on the Use of Technology to Recruit, Groom and Sell Domestic Minor Sex Trafficking Victims*. Thorn, 2015.

Tsagourias, Nicholas. "The Legal Status of Cyberspace." In *Research Handbook on International Law and Cyberspace*, edited by Nicholas Tsagourias and Russell Buchan, 13–29. Camberley, UK: Edward Elgar Publishing, 2015.

Turner, Catherine. *Out of the Shadows: Child Marriage and Slavery*. Anti-Slavery International, 2013.

UK Department for Digital, Culture, Media & Sport and Home Office. *Online Harms White Paper* (CP57). Crown Copyright, 2019. www.gov.uk/government/consultations/online-harms-white-paper/online-harms-white-paper.

UNICEF Innocenti Research Centre. *Handbook on the Optional Protocol on the Sale of Children, Child Prostitution and Child Pornography*. Florence: UNICEF, 2009.

UNICEF, the Global Compact, and Save the Children. *Children's Rights and Business Principles*. 2012.

United Nations. Statute of the International Court of Justice (1945).

———. Vienna Convention on the Law of Treaties. May 23, 1969. U.N.T.S. 1155.

United Nations Commission on Human Rights. "Norms on the Responsibilities of Transnational Corporations and Other Business Enterprises with Regard to Human Rights." E/CN.4/Sub.2/2003/12/Rev.2. August 26, 2003.

———. "2004/116. Responsibilities of Transnational Corporations and Related Business Enterprises with Regard to Human Rights." April 20, 2004.

United Nations Committee on the Elimination of Discrimination against Women and CRC. "Joint General Recommendation no. 31 of the Committee on the Elimination of Discrimination against Women/General Comment no. 18 of the CRC Committee on Harmful Practices." CEDAW/C/GC/31-CRC/C/GC/18. November 14, 2014.

United Nations Committee on the Rights of the Child. "Concluding Observations on the Combined 5th and 6th Periodic Reports of El Salvador: CRC." CRC/C/SLV/CO/5–6. November 29, 2018.

———. "Concluding Observations on the Combined Fifth and Sixth Periodic Reports of Costa Rica." CRC/C/CRI/CO/5–6. March 4, 2020.

———. "Concluding Observations on the Combined Fifth and Sixth Periodic Reports of Australia." CRC/C/AUS/CO/5–6. November 1, 2019.

———. "Draft General Comment no. 25 (202x): Children's Rights in Relation to the Digital Environment." CRC/C/GC/. August 13, 2020.

———. "General Comment no. 12: The Right of the Child to Be Heard." CRC/C/GC/12. July 20, 2009.

———. "General Comment no. 13 (2011): The Right of the Child to Freedom from All Forms of Violence." CRC/C/GC/13. April 18, 2011.

———. "General Comment no. 14 (2013) on the Right of the Child to Have His or Her Best Interests Taken as a Primary Consideration (art. 3, para 1).*" CRC/C/GC/14. May 29, 2013.

———. "General Comment no. 16 (2013) on State Obligations Regarding the Impact of the Business Sector on Children's Rights." CRC/C/GC/16. April 17, 2013.

United Nations Convention on the Rights of the Child. "General Comment no. 25 (2021) on Children's Rights in Relation to the Digital Environment." CRC/C/GC/25. March 2, 2021.

———. "Guidelines Regarding the Implementation of the Optional Protocol to the Convention on the Rights of the Child on the Sale of Children, Child Prostitution and Child Pornography." CRC/C/156. September 10, 2019.

United Nations Economic and Social Council. "Supplementary Convention on the Abolition of Slavery, the Slave Trade, and Institutions and Practices Similar to Slavery." April 30, 1957. U.N.T.S. 3822.

United Nations General Assembly. Resolution 68/167, "The Right to Privacy in the Digital Age," A/RES/68/167 (January 21, 2014).

———. Resolution 70/1, "Transforming Our World: The 2030 Agenda for Sustainable Development," A/RES/70/1 (October 21, 2015).

———. Resolution 70/237, "Developments in the Field of Information and Telecommunications in the Context of International Security," A/RES/70/237 (December 30, 2015).

———. Resolution 73/179, "The Right to Privacy in the Digital Age," A/RES/73/179 (January 21, 2019).

———. "Addendum: Interpretative Notes for the Official Records (*Travaux Préparatoires*) of the Negotiation of the United Nations Convention against Transnational Organized Crime and the Protocols Thereto." A/55/383/Add.1. November 3, 2000.

———. "Chapter V: Peremptory Norms of General International Law (*jus cogens*)." In *Report of the International Law Commission: Seventy-First Session*, 141–208. New York: United Nations, 2019.

———. "Convention on the Rights of the Child." September 2, 1990. U.N.T.S. 1577.

———. "Developments in the Field of Information and Telecommunications in the Context of International Security." A/72/315. August 11, 2017.

———. "Developments in the Field of Information and Telecommunications in the Context of International Security." A/74/120. June 24, 2019.

———. "Group of Governmental Experts on Developments in the Field of Information and Telecommunications in the Context of International Security." A/68/98.* June 24, 2013.

———. "Group of Governmental Experts on Developments in the Field of Information and Telecommunications in the Context of International Security." A/70/174. July 22, 2015.

————. "Group of Governmental Experts on Developments in the Field of Information and Telecommunications in the Context of International Security." A/65/201. July 30, 2010.

————. "International Covenant on Civil and Political Rights." March 23, 1976. U.N.T.S. 999.

————. "Optional Protocol to the Convention on the Rights of the Child on the Sale of Children, Child Prostitution and Child Pornography." January 18, 2002. U.N.T.S 2171.

————. "Promotion and Protection of the Right to Freedom of Opinion and Expression, David Kaye." A/71/373. September 6, 2016.

————. "Protocol to Prevent, Suppress and Punish Trafficking in Persons Especially Women and Children, Supplementing the United Nations Convention against Transnational Organized Crime." December 25, 2003. U.N.T.S. 2237.

————. "Report of the Secretary-General: Developments in the Field of Information and Telecommunications in the Context of International Security." A/71/172. July 19, 2016.

United Nations Human Rights Committee. "CCPR General Comment no. 16: Article 17 (Right to Privacy): The Right to Respect of Privacy, Family, Home and Correspondence, and Protection of Honour and Reputation." April 8, 1988.

————. "Concluding Observations on the Fifth Periodic Report of Portugal." CCPR/C/PRT/CO/5. April 28, 2020.

————. "General Comment no. 31 [80]: The Nature of the General Legal Obligation Imposed on States Parties to the Covenant." CCPR/C/21/Rev.1/Add.13. May 26, 2004.

————. "General Comment no. 34, Article 19: Freedoms of Opinion and Expression." CCPR/C/GC/34. September 12, 2011.

United Nations Human Rights Council. Resolution 17/4, Human Rights and Transnational Corporations and Other Business Enterprises, A/HRC/RES/17/4 (July 6, 2011).

————. Resolution 20/8, "The Promotion, Protection and Enjoyment of Human Rights on the Internet," A/HRC/RES/20/8 (July 16, 2012).

————. Resolution 26/13, "The Promotion, Protection and Enjoyment of Human Rights on the Internet," A/HRC/RES/26/13 (July 14, 2014).

————. Resolution 31/7, "Rights of the Child: Information and Communications Technologies and Child Sexual Exploitation," A/HRC/RES/31/7 (April 20, 2016).

————. Resolution 32/13, "The Promotion, Protection and Enjoyment of Human Rights on the Internet," A/HRC/RES/32/13 (July 18, 2016).

————. Resolution 38/7, "The Promotion, Protection and Enjoyment of Human Rights on the Internet," A/HRC/RES/38/7 (July 17, 2018).

————. "Impact of Coronavirus Disease on Different Manifestations of Sale and Sexual Exploitation of Children: Report of the Special Rapporteur on the Sale and Sexual Exploitation of Children, Including Child Prostitution, Child Pornography and Other Child Sexual Abuse Material, Mama Fatima Singhateh.*" A/HRC/46/31. January 22, 2021.

————. "Promotion and Protection of the Right to Freedom of Opinion and Expression, Frank La Rue." A/69/335. August 21, 2014.

————. "Report of the Special Rapporteur on Contemporary Forms of Slavery, Including Its Causes and Consequences, Urmila Bhoola." A/73/139. July 10, 2018.

————. "Report of the Special Rapporteur on Contemporary Forms of Slavery, Including Its Causes and Consequences, Urmila Bhoola." A/HRC/39/52. July 27, 2018.

————. "Report of the Special Rapporteur on the Promotion and Protection of the Right to Freedom of Opinion and Expression, Frank La Rue." A/HRC/17/27. May 27, 2011.

————. "Report of the Special Rapporteur on the Promotion and Protection of the Right to Freedom of Opinion and Expression, David Kaye." A/HRC/32/38. May 11, 2016.

————. "Report of the Special Rapporteur on the Promotion and Protection of the Right to Freedom of Opinion and Expression, David Kaye." A/HRC/35/22. March 30, 2017.

————. "Report of the Special Rapporteur on the Promotion and Protection of the Right to Freedom of Opinion and Expression, Frank La Rue." A/HRC/23/40. April 17, 2013.

————. "Report of the Special Rapporteur on the Promotion and Protection of the Right to Freedom of Opinion and Expression, David Kaye." A/HRC/29/32. May 22, 2015.

————. "Report of the Special Rapporteur on the Sale of Children, Child Prostitution and Child Pornography, Maud de Boer-Buquicchio." A/HRC/28/56. December 22, 2014.

————. "Report of the Special Representative of the Secretary-General on the Issue of Human Rights and Transnational Corporations and Other Business Enterprises, John Ruggie." A/HRC/17/31. March 21, 2011.

————. "The Right to Privacy in the Digital Age: Report of the Office of the United Nations High Commissioner for Human Rights." A/HRC/27/37. June 30, 2014.

————. "Surveillance and Human Rights: Report of the Special Rapporteur on the Promotion and Protection of the Right to Freedom of Opinion and Expression." A/HRC/41/35. May 28, 2019.

United Nations Office on Drugs and Crime. *Abuse of a Position of Vulnerability and Other "Means" within the Definition of Trafficking in Persons: Issue Paper.* New York: United Nations, 2013.

————. *Anti-Human Trafficking Manual for Criminal Justice Practitioners: Control Methods in Trafficking in Persons (Module 4).* New York: United Nations, 2009.

————. *Anti-Human Trafficking Manual for Criminal Justice Practitioners: Definition of Trafficking in Persons and Smuggling of Migrants (Module 1).* New York: United Nations, 2009.

————. *Anti-Human Trafficking Manual for Criminal Justice Practitioners: Indicators of Trafficking in Persons (Module 2).* New York: United Nations, 2009.

————. *Comprehensive Study on Cybercrime.* New York: United Nations, 2013.

———. *The Concept of "Exploitation" in the Trafficking in Persons Protocol: Issue Paper*. Vienna: United Nations, 2015.

———. "COVID-19 Pandemic and Its Impact for Victims and Survivors of Trafficking in Persons." www.unodc.org/unodc/en/human-trafficking/Webstories2020/covid-19-pandemic-and-its-impact-for-victims-and-survivors-of-trafficking-in-persons.html.

———. *Global Report on Trafficking in Persons 2018*. New York: United Nations, 2018.

———. *Global Report on Trafficking in Persons 2020*. New York: United Nations, 2021.

———. *Guidance Note on "Abuse of a Position of Vulnerability" as a Means of Trafficking in Persons in Article 3 of the Protocol to Prevent, Suppress and Punish Trafficking in Persons, Especially Women and Children, Supplementing the United Nations Convention against Transnational Organized Crime*. New York: United Nations, 2012.

———. *Issue Paper: The Role of "Consent" in the Trafficking in Persons Protocol*. Vienna: United Nations, 2014.

———. *Legislative Guides for the Implementation of the UN Convention against Transnational Organized Crime and the Protocols Thereto*. New York: United Nations, 2004.

———. *Study on the Effects of New Information Technologies on the Abuse and Exploitation of Children*. New York: United Nations, 2015.

U.S. Department of Justice. *The National Strategy for Child Exploitation Prevention and Interdiction* (no. 249863). Washington, DC: U.S. Department of Justice, 2016.

———. *Voluntary Principles to Counter Online Child Sexual Exploitation and Abuse*, 2019. www.justice.gov/opa/press-release/file/1256061/download.

U.S. Department of State. *Report on U.S. Government Efforts to Combat Trafficking in Persons*. Washington, DC: U.S. Department of State, 2019.

———. *Trafficking in Persons Report*. Washington, DC: U.S. Department of State, 2013.

———. *Trafficking in Persons Report*. Washington, DC: U.S. Department of State, 2016.

———. *Trafficking in Persons Report*. Washington, DC: U.S. Department of State, 2017.

———. *Trafficking in Persons Report*. Washington, DC: U.S. Department of State, 2020.

Virtual Global Task Force. *VGT Online Child Sexual Exploitation: Environmental Scan Unclassified Version 2019*, 2019.

Voronova, Sofija, and Anja Radjenovic. *The Gender Dimension of Human Trafficking*. European Parliament, 2016.www.europarl.europa.eu/thinktank/en/document/EPRS_BRI(2016)577950.

WeProtect Global Alliance. *Global Threat Assessment 2018: Working Together to End the Sexual Exploitation of Children Online*. London: Crown Copyright, 2018.

———. *Global Threat Assessment 2019*. London: Crown Copyright, 2019.

Whittle, Helen C., Catherine Hamilton-Giachritsis, and Anthony R. Beech. "Victims' Voices: The Impact of Online Grooming and Sexual Abuse." *Universal Journal of Psychology* 1, no. 2 (2013): 59–71.

Wiessner, Siegfried. "The New Haven School of Jurisprudence: A Universal Toolkit for Understanding and Shaping the Law." *Asia Pacific Law Review* 81, no. 1 (2010): 45–61.

Witting, Sabine. "'Cyber' Trafficking? An Interpretation of the Palermo Protocol in the Digital Era." Völkerrechtsblog. https://voelkerrechtsblog.org/cyber-trafficking-an-interpretation-of-the-palermo-protocol-in-the-digital-era/.

Wolak, Janis, and David Finkelhor. *Sextortion: Keys Findings from an Online Survey of 1,631 Victims*. Crimes against Children Research Center / Thorn, 2016.

World Health Organization, UNICEF, UNESCO, UN Special Representative of the Secretary-General on Violence against Children, and End Violence against Children. *Global Status Report on Preventing Violence against Children*. Geneva: World Health Organization, 2020.

Index

256   *Index*

European Union (EU), 28, 53–54,
   55n22, 110–11, 192–94
European Union Agency for Law
   Enforcement Cooperation (Europol),
   72, 80–81, 87, 125–27, 133,
   153, 199–200
Europol. *See* European Union Agency
   for Law Enforcement Cooperation
Evens, Charles, 88
exploitation, 41, 44, 46, 110–11, 115,
   126; CSAM with act and purpose of,
   79–81; defined, 48–49, 50–53; illegal
   child adoption for, 94–95; Internet-
   facilitated contact, 73, 89–90;
   Internet-facilitated noncontact,
   73–75; jurisprudence perspective
   and online, 149–52; livestreaming of
   child sexual abuse and, 84–87, 221;
   NCMEC, xvii, 82, 125, 195, 199;
   sexual, 49–51, 91–93, 109, 220. *See
   also* child sexual exploitation
extortion, online sexual coercion, 82–83

Facebook, xvii, 83, 199–200
face-to-face (in-person) meetings, 90,
   106, 112, 192
families, dysfunctional, 124–25
FBI, 193, 199–200
findhotescorts.com, 137
Finland, 64, 161–62
First World Congress against
   Commercial Sexual Exploitation of
   Children, 51, 219
Florida, 128
forensics, 79, 85, 201–202, 206
forum sites, 87
FOSTA (Allow States and
   Victims to Fight Online Sex
   Trafficking Act), 195
Fourteenth Amendment, 6, 30n25
France, 4, 24–26, 34n89, 64
freedom, 3, 5, 17, 27, 80
freedom of expression, 154–61
Freenet, 132
Fugitive Slave Clause, 4

gaming community, 124
GCA (Global Cybersecurity Agenda), 62
GCI (Global Cybersecurity Index), 95
GDPR (General Data Protection
   Regulation), EU, 193–94
gender, 2, 6, 47, 89, 92, 122, 227
General Comment no.13, CRC,
   45–46, 233n31
General Data Protection Regulation
   (GDPR), EU, 193–94
general declaration, UN, 2010–11
general parameters for restrictive
   measures on the right to freedom
   of expression and privacy in online
   environments, ICCPR, 154–59
general provisions, articles 1–5, 219–21
Genesis, 10
Geneva Declaration on the Rights of the
   Child (1924), 10–11
Germany, 134
GGE (Group of Governmental Experts),
   UN, 184–85
girls, 46, 92, 106, 122, 128, 131; with
   dysfunctional families, 124–25;
   Internet-facilitated grooming
   of, 113–14
Global Cybersecurity
   Agenda (GCA), 62
Global Cybersecurity Index (GCI), 95
Global Report on Trafficking in Persons
   (UNODC), 79, 113, 124, 130, 139
Gnutella, 80
Goldschlag, David, 134
Google, 132
government, 72, 150, 186
Greece, 64
grooming of children, Internet-
   facilitated, 118n18, 223; criminal law
   dimensions, 108–16; cybergroomers,
   106–7, 109–10, 112, 114; EU with
   sexual exploitation and, 192–93;
   online, 105–8; recruitment into sex
   trafficking, 113–16; secrecy of online
   relationships, 116–17
Grotius, Hugo, 3

offenders: with anonymity and freedom, 80; CSAM, 139–40, 161, 171; cyberoffenders, 43, 82, 106–7, 109, 121, 131, 135, 197; end-to-end encryption protecting, 201–202; life imprisonment for, 133, 197; men as, 75; network of, 90; perpetrators, xviii, 45; prosecuting online child sexual exploitation, 213–14; self-esteem of, 139. *See also* perpetrators

offenses: cyber-dependent, 70; ISPs and reporting responsibilities, 197; preparatory act with sexual, 112–13

Office of the United Nations High Commissioner for Human Rights (OHCHR), 127, 172

offline: abuse, 112, 119n37; grooming and trust, 106; sexual offenses, 112–13

OHCHR (Office of the United Nations High Commissioner for Human Rights), 127, 172

Onion Router (Tor), 81, 132, 133–34

online: ads, 89, 138–39, 161–62; buyers, 43, 48; "close online relationships," 125; CSAM, 74–75; enticement of children, 110, 195; exploitation in policy-oriented jurisprudence perspective, 149–52; grooming of children, 105–8

online child protection policy: with acts related to CSAM, 213; global, 211–13; national law harmonized, 212

online child sexual exploitation: with camouflaged identities, ix, 71, 83; child victims with vulnerabilities and, 124–27; customary law norm and prohibition of, 187–88; online sex trafficking, modern slavery and, x; forms of, xx; policing, 205–13; prosecuting offenders of, 213–14

online sex trafficking, x, xxi, 135; of children, 44, 50, 53, 69, 172, 213–19; protection of child victims of,

226–27. *See also* Internet, *indicia* of slavery on

OP-CRC-SC (Optional Protocol to the Convention on the Rights of the Child on the Sale of Children, Child Prostitution and Child Pornography), xix, 180n106, 180n113, 217, 237n115; article 9(5), 214; draft treaty sample and, 215; grooming and, 109, 115; international legal instruments, 13–14; Internet-facilitated contact exploitation and, 90; Internet-facilitated noncontact act exploitation and, 73–75; livestreaming and child pornography, 86; Operational Principle 24, 182n137; preamble, 180n113; respect and, 170; sexual exploitation and, 50–51; victim-centered approach, 129

Operational Principle 24, OP-CRC-SC, 182n137

Operation Atlas, VGT, 200

Operation Basket, VGT, 200

Operation Endeavour, VGT, 86, 200

Operation Globe, VGT, 200

Operation Pacifier, FBI, 199, 200

Operation Rescue, VGT, 200

Operation Torpedo, FBI, 199

opinio juris (acceptance as law), 189–91, 203–4

Optional Protocol to the Convention on the Rights of the Child on the Sale of Children, Child Prostitution and Child Pornography. *See* OP-CRC-SC

organized crime, 55n21, 71, 90; groups, 80, 116, 130, 131, 135–37; UNTOC, 20–21, 116, 120n60, 135–37, 219

Organized Crime Convention, 55n21

Owen, Gareth, 132

ownership: of children, 43, 47–48; exploitation and, 94; *indicia* of, 28; powers of, 17, 39, 95, 183; right of ownership over a person, 17–18, 23, 26; with tattoos, 27. *See also* slavery

About the Author

Beatriz Susana Uitts is a human rights lawyer and researcher. She holds a Doctor of the Science of Law (JSD) degree and a Master of Laws (LLM) degree in intercultural human rights from St. Thomas University College of Law in Miami Gardens, Florida, and a juris doctor (JD) from Pontificia Universidad Javeriana in Bogotá DC, Colombia. She is the founder and director of Human Trafficking Front, an organization dedicated to studying and preventing issues related to human trafficking and modern slavery through education, research, and community engagement. She is an associated expert at the John J. Brunetti Human Trafficking Academy at St. Thomas University. She has appeared on national media and has been a guest lecturer in the field of human trafficking at national and international levels. Her research focuses on trafficking in persons, human rights, and the relationship and connections between technology and exploitation. Her legal and advocacy work, undertaken for academic, governmental, and nongovernmental organizations, includes strengthening responses of the criminal justice system to human trafficking; enhancing coordination of services to victims of violence, including domestic violence and human trafficking; and serving and mentoring unaccompanied immigrant youth. She has served as petitioner attorney before the Inter-American Commission on Human Rights in Washington, DC.